From the House to the Streets

From the House
to the Streets

The Cuban Woman's

Movement for

Legal Reform,

1898–1940

K. LYNN STONER

DUKE UNIVERSITY PRESS

Durham and London 1991

Third printing, 1997
© 1991 Duke University Press

All rights reserved.
Printed in the United States of America
on acid-free paper ∞

Library of Congress Cataloging-in-Publication Data
Stoner, K. Lynn.
From the house to the streets : the Cuban woman's movement for
legal reform, 1898–1940 / K. Lynn Stoner.
p.   cm.
Includes bibliographical references and index.
ISBN 0–8223–1131–3. —ISBN 0–8223–1149–6 (pbk.)
1. Women's rights—Cuba—History.   2. Women—Legal status, laws,
etc.—Cuba—History.   3. Feminism—Cuba—History.   I. Title.
HQ1236.5.C9S76   1991
305.42'097291—dc20   90–48182
                                                                  CIP

For my parents
Henry H. and Frances P. Stoner

Contents

Tables

Acknowledgments

⚓

This book has been ten years in the making, and it is the result of many people's efforts in both Cuba and the United States. It began as a doctoral dissertation at a time when travel to Cuba was possible under tourist visa but little contact between academic communities existed for facilitating graduate research. Choosing to study Cuban women took an act of faith that only a naive graduate student would have made. Yet Cubans living in this country assured me that a dynamic and effective Cuban woman's movement had existed and that there was sufficient historical evidence in the United States to complete the dissertation. Miguel Solís, now retired, was a bibliographer at Indiana University's Lily Library who encouraged my study of the woman's movement by suggesting starting points and sources. Armando González, retired Assistant Chief of the Hispanic Law Division of the Library of Congress, gave countless hours of advice about the use of legal documents and clarified obscure legal terms. Pablo Calvan, librarian in the Library of Congress microfilm reading room, took an active interest in my sources and enjoyed sharing my rich materials and interpreting *cubichismos* not found in dictionaries.

In the early stages of research three Cuban feminists were still living, and they graciously agreed to help me write a history of the feminist movement. They knew this book would be a testimony to their work as young women, so they listened to my questions, searched for documents, and answered me honestly. María Gómez Carbonell, the first female house representative and senator in Cuba, met with me once and wrote several letters in response to questions about her perspectives on feminism during the 1920s and 1930s. Ana Moya de Perrera, the superintendent of public schools in Havana province during the 1950s, shared information she had collected for a book on Cuban women she never wrote. Elena Mederos de González, a feminist and a social reformer, was my most important guide. She was a woman of great integrity who worked for the benefit of Cuban women, culture, and social justice. In her last years she became my friend. She taught me about Cuba and the woman's movement there, but her greatest messages were about life and ultimately about death.

Other Cuban exiles led me to documents that enriched my work. Rosa Abella and Lesbia Varona at the University of Miami opened their resources to me, and they have been waiting too long for the publication of this work. Dr. Asunción Lavrin, the pioneer of Latin American women's history, has been a loyal colleague and friend. Few areas of research have been opened by a more generous scholar, who never failed to share material, ideas, and encouragement. Her elegance and kindness set a high standard for those of us who share her enthusiasm for women's history.

Cubans living in Cuba have aided in the final stages of this work. In 1985 I had the good fortune to meet Margy Delgado and Rita Pereira of the Federation of Cuban Women, who took a lively interest in my work. They invited me to return to Cuba more than once to complete new research in the José Martí Nacional Library and the National Archives. The new sources improved the book immeasurably. At the José Martí National Library Tomás Fernández Robaina turned the stacks inside out for me, and his own vast knowledge about sources on Cuban women enabled me to amass materials quickly. Francisco García, the micro-filmer, suffered countless hours copying my archival documents, and without his labor this book would have been impossible. At the National Archives Emma Rita Gutiérrez worked overtime to make sure that I saw the materials I needed and secured permission for me to have them copied. Nydia Sarabia and Armando Caballero, two historians, discussed my work with me, helping me conceptualize a past they remember.

I am indebted to all these people, who happen to share a common birthplace. Despite their differing views about political order and thirty years of isolation from one another, they share many qualities. Cubans on both sides of the Florida Straits have a high regard for scholarly integrity and intellectual honesty. All have aided my research, and none has tried to influence my analysis or withhold information. Both communities lament that a gringa, and not a Cuban, is writing this history, but they nonetheless applaud my work and encourage me with that ebullient Cuban enthusiasm.

Other people helped enormously with this book. Dr. Paul M. Siegel, Chief of the Education Branch of the Census Bureau, has watched this book mature for ten years. Conversations with him have clarified my thinking about some points, and he aided with statistical analyses on the divorce tables and the prosopography surveys. Most important has been his unwavering confidence that I would finish this task. Dr. Robert Levine, Chairman of the Department of History at the University of Miami, and Dr. Philip Vandermeer, associate professor at Arizona State

University, also advised me on the survey. Dr. Donna J. Guy, Director of the Latin America Area Center and associate professor of history at the University of Arizona, has challenged me to analyze the juxtaposition of Cuban and U.S. feminisms and to draw a connection between modern imperatives of state rule and new roles for women. Her contributions have sharpened my focus of analysis. Dr. Louis A. Pérez, professor at the University of South Florida, taught me that history is both a science and an art. His high standards for historical documentation and analytical explanation and his ear for artful writing improved the quality of this work. My mother, Frances P. Stoner, read a final version of this manuscript and made a number of valuable suggestions. Steven D. Koppe cheerfully transferred my manuscript into WordPerfect and made editing corrections. Larry Malley, Director and Editor-in-Chief at Duke University Press, has been the perfect editor.

My travel to Cuba has been supported by various grants from Arizona State University and Kansas State University. While in Cuba a number of friends made my stay not only joyful, but meaningful. Ramona, María López la Rosa, and Nereida Pereira Rodríguez were my compañeras in the FMC guest house. To my friends Alberto, Norma, Rafael, Raul, Lyly, Mily, Maday, Quiqui, Aniceto, and Selma, thank you for inviting me into your hearts and homes. And to the Hartley Campbells especially, thank you for accepting me as a member of your family and sharing with me your wealth of laughter, love, dignity, and wisdom. Our connections will not end with this book.

My parents, Henry H. and Frances P. Stoner, have been constant sources of support throughout my graduate and academic careers. Their achievements as professionals and global citizens have set high standards for discipline and integrity toward which I strive. Their examples of zest, curiosity, achievement, and social awareness continue to delight and amaze me.

Although many people have helped with this book, the final responsibility for its contents is my own.

Preface

❦

This is a study of feminists and a feminist movement in Cuba between 1902 and 1940. It explains how a small group of women helped to shape broad legal reforms in only thirty-five years. At the same time it describes the version of feminism that these women adopted, with all its internal contradictions, and contrasts it to the model of feminism North Americans were transporting to Cuba. It emphasizes the mentalité of Cuban protagonists in the struggle for women's rights as well as the surrounding events that enhanced their power to mold national values. In short, this study attempts to portray the Cuban feminist movement in its nationalist context and in its own words. It also demonstrates how feminism, emerging in Cuban society during the formative years of the republican period, drew from traditional notions of femininity and a rejection of gender equality to advance a cause that assumed that women's roles were necessary for social progress.

Histories of feminism have progressed from those that concentrated only on declared feminists and their campaigns to those that acknowledge the reformist efforts of women outside feminist circles. Breaking down the woman's movement into its components and constituents, or deconstructing feminism, has preoccupied North American women's historians for the last decade. As a result, we know that there are many interpretations of feminism and many women activists who did not call themselves feminists who nevertheless promoted women's causes and rebelled against social injustice.[1]

Nancy Cott and Paula Baker demonstrate how North American women, motivated among other things by domestic values, were consistently active in political and community life. That is, women's orientations in the home fed their sense of social action. By the nineteenth century women were involving themselves in slave emancipation and temperance, both moral issues appropriate for domestic, feminine involvement. The woman's movement that emerged at Seneca Falls in 1848 drew from the struggle to emancipate slaves because in that struggle women saw the parallel between their own conditions and the noncitizenship of slaves and because they had learned to organize a popular movement. The politics of domesticity were central to the woman's movement until the beginning of the twentieth century when for reasons of political efficacy the National Women's Party narrowed feminist objectives to suffrage and omitted earlier interests in family issues, labor inequities, education, social welfare, and prostitution. This complex development of feminism in the United State raises the question for all scholars about who feminists were: women in a narrowly focused woman's movement and/or women in broader movements, such as the antislavery movement, who promoted other kinds of change that per force had to address women's issues.

All feminist movements by definition rejected conditions of gender bias. The means and the definition of struggle, however, differed from society to society. Reactions to oppression and submission depended upon the nature of gender inequality, culturally based prejudices, as well as conventions of female empowerment within a cultural group. Hence, Cuban feminism, while sharing some objectives with other national feminist movements, also was culturally centered. Karen Offen's work on the comparison of French and U.S. feminism supports the argument for the cultural relativity of feminism.[2] She posits that nationalist sentiments and regional cultures shaped the language, sources of empowerment, and final objectives of French feminism. She counterposes French feminism with feminism in the United States where prevailing values rested on individual rights and social equality, inspiring feminists to seek individual freedom. Conversely, in France, Offen chooses to term feminism "relational feminism," because feminists viewed themselves in community with others. They sought a power in gender difference and not equality, in womanliness, and in shared authority with men. Offen's conclusions more nearly match my own, and, more importantly, explain why many Cuban feminists were uncomfortable with the North American model. The Cubans went to some trouble to explain shared aspirations and important distinctions with North American activists such as Doris Stevens and Carrie Chapman Catt, the two North American feminists best known in Cuba.[3]

Too much could be made of a comparative analysis of Cuban and U.S. feminism except that the United States dominated Cuba between 1898 and 1940. Four military occupations, amounting to ten of Cuba's forty-two years of independence from Spain, placed in question the meaning of Cuban sovereignty. Land fell increasingly to foreign landholders who generated profits for themselves by underpaying Cuban laborers and buying up foundering estates. The United States, England, and Spain controlled banking; the United States owned the nickel mines; sugar, Cuba's main export, was controlled by U.S. interests; and Cuban citizens and the country became cheap labor and debtors.

U.S. domination went beyond the obvious political, military, and economic dimensions of foreign rule. Prolonged contact between Cuban and U.S. societies insured cultural associations. Cubans increasingly adopted U.S. standards of beauty and dress, baseball and boxing arenas brought together athletes from both countries in hotly contested championships, and Hollywood movies dazzled Cuban audiences and challenged their standards of morality and romance. U.S. feminists took an interest in the liberation of Cuban women and attempted to impose U.S. standards for feminism. More than any other Latin American feminist movement, Cuba's had to contend with delegations from the north attending their conventions, insisting on winning the vote, and working to put women in public office, while deemphasizing the importance of motherhood. Cuban reaction to U.S. feminism was mixed. Some activists agreed that electoral rights were central to liberating women. Others believed plebiscites failed to resolve problems of poverty, male domination, and an egalitarian society, and that accepting the U.S. model was another form of acquiescing to imperialism. Although divided on some issues, nearly all Cuban feminists insisted upon a reverence for motherhood and a desire to complement men's lives. Rightly or wrongly, many Cubans believed that by conserving femininity and making it central to feminism, they distinguished themselves from their North American counterparts.

Class and race divisions set Cuban feminists apart from poor women and women of color. Lower-class women, mulattas, and black women had always lived and worked on the streets. Poverty, ill health, sexual exploitation, and disrespect for people of their class and race all hampered their living prosperous lives. Gender discrimination was only a part of their misery. Social complexities did not, however, deter white, middle- and upper-class women from assuming power in the name of all women. Cuban women who called themselves feminists generally came from the privileged classes, and they basically sought power for themselves. They were nonetheless aware of racial and class issues, and they encumbered themselves with the responsibility of speaking for the lower classes. Women of the lower classes organized but rarely under the banner of feminism. This is not to say that female trade unionists, for example, should not be called feminists. Anyone with a program for fair and egalitarian gender relations could claim that label. But while women were labor organizers, strike leaders, heads of opposition groups, and combatants against dictatorship, many refused to give gender issues top priority. I have chosen to examine the activities and identities of women who called themselves feminists and who belonged to feminist organizations.

Deliberately, then, I have chosen to study self-avowed feminists, who specifically adopted the terms *feminismo, feminista,* and *la revolución femenina,* or they advocated *la liberación de la mujer* and *el sufragio feminino.* They belonged to women's organizations whose main purpose was to pursue women's rights and improve their chances for self-determination. As a result, I have ignored many other women who certainly contributed to the struggle for expanded women's rights. I do not pretend to portray feminists as the only people interested in women's rights, but only one of several groups. Women's historians are now showing how complex women's movements were, and Cuban society has never been wanting for complexities. But I could not, on the basis of my evidence, give equal attention to all these groups. Women participants in the student movements, women who led labor guilds, black women who participated momentarily in the Independent Colored Party in 1912—all of these need to be studied to give a fuller view of the vitality and fervor of women during the prerevolutionary period. At best, I have shown how some of the groups influenced and, at times, participated in the feminist movement. I have only done what my sources will bear, which is to describe, in detail, the values and visions of a small group of women and men who were powerful beyond their numbers and who put Cuba well ahead of other nations in its legal regard for women.

I began this study with the intention of explaining how women won so many legal rights within so short a period of time. I ended with that explanation and more. This book is about the mentalité of privileged women within the feminist movement, the values of the men who supported them, and a broad definition of Cuban feminism articulated by this particular group. Mentalité, perhaps the most immeasurable but important motivation behind human action, is that composite of values, beliefs, mores, superstitions, and behaviors that direct a group of people to act. Information about mentalité cannot be gleaned from a particular source or a single methodology. My most reliable sources are texts (speeches, personal letters, journal essays, radio broadcasts, and memoirs from women's congresses) that record in their own words feminists' senses of what they wanted, who they opposed, and how they would act. I also have records of what men believed they were doing when they supported reforms for women. More indirect, anthropological studies discuss Cuban gender values and provide a background for feminist responses. Census data and sociological studies measure the circumstances in which the feminists lived. Thus, this is an interdisciplinary examination of the feminist movement.

Ascertaining a clear, linear definition of Cuban feminism was unfeasible, but describing the complex, often self-contradictory ideals contained in the movement is possible. Women joined the movement to force agendas that often differed from those of their colleagues. Conservative feminists wanted the vote, beautification of Havana, and improved health standards for women and children. Moderates advocated women holding public office and pushed state welfare along with a broad commitment to human rights, good employment for women, and an equitable distribution of wealth. Radicals rejected U.S. domination and advocated an overthrow of the capitalist state and the installation of a socialist system that would treat women and men equally. Factionalization occurred between groups of feminists, but it also existed within the life of a single individual. Ofelia Domínguez Navarro, for example, the leader of the social feminists, changed from a woman willing to imitate the North American model to the harshest critic of U.S. feminism.

To understand Cuban feminism in all its forms, it is important to bear in mind that Cubans have always been able to assimilate dualities such as the sacred and profane (Roman Catholicism and *santería*), *machismo* and *marianismo*, and equality and separateness without the attendant blow to linear logic. These dualities allowed certain advances that have yet to occur in the United States, such as protective labor legislation and an equal rights law. The North American reader should not see these dualisms as a fault in my reasoning or irrational Cuban behavior. Duality simply is a fact of life and certainly a reality for most people. It happens to be overt in Cuba.

Any study of social and political movements in twentieth-century Cuba requires a careful definition of terms. *Feminist* and *feminism, woman's movement, conservative, moderate, reformer, progressive, Marxist, radical,* and *revolutionary* are false cognates in North American English. Feminism in general is an ideology that assumes the importance and centrality of women in their society. It is a movement that intends to claim for women the rights and power due them as members of a community. It is also a reaction to unique cultural and historical circumstances and, therefore, is not monolithic.

Cuban feminists claimed new authority for women, but they did so within their social and historical context. After independence, colonial institutions such as the Catholic Church and authoritarian government became targets for change. Modern state and social formations created new roles for women and raised questions about women's rights. Feminists organized to empower women in an emerging nation, and they took on the role of state builders. They concentrated as much on tearing down Spanish colonial structures as progressing along the same lines as other feminist movements. Patriotic sentiments, still passionate after the wars of independence, reverberated in feminist speeches, and José Martí's calls for social justice prepared feminists and Cuban politicians for a women's movement.

Modern political philosophies informed Cuban feminism, but traditional images became its symbols. Democratic principles initiated demands for the vote. Marxism gave direction to the rights of women workers, and the advent of the welfare state promised protection for poor women. Along with these modern philosophical ideas, feminists evoked the image of the Mother Mary, even as they attacked the Church, and used her attributes of purity and morality to define their cause. Feminists were also slow to identify the patriarchy or a class society as the root of women's oppression.

The term *feminism* was troublesome even for Cubans who defined themselves as feminists, because North Americans, the French, and the English had given it meanings that Cubans could not accept. Some elements in the Cuban movement rejected U.S. leadership in an international suffrage campaign because they viewed it as another instance of U.S. imperialism. Cuban feminism emphasized the importance of motherhood, as did many North Americans, but Cuban feminists demanded a reverence for motherhood and viewed it as the only stepping stone to power. Thus, Cuban feminism was pro women, pro family, pro motherhood, and pro children.

Feminist studies in the United States separate the woman's movement there into at least two political groups: feminists and suffragists. The feminists, characterized by Elizabeth Cady Stanton and the American Women's Suffrage Party and Jane Addams, sought a broad array of women's rights. Motherhood counted as a central focus for these women, as did welfare and work rights. Suffragists, represented by Alice Paul and the National Women's Party, narrowed their demands to the vote. Using the same nomenclature might be less confusing to U.S. scholars, but it blurs the political alliances Cuban feminists and suffragists were making with political parties. Therefore, I have chosen to call all women's activists feminists and group them by their political affiliations, for example, conservative feminists, moderate and progressive feminists, and socialist feminists.

Political terms such as *conservative* and *moderate* had no clear ideological meaning during the formative years of the Republic. Other than the Cuban Communist Party, with its established party line, political organizations espoused few political ideologies, and these organizations were often used by members who selfishly sought power and wealth. Individuals frequently changed from one party to another to enhance their fortunes, and not as an expression of political ideals. Therefore, political terms did not originate in classical meanings.

Some terms must, nonetheless, be used to indicate political positions. Central to most political agendas was the intention to reform Cuba's political structures and address, if not change, issues of racial discrimination and social justice. Conservatism in Cuba would have meant to return to the colonial past, a position that had few advocates. The question of reform was one of the extent to which individuals were willing to change, and not a blockage of change. Most Cubans favored modernization, democratic rule, and a modicum of social reform. Some conservatives wished to retain Catholic values and class and racial divisions. Conservative feminists primarily wanted the vote, though they paid some attention to health, education, and welfare services. Progressive feminists worked to alter aspects of social order and to require the state to take on matters of social welfare and provisions for the poor, but they left in place class structures, prevailing racist practices, and the patriarchy. Progressive feminists believed that democracy was possible in Cuba and that women were in a position to make significant contributions. They criticized the Church, but they did not attack conventions of male domination, and they believed that new laws would insure social reform. Most of the feminists belonged to this group.

Marxist and revolutionary activists advocated the restructuring of Cuban society to allow workers either to own the means of production or take political power to improve their lives. Students, intellectuals, workers, and a faction of the feminist movement belonged to this group. Revolutionary feminists by 1930 opposed suffrage because they believed that it would involve women in corrupt government. They worked to organize women in labor unions and defend dissidents of either gender against imprisonment, exile, and execution. They also supported women's issues before the socialist leadership to ensure that women's labor and maternity concerns were addressed.

Appropriate terminology denoting Cuban class ordering is no less difficult to implement because classifications such as upper, middle, and lower class, as well as elite, bourgeoisie, and proletariat have political connotations and applications that confuse the Cuban situation. That Cuba was a society of hierarchy through the early republic is unquestionable. But Cuba was experiencing tremendous flux and change in the composition of those orders. This transition makes it difficult to label groups without supplying appropriate definitions.

For the sake of simplicity, the terms *lower, middle* and *upper class* are used to designate socioeconomic ordering of Cuban society and the positioning of feminists therein. Most feminists were middle- and upper-class women: they or their families had wealth and position and were from the landholding elite, the professional class, or political families (see chap. 4). Feminists also behaved as middle- or upper-class people, since they expected to be heard and they intended to wield influence. They also educated and cared for the less fortunate. Perhaps the most conclusive indication for the feminists' class affiliation are their own opinions of their position. In speeches to congress and in newspaper and journal articles, feminists referred to themselves as members of the intelligentsia and the middle and upper classes.

Feminists were committed to giving women important functions in Cuba's emerging national order. They recognized women's historical contributions to Cuban society, and they wished to expand those contributions into public duty. Legal reform seemed the best means to ensure women their rights and protection, and a feminist leadership formed to articulate new values and oversee the needs of powerless women. Common ends, however, did not imply a unified movement. Diversity characterized the Cuban feminist movement as moderate, progressive, and social feminists fought old social standards and each other. Aided by their social advantages, feminists of all political persuasions successfully convinced politicians to alter legal codes to accommodate women's needs.

Introduction

᭐

In the two generations following Cuba's independence from Spain, women's rights became part of the Cuban political consciousness. Nationalist sentiments stirred by José Martí's pronouncements for social justice gave all Cubans, including women, hope that liberty, equality, and social justice might extend to them. Between 1902 and 1940 feminist organizations formed and worked to influence the direction of legislative decisions made by politicians, all of whom were men. Feminists held congresses, petitioned politicians, formed coalitions with a variety of men's activist groups, demonstrated in the streets, addressed the public in newspapers and on radio, built childbirth clinics, organized night schools for women, developed women's health programs, and established links with international feminist groups. As a result, by 1940 feminists had helped pass a corpus of legislation that was, in terms of its provisions for women, one of the more progressive in the world.

The Cuban feminist movement emerged during a period marked by controversy and instability. A restive population eager to modernize attacked colonial institutions such as the Catholic Church, Spanish laws, patriarchal privilege, social ordering, and a plantation-centered economy. Nationalists responded to the U.S. occupation and hegemony over the island. U.S. principles of capitalist materialism and individual rights clashed with Spanish notions of corporate privilege and community interdependence. Few agreed about the direction the Cuban government should take, but most Cuban political leaders concurred that modernization implied public education, some individual freedoms, elections, and attention to social reform. To those ends, they set about altering Spanish law. But elected officials were corrupt and weak, which cast doubt on whether laws had meaningful jurisdiction. By 1910, when political leaders had proved themselves unable or unwilling to bring honest democratic government to Cuba, students, workers, and women took to the streets to demand reform, and discord and violence became a means of conducting politics.

In this atmosphere of violence feminists began to present their demands to Cuba's political leaders and the people. Political instability in the 1920s and 1930s might have discouraged a more timid group, but in this case the chaos enhanced rather than inhibited their efforts. Disorder meant that no faction held control and feminists could act as effective power brokers during periods of instability. The majority of feminists were political reformers whose demands required legal changes but not economic and political restructuring that was being urged by radical students and workers. In a time of irresolution, politicians enacted reforms to amass a following and demonstrate their reformist intentions. Feminists both led and followed. They produced a political agenda, and they supported those officials who honored their demands. As a result, feminists attained more legal rights for women than they otherwise might have won.

Feminist leaders were privileged women, comfortable with their social and political advantages. By concentrating on legal reform as a means of correcting social inequities, they interacted with politicians in the name of marginalized women. Their personal resources went toward building health and educational institutions for poor women and children, and their purpose was to ensure that the state establish health, education, and welfare agencies. They believed that democracy was not only workable in Cuba, but that it was the ideal means by which all women could effect social change. Cuban feminists, in fact, viewed themselves as the matriarchs of Cuban society, with a guaranteed position equivalent in importance to that of the men who governed.

Cuban feminists did not directly attack the patriarchy as the source of women's oppression, nor did they wage a serious campaign for women's social equality. Instead, they used their femininity in pursuit of their goals, the most important of which was general recognition that motherhood was women's divine right and that it justified their exercising political authority in nationalist Cuba. In short, they hoped to create a space for women in national and state governments as the overseers of welfare without displacing men who managed business, international relations, and other matters of state. The Spanish adage *El hombre está hecho para la calle y la mujer para la casa* (Men are made for life in the streets, women for life within the home) was unacceptable to feminists who took to the street in protest of their legal disadvantages and brought the home into politics by making women's domain the administration of women's, children's, and family rights.

The feminists' success rested on their boldness and insightfulness, to be sure, but they could not have had the impact they did if Cuba were not undergoing a transition from a colony to a modern state. That period was reformist in nature, but it was a process that brought together in dynamic conflict revolutionary, moderate, and conservative forces. Social militancy, political instability, and revolutionary ideals provided the backdrop for feminist activism. Although the majority of feminists were progressives, preferring evolutionary reform to violent overthrow of government or the dictatorship of a proletariat, they nonetheless took their rhetoric from radical ideals. The connection between Cuban revolutionary ferment and the feminist movement was unmistakable.

The Cuban woman's movement (1902–40) is one of the most ignored phenomena in modern Cuban history. From the first moments of the struggle for independence through the writing of the progressive constitution of 1940, politically aware Cubans recognized women's contributions to national identity and the formulation of nationalist values. Many Cubans who lived in that era remember the feminists and still recall their names and actions. Popular journals and newspapers chronicled their activities and gave them space in regular columns. That the movement has been forgotten is in part due to a common tendency to devalue women's activities. But the loss of information is also due in part to the drama and division over the 1959 Cuban Revolution, which has drawn attention away from the earlier, and more moderate, efforts of a small group of women.

The success of the Cuban Revolution in redefining women's economic and political roles in no way diminishes the earlier movement. The Revolution built on the successes of earlier campaigns, extending to all women the rights that had been accorded to only a few. In the early years feminists identified many injustices in Cuban patriarchal society, but their efforts changed only the law. Cuban women today continue the struggle at the mass level, and they share with their more moderate predecessors a devotion to the concept and the experience of motherhood and a commitment to find power in femininity.

The Cuban feminist movement was dramatic and effective. It contrasted with feminist movements elsewhere because of its roots in national independence, its confrontation with U.S. hegemony, its cultural setting, and the individuals who led the movement. That the law and a public consciousness about women's rights changed rapidly over thiry-eight years caused one Peruvian ambassador to Cuba to describe the feminists as "those amazing women."

This book examines the motivations of the feminists and Cuban lawmakers as they strove to build a new state through legal reform. As such, it reconstructs and interprets the mentalité of the ruling elite during the formative years of the Cuban republic in order to explain why so many reforms occurred so quickly and to define the terms and actions the protagonists used to accomplish their goals.

Breaking the Mold

Each generation bequeaths its descendants values and habits to accept or reject. The women who fought in the Cuban Wars of Independence presented their daughters with examples of heroism, durability, integrity, ingenuity, self-sacrifice, and combativeness during the campaigns against Spanish rule. The *mambisas* forged a new model for middle- and upper-class women of the twentieth century by breaking the mold of prescribed behavior for proper Cuban ladies who before 1868 were uneducated and dependent upon men. Mambisas, while remaining wives and mothers, left the protection of their homes, went into the *manigua,* and took up arms in support of national sovereignty.[1] The protracted guerrilla wars increased the difficulties of daily existence that women could not escape. Engulfed in the struggle to survive, women of all classes expanded their capabilities to include nursing, gunrunning, supplying provisions, fund raising, publishing, and fighting. Their war efforts proved to men and, more importantly, to the women themselves, their worthiness as full citizens in independent Cuba.

The actions of the mambisas contrasted sharply with the activities of proper Cuban ladies who lived only two decades before.[2] Social prescription for the highly bred in 1848 held that women were most desirable when weak, beautiful, and submissive. Men were their tutors in every matter save domestic work. If women received any education at all, it was in Church catechism to enhance their virtues as mothers. Men feared that women uninstructed in religious fundamentals risked becoming perverted, frivolous, and gossips. They might even fall into the disagreeable habit of reading "adventurous love stories" that would give them the illusion that love could possibly offer pleasure or enchantment. Such an illusion might lead them away from the brutal reality that marriage "was the painful job of having children."[3] Women's education was based upon the principles that they should not use their intellects and that their place was having children and doing domestic work in the home.

Escaping the confinement of marriage was impossible for women and men. The family was the social base that united a people and preserved class and familial authority. It bound men to men through extended family ties. Society functioned according to power linkages between family groups, and each group succeeded or failed according to its ability to control wealth and to protect family and friends under the direction of the patriarch. Conversely, the family-based society was closed to interlopers or newcomers seeking power and wealth.

Marriage, ideally, was a panacea for all that was bad in society. It was a paradise for parents and children. It liberated women from working for a living as domestic servants, street vendors, or prostitutes. Parenthood increased social sympathy. Every member of society worked to enhance the well-being of the family. The husband and head of household, under the *patria potestad,* was the sole administrator of wealth and family relations. The husband and wife helped one another in time of need.[4] Children were guaranteed protection, shelter, food, and sustenance. They also inherited what estate there might be. As adults, the children insured their aging parents against want, hunger, and loneliness. Theoretically, then, society progressed according to family economies and within family units and not according to a government's economic strategies.

Within marriage and parenthood, women were inferior to men. Women were mothers and expected to be generous, tender, merciful, soft, timid, and compassionate. Their only acceptable public function was to help children and disadvantaged women through Catholic charity organizations where the Church could oversee their work.

Many privileged women strove to be exemplary wives and mothers, though not always of their own volition. Their behavior was prescribed by Church teaching, social custom, and man-made laws. Religion and education reinforced their family orientation, while the penal code allowed husbands to kill unfaithful wives with impunity.[5] Just as Cuban society under Spanish domination was subject to violent suppression for social and political restlessness, women were subject to violent repression for challenging their subordination to men.

Women outside the privileged classes suffered under the same principles of subordination but lacked the protection that money and power provided. For many women, poverty meant arduous work and living on the verge of starvation. The sanctity of marriage and men's protection eluded many because poor men could not maintain their families. Racial and class distinctions placed an inferior value on black, mulatto, and poor women's lives. While the Catholic Church attempted to impose moral behavior on all women regardless of race and class, social custom—namely, concubinage and unsanctioned unions—determined that many poor women of any race would be unwed mothers and workers outside

Mercedes de Santa
Cruz y Montalvo, con-
sidered to be Cuba's
first feminist writer.
Taken from *La mujer,*
May 31, 1930. The
Stoner Collection,
Roll 7.

the home.[6] For these women, marriage, religion, notions of the "bello
sexo," the arts, charity, tenderness, and deference to men had no place.

Some privileged women ignored prescribed behavior and became
recognized intellectuals before the end of the century.[7] The better
authors, however, spent much of their lives in Europe. One of Cuba's
protofeminists, Mercedes Santa Cruz de Montalvo (La Condesa de
Merlin), resided in France through the greater part of her life, having left
Cuba at the age of twelve. Her writing reflects her womanly sentiments
and Cuban roots. Perhaps in response to Descartes' enlightened phrase
"I think, therefore I am," she said, "I think because I feel, and I write
because I think. Herein lies my art." The Condesa's greatest contribution
was her unbridled sentiment and her unapologetic respect for a feminine
perspective.

The Condesa wrote prose about Cuba and her life. In 1833 she
published in Paris *Mis doce primeros años,* which was about her early
childhood in Cuba. Later she wrote *Sor Inés o Santa Rosa,* which was
published along with *Mis doce primeros años* as *Memorias de una criolla.*
In 1833 she published in two volumes *Ocios de una mujer de gran*

Marta Abreu, a
wealthy benefactress
who built public
works, hospitals, and
schools in Santa Clara.
Taken from *La mujer
cubana*, p. 28.
The Stoner Collection,
Roll 1.

mundo o Lola y María, Marquis de Foudras, a book that she claimed was essential reading for any woman who aspired to excellence in any given field. Her greatest work, *La esclavitud en Cuba,* was written in 1849. After her return to Cuba in 1851, the Condesa published in Paris three volumes about Cuba entitled *Viaje a la Habana.*

Gertrudis Gómez de Avellaneda, Cuba's greatest nineteenth-century writer, wrote on a broad range of topics, most notably on slavery, independence, and the alienation of modernization. Born in Camagüey in 1814, La Avellaneda suffered the loss of her father at an early age and rejection by her first fiancé. Disillusioned with life, she emigrated to Spain where she continued to write novels, poetry, heroic legends, and plays. Her literature rarely reflected the frustrations of a woman intellectual, which for her must have been significant. She was denied a chair in the Spanish Royal Academy because she was a woman.

Upon returning to Cuba in 1859, La Avellaneda edited a woman's journal, *Album Cubano de lo bueno y lo bello* (1859–64), that encouraged women to enter the arts. She contradicted popular assumptions about woman's intellectual and spiritual weakness by using contemporary beliefs about women's moral superiority and sentimentality. She argued that women were superior to men in every way. Because women could reason and feel, and men could only reason, women were better able to lead than men. Women, she insisted, produced a higher percentage of memorable leaders from all female leaders than men did. She believed that women possessed capable intellects, and she resented their exlusion from advanced education and learned societies.

La Avellaneda's attention to gender issues comprised a minor fraction of her literature, and her approach to the topic was indirect and cautious. She sometimes wrote pieces that confirmed women's weaknesses and fragility. La Avellaneda's message to women was contradictory. La Avellaneda challenged male domination of the arts and the Spanish Royal Academy by the very act of writing well and she urged women to do the same. But she warned against competition between women and men based on her perception of women's feminine weakness.[8]

Prescribed behavior notwithstanding, elite creole women were among the first to oppose Spanish rule publicly. In 1807, in response to the capture of Carlos IV and Ferdinand VII by Napoléon Bonaparte and fearing republican unrest, the Spanish government in Havana cracked down on Cuban stirrings for economic and social freedoms. Some Cuban women exhibited their commitment to republican ideals and their outrage at repression by cutting their hair short to distinguish themselves from the Spanish contemporaries.[9] Several decades later, during the filibustering campaigns of Narciso López, Marina Manresa was executed for conspiring to receive rebel troops in Camagüey. Pepilla Arango hid patriots on her ranch. Rita Balben was active in a plot against her own husband. Both Arango and Balben were exiled.

Gaining political independence from Spain was an arduous struggle spanning three decades from 1868 to 1898. Its toll, both in terms of lives lost and economic dislocation, was staggering. In the years preceding 1868 and following 1898, Cuba's population increased steadily. In 1861, before the outbreak of rebellion, the annual growth rate was 0.9 percent. In 1877, the last year of the Ten Years War, population growth had diminished to 0.3 percent. In 1887, after nine years of peace, the growth rate increased to 0.8 percent, but, after the final war in 1899, the population had decreased to a negative 0.25 percent. In the last year of that war (1897–98) starvation and disease killed one out of four Cubans, women as well as men (see table 1). The strain of military conflict and repressive political tactics changed the lives and personal expectations of

Table 1   Total Population Growth, 1774–1931

Year	Population	Annual Rate of Change
1774	171,620	—
1792	272,300	1.72
1817	572,363	1.36
1827	704,487	2.40
1841	1,007,624	2.07
1861	1,396,530	0.90
1877	1,509,291	0.31
1887	1,631,687	0.80
1899	1,572,797	−0.25
1907	2,048,980	4.88
1919	2,889,004	2.75
1931	3,962,344	2.58

Source: Calculated from Commission on Cuban Affairs, *Problems of the New Cuba* (New York: Foreign Policy Association, 1935), 25.

all Cubans, but in particular it altered women's expectations of themselves.

Cuba's first call to independence in 1868 required general public support and a sense of nationalism.[10] The Ten Years War, though drawing on forces from all social and economic strata, was led by members of the creole class interested in eliminating Spain's restrictive trade measures and establishing self-rule. Their strategy was to defeat the Spanish with a guerrilla army. Insurgent forces could not win set piece clashes against the superior arms and training of Spanish troops. Thus, the first military encounter at Bayamo characterized the Ten Years War, when it pitted Spanish cavalry and infantry with muskets and cannons against untrained campesinos with machetes. The Spaniards, who had themselves fought guerrilla campaigns against Joseph Bonaparte between 1807 and 1814 and rebellions in their north African colonies, knew exactly how to contain such an effort. By 1870 they had burned and destroyed the land and plantations where the insurgents operated with the intentions of starving them out of the *manigua* and forcing them to surrender.

By destroying civilian homes and farmland, the Spanish forced women and children out of their safe positions away from war fronts. In the first call to the machete, some mambisas went to the manigua to fight alongside their husbands and fathers. Whether in villages or with the

Cuban colonos being moved off their land so that the land would be rendered unproductive for the Cuban guerrilla army. Drawing by Frederic Remington, in Richard Harding Davis, *Cuba in War Time* (New York: R. H. Russell, 1898), p. 21.

army, women also served behind the lines as nurses, correspondents, spies, contraband arms traders, manufacturers of provisions, writers, and examples to men of the sacrifice that all would make for independence.

James O'Kelly, a *New York Herald* reporter writing from Cuba in 1871, described how the mambises carried out their war against the Spanish and how the Spaniards' retaliation affected patriot women. O'Kelly quoted Carlos Manuel Céspedes, the president of *Cuba Libre,* when he described the Spanish proclamation of the terms of war:

> In the beginning we acted with too much generosity, setting at liberty the Spanish prisoners, even after the proclamation of the Spanish government announcing that all taken in arms would be shot, and that even the women captured in the insurgent districts would be subject to ten years' imprisonment or deportation to Fernando Po (one of Spain's political prisons in Africa). Several times I have made efforts to induce the Spanish government to carry on the war in a civilized manner, but without results.[11]

The mother/patriot symbolized Cuban sacrifice and endurance. Separatist women taught their children the value of national independence.

Pictures published in magazines of the day displayed strong, beautiful young mothers pointing the way for young men and children who clung to their dresses. Mariana Grajales, the mother of ten fierce patriot soldiers, one of whom was Antonio Maceo, became the legendary model of motherhood and patriotism. She and her sons fought in the Ten Years War, the Little War (1879), and the War of 1895, and she became a part of Cuba's pantheon of war heroes. José Martí called her *La Leona*. She taught her sons how to use the machete, and she instilled in them dreams of a sovereign Cuba devoid of slavery. With all but her youngest son at the front, she received news of the oldest's, Miguel's, death. Reportedly she turned to the youngest and said, "Y tú, muchacho, empíñate, que ya es la hora de que pelees por tu patria" (And you, son, stand tall, for the time has come for you to fight for your country).

Mariana Grajales also joined the men on the front. Together with Antonio Maceo's wife, María Cabrales, she helped nurse the wounded and feed the troops. These two women won the admiration of José Martí when he observed them entering the battlefield to rescue the wounded Antonio with only the gunfire of José Maceo to cover their retreat. They inspired his epic remark: "Fáciles son los héroes con tales mujeres" (It is easy to be heroes with women such as these).

The mambises expected no mercy from the Spanish. To reduce the number of rebels killed and maintain confidence within the ranks, they promised to carry away their wounded to hospitals scattered throughout the manigua and staffed by women. The patriots bound themselves together in expressed solidarity through "El Silencio," a secret society that pledged never to abandon a soldier and to rescue their wounded, even if it meant passing behind enemy lines.[12] The hospitals became a popular target for the Spanish forces, because they could find weakened soldiers and women and children whom they could eliminate with little effort. O'Kelly wrote about the mambises:

> The Mambis have maintained a struggle as glorious as the Suliote or Cretan wars against the Turk, and in all history there are no more gallant struggles than these, but modern society is such a sham that it can see nothing great in the struggle of a weak people holding out against fearful odds; sacrificing fortune, family, and life; perishing by sabrestroke, and bullet, and disease; seeing their wives and children hunted like beasts of the forest, sinking with fatigue and hunger, dying miserably in the savage woods; and amid all their suffering and desolation remaining unshaken in their resolve to conquer or to die. Yet all human history cannot furnish a greater example of heroic purpose. Thermopylae was not but the passing effort of an hour, whereas the heroism of the Cubans has been constant, and displayed in a hundred fields.[13]

Mariana Grajales, the
mother of Antonio Maceo
and a symbol of the Cuban
independence struggle.
Taken from *La mujer cu-
bana,* p. 11. The Stoner Collection, Roll 1.

Some nationalist women used their influence as writers to spark nationalist sentiments. They exhorted Cubans to take up arms, and they wrote
poetry and patriotic songs for the independence cause. Sofía Estevez
urged her compatriots to defeat the Spanish in the following verse:

> But now is the time that Cubans
> Rise up against the executioner
> And lay aside fearlessly the yoke
> That he placed upon their hands.
> Curse his inclemency,
> We wish death to his existence,
> We offer up our prayer to God,
> Let Cuba become free,
> And long live her independence![14]

Besides being conspirators, combatants, and inspirational writers,
women also created homes for the soldiers. They moved into the
manigua where they continued family life despite the complications of
war. Living in the manigua meant belonging to a community of a few
families and inhabiting a cluster of *bohíos* (peasant houses), in mountains
where the difficult terrain discouraged attacks from Spanish forces.[15]
Under these circumstances, women contributed to the liberation effort

by making hammocks, nursing the wounded, growing and foraging for food, fighting and spying, and supplying emotional support for the independence effort. According to O'Kelly, all the rebels were poorly, but not miserably, dressed. Yet, even in poverty, the mambisas did not lose their eye for feminine style. They would don a ribbon or a kerchief that accented a coquetishness which even their rude surroundings could not suppress.[16]

In the manigua men and women shared the struggle to survive and developed new family arrangements. Men hunted game, dug tubers, and cut cane. Women made clothing, cooked, washed, and cared for the children. There was no concept of community property. Each person was the owner of her/his possessions, and each person distributed the fruits of labor as circumstances warranted. This arrangement generated a respect for private property, regardless of the owner's gender, and challenged the old concept of the father's authority over family property.[17] Women's right to control their own property without a prenuptial agreement was established first in the manigua. After independence, as Cubans rewrote laws, women's control over property became law in 1917.

Although certain notions of equality evolved in the manigua and Cuban men respected women for their sacrifices, some mambisas were aware of their inferior social status. Ana Betancourt de Mora, patriot and member of a landholding family, spoke of women's rights on April 10, 1869, at the Constitutional Congress at Guáimaro. The rebels were in the process of writing the *Bases de la revolución* to select their governing body and outline the principles of self-rule. Ana Betancourt substituted for her ailing husband and addressed the Congress in a short, dramatic speech. Cuban independence, Betancourt argued, meant the rejection of slavery and racial discrimination and the overthrow of Spanish rule. But she demanded more. Betancourt exhorted the Assembly to examine the problem of women's subjugation:

> Citizens: The Cuban woman, from the dark and tranquil corner of her home, has waited patiently and with resignation for this sublime hour in which a just revolution will break her yoke, will untie her wings. Everyone has been enslaved in Cuba: families, people of color, and women. You will fight to the death if necessary to destroy racial slavery. Racial slavery no longer exists. You have emancipated men of servitude. When the moment arrives to liberate women, Cuban men, who were subjugated in familial and racial slavery, will also dedicate their generous souls to women's rights. For women, who today and in wartime are their sisters of charity even while they are denied their rights, will tomorrow be men's exemplary companions.[18]

Ana Betancourt, the
first woman to speak
out for women's eman-
cipation in the 1869
Constitutional Con-
gress. Taken from *La
mujer cubana,* p. 20.
The Stoner Collection,
Roll 1.

Despite Ana Betancourt's courageous speech, the Assembly did not consider women's rights in the *Bases de la revolución.* Though representatives at the congress spoke well of women's heroic deeds, the notion of full constitutional rights to women was unprecedented. The rebel government directed its efforts toward establishing national sovereignty with limited democratic participation. From the representatives' perspective, women were adequately represented through the legal power of men. Patriots believed, moreover, that women had redefined their social positions by disproving that they were frail and incompetent.

While men consigned women to secondary civil status, women continued to prove themselves men's equals in the independence struggle. The Spanish punished women for their cooperation with insurgent forces with exile, incarceration, or execution. Cubans began referring to their struggle as the "War of Women" and the "Family Wars" precisely because of the sacrifice women made.

Expatriate women continued to wage war against Spain by organiz-

Club "Discípulas de Martí," a revolutionary club in Tampa. Taken from J. J. E. Casasus, *La emigración cubana*, p. 269.

ing nationalist clubs, writing and publicizing in favor of independence, and collecting funds. During the Ten Years War, Emilia Casanova de Villaverde founded the Liga de las Hijas de Cuba in New York. In New Orleans the Hijas del Pueblo was formed, and in Havana the Comité Central de Señoras had to meet secretly. Their work was to raise funds for the insurgent army and expose Spain's war tactics to critical world powers such as the United States.

The Ten Years War ended without victory for either side. Unacceptable terms in the Zanjón Pact provoked the Little War (1879–80), and more women's revolutionary clubs formed. One club in particular, the Hijas de le Libertad, had chapters in Key West and cities in Cuba.

The War of 1895 could not have been successful without the proliferation of women's revolutionary clubs and their absorption into the Cuban Revolutionary Party (PRC)—the umbrella revolutionary organization created by José Martí. By 1897 forty-nine women's revolutionary clubs had joined the PRC and comprised 25 percent of all revolutionary clubs.[19] Women represented 37 percent of the delegates to the PRC by 1898 and formed a membership of about 1,500.[20] Other women organized clubs independent of the PRC that worked for Cuban sovereignty. There were also men's and women's clubs.

Club José Martí, founded in 1895 to support the patriot cause against Spain.
Taken from Partido Comunista de Cuba, *La mujer cubana en cien años de lucha, 1868–1968* (Havana: n.p.), p. 28. The Stoner Collection, Roll 1. Apparently
this photograph is held by the Bacardi Museum in Santiago de Cuba.

Women's revolutionary clubs set precedents for future generations of
Cubans. Although the clubs were represented at PRC meetings by men
chosen by the female membership, women initiated their own programs
and voted on policy and leadership. Electoral experience prompted the
women in the Club Hijas de la Libertad to ask the PRC to allow women to
elect female representatives to that body. The Key West branch of the
PRC did not rule on the matter, citing insufficient authority as its
reason.[21]

Women were also combatants during the Wars of Independence.
Heroines of the Ten Years War entered the conflict not as individuals
fighting for women's rights but as wives, mothers, sisters, and daugh-

Bernarda Toro (Manana), the wife of Máximo Gómez and the mother of Panchito Gómez. Taken from *La mujer cubana*, p. 11. The Stoner Collection, Roll 1.

ters who joined the men in their families in the war effort. Their sacrifice and bravery inspired men to endure hardship and continue a war costly in human lives and property lost. Legends about the better-known mambisas have become part of the Cuban national identity, and they symbolized the efforts of nameless heroines who fought. Mariana Grajales and María Magdalena Cabrales Isaac, the mother and wife of General Antonio Maceo, fought all three wars with the general. Bernardo Toro, the wife of General Máximo Gómez and mother of Panchito Gómez Toro, worked with revolutionary clubs abroad to support the war effort.

Dominga Moncada, the mother of Guillermon Moncada, was the object of Spanish aggression for her own contributions to rebel insurrection. Dominga Moncada was a child of free Blacks who learned midwifery at an early age. She lived in free union with a Spanish businessman and had one daughter by him, though he refused to give the daughter his name. Moncada sustained herself and her children (she had two sons by a previous association) as a midwife and, like Mariana Grajales, taught her sons to fight for independence.

Moncada was fifty-eight years old when the Ten Years War began, and she volunteered to serve as a nurse. She also brought mail to the troops encamped around her farm. In 1871 the Spanish arrested her for seditious activities and took her to the Morro Castle in Santiago de Cuba. While she was imprisoned, the Spanish tried to exchange her for her son Guillermon, who was an important rebel leader in Oriente, but she refused to allow the trade to take place.

Moncada's heroism did not end then. During the Little War the Spanish government looked for ways to expel insurrectionists. It exiled major leaders and their families, guaranteeing them safe passage on British frigates. Filled with exiles and one day from shore, the *Thomas Brooks* was overtaken by a Spanish gunship, *El Bazan*. The Spanish captain commandeered the Cuban refugees, ignoring their documents guaranteeing safe passage. The men were taken to prisons in Africa and Spain, and their families were put ashore at Santiago de Cuba. The Spanish made an exception, however, for Dominga Moncada's family. She, three younger women, and children under the age of eleven were set adrift in a rowboat somewhere between Jamaica and Cuba. They had to find their way to safety on Cuba's southern shore. Moncada, then seventy, did most of the rowing. When the small group landed near Santiago de Cuba, they were captured by a Spanish marine detachment and taken to Morro Castle in Santiago. At the prison Moncada convinced the Spanish authorities to release the other women and the children and imprison her, since she was known to Spanish authorities as a revolutionary and the others were not. In Santiago's Morro Castle she nursed her son, who had contracted tuberculosis, until his death. She lived to see Cuban independence and died in 1905 at the age of ninety-five.[22]

Women's involvement in the Ten Years War became a symbol of Cuban sacrifice and heroism. Men believed that women's suffering was worse than their own because women were unaccustomed to guerrilla warfare and exposure to hardships outside their homes. Stories of women's tribulations focused on the tragedy of losing children to war, the life-threatening experience of giving birth in the manigua, and the panic of running before Spanish troops through the countryside clutching their children and not knowing where their men were. The image also included women who fought with guns, served as spies, and smuggled arms, and in the end died like men. Death was the ultimate sacrifice and the highest symbol of Cuban patriotism.

The Ten Years War ended in 1878 in a stalemate. The Pact of Zanjón, which was signed by Spanish representatives and Cuban Autonomists, provided for Cuban deputies in the Spanish court and a timetable for the emancipation of slaves. Almost immediately, Cubans criticized the treaty because it did not give them the autonomy they had sought. Patriots were disillusioned with the curtailment of self-rule and refused to vote in the local elections of 1879. Cuban grievances erupted into armed conflict again in 1879 when Major General Calixto García Iñiguez led a short-lived rebellion known as the Little War. The rebel defeat in 1880 convinced Cubans that only a full-scale revolution would liberate them from Spain, yet the rebels quarreled over the objectives of a newly independent nation. They were, moreover, exhausted and scattered in exile.

The rebel cause lay dormant until the dispersed patriots unified under José Martí. Martí called Cubans to arms in the Montecristi Manifesto in 1895. He appealed to Cubans as revolutionaries who would accept nothing less than complete independence from Spain and formed the Cuban Revolutionary Party as a multiclass patriotic front. The broad-based party joined old landholders with tobacco workers and agricultural laborers. José Martí promised a Cuba Libre that would advance beyond any current examples of social justice. Cuba would be for Cubans, and Cubans, he insisted, were obliged to rectify the evils of slavery, institutions of domination, excesses of power, abuses of religion, and effects of racism. Martí raised Cuban expectations and dreams of noble sovereignty and warned his compatriots to resist U.S. dominance.

Under these revolutionary precepts, Cubans again gathered for war. This time, however, the patriots were imbued with ideals and purposes that transcended creole interests. Every Cuban envisioned a socially just nation, and men and women again committed themselves to the end of Spanish rule. On February 24, 1895, with the "Grito de Baire," separatists rose up in arms, and revolutionary forces returned to the manigua for the final struggle.

The mambisas fought as they had in the Ten Years War—as patriotic wives and mothers who supported their husbands' cause and who urged their sons to fight for Cuba Libre. But they also undertook new roles. Some assumed a new stance as protagonists in the independence cause without the leadership of men in their families. They responded to Martí's calls for patriotic sacrifice and commitment to social justice. Scores of women enrolled in the Liberation Army. Many served as soldiers and achieved commissioned status. An estimated twenty-five women held officer rank, including one general, three colonels, and more than twenty captains.[23] They continued as conspirators, messengers, fund-raisers, nurses, and writers as well as cooks and seamstresses. Their activities were broader and more militant after 1895 than during the Ten

Years War. The mambisas moved into the masculine sphere of military affairs and won men's respect for their efforts.

José Martí did not emphasize women's positions in the new society, nor did he indict social injustices affecting women with the same vehemence as he did the evils of racism, slavery, and the dangers of North American imperialism. He did acknowledge women's contributions to independence, however, by making them symbols of national sovereignty. His most passionate poems about independence and women portrayed women as mothers.

Martí's images of women idealized the woman/mother and the woman/revolutionary, and he formed links between the two roles. Mothers who sent their sons into battle symbolized the firm commitment Cubans had to independence, and the old woman, the mother who had seen her husband and sons die and who remained faithful to Cuba Libre, assured Cubans that they would triumph:

> the old woman still wears next to her heart the badge that glistened on Ignacio Agramonte's hat, a badge that had seen a lot of use. The brave Cuban woman had offered him the embroidery of her own hands, the courteous hero helped her dismount and he tore off his hat the symbol that faithful old woman has kept. Everywhere, with their simple mantillas and their lovely gray hair these old women who do not tire of us, these mothers who created the sons who opened the road where the merciful grass covers the graves of their parents, these widows with a firm step who do the chores in the house of the exiled, with the medal of their dead husbands on their breasts, who follow the flag for which he died. These women who in their amber boxes keep the insignia that defied the bullets of the enemy so many times. How can men tire when women are tireless?[24]

Women produced the patriots and they taught heroism and nationalist dedication. They stood for human justice rooted in women's natural instinct to create and preserve life. They represented dignity and fidelity to the patriotic cause, and they legitimized nationalist insurgency.

As the rebel cause gathered force, the Spanish assigned General Valeriano Weyler to put down the insurrection. Having been trained in Spain's colonial wars in northern Africa, Weyler was known for his cruel efficiency in suppressing insurgents. His only hope for defeating the Cuban popular uprising was to punish those who sided indirectly or directly with the rebels. He emulated his predecessors in destroying the countryside, only Weyler was more thorough. General Weyler torched farmlands and drove the rural population into concentration camps. The Spanish troops oversaw the genocide of Cuban civilians, who died of starvation and disease by the thousands.

This tactic roused those who had not been moved by José Martí. The old mambisas and their younger sisters willingly fought because, under Spanish rule, their lives were as meaningless as their deaths. Dying in battle was certainly more noble than starving to death in concentration camps. Examples of heroism now included a significant number of women soldiers.

Magdalena Penarredonda y Doley, called La Delegada, fought through all the wars of independence and rose to the rank of general. Born in 1846 to a Spanish father and French mother, she had to choose between enlightened thought on the rights of man taught by her mother and the familiar ruling order of the Spanish that her father represented. As a child, Magdalena sided with the mambises. At the age of five she freed a rebel arrested by her father. When she was a teenager, she cut her hair as an expression of solidarity with women in Camagüey who were protesting Spanish rule. Her father incarcerated her and her sisters until their hair grew long again.

Her brothers also supported the mambises. They informed Cubans of Spanish battle plans, information they obtained in their father's home. The assassination of one of Magdalena's brothers for his nationalist activities underscored the tragedy of the family's divided allegiances, and she could not forget the conditions of her brother's death. During the Ten Years War she served as a delegate of the New York Revolutionary Club in Pinar del Río. By 1893 she became more deeply involved in conspiracy and in publishing for the independence cause. That year she wrote about her brother's death to inspire Cubans to act against Spanish repression. As a result, Magdalena had to flee to New York, where she met José Martí and joined the Cuban Revolutionary Party. Her exile lasted only a few months, and Magdalena returned to Cuba with renewed zeal. She continued to make trips to New York to do party work, and she remained in contact with Martí.

When the War of 1895 began, La Delegada, as she was then called, doubled her efforts to aid the rebel cause. She secretly collaborated with Antonio Maceo's and Máximo Gómez's military actions in Pinar del Río. She knew the terrain, and her connections with Spaniards gave her access to sensitive information on military movements. In 1896 she was identified as a traitor, and she went to jail in the Casa de las Recogidas in Havana. There she loudly protested the conditions of the jail, and the prison warden had to remind her that she was a prisoner, not a member of the court. She became the leader of the prisoners, both criminal and political, and they began to insist on humane treatment. She was released from prison only after the rebels defeated the Spanish in 1898.[25]

Paulina Ruiz, a flag bearer
and fighter during the War
of 1895. Taken from Grover
Flint, *Marching with Gomez*
(Boston: Lamson Wolffe,
1898), p. 86. Illustration by
author and signature is
Ruiz's.

Blacks and Whites fought side by side during the War of 1895, and
women of both races distinguished themselves and their country
through their war efforts. Maria Hidalgo Santana, a poor black woman
from Matanzas, presented herself before rebel Brigadier General José
Lacret Morlot and asked for a position among his troops. The surprised
general agreed, even though she carried no gun. In the Battle of Jicarita,
near the town of Bolondron, the flag bearer was shot dead. Maria
Hidalgo Santana rushed forward to carry the flag at the head of the
attacking infantry where the fighting was heaviest. The rebel forces won

the battle. As the troops regrouped, she fell from her horse and was unconscious; she had been shot seven times. As it turned out, the bullet wounds were not fatal, and she survived to fight in eight major battles. She was known as the Flag Bearer and the Heroine of Jicarita, and was elevated to the rank of captain. She died fighting in the battle of Vieja Bermeja.[26]

The three-year campaign shaped Cuban ideals and established a pantheon of heroes and martyrs. Women had established their place among the independence heroes. A letter in 1897 written by General Federico Cavada, a member of the Revolutionary Army, reflects the male leadership's respect for the mambisa.

> I do not know if these disturbing reports about Cuba are sad or kind. They are sad because they report the patriots' crude suffering. They are kind because they record for history the heroism and denial that Cubans have had to endure in order to be free.
>
> Our women in particular merit applause and sympathy from every sensitive and generous heart. Hidden in the darkness of the forest, suffering hunger, naked and ill, exposed to the brutal rage of inhuman fighting that pursued them incessantly and that mistreated them mercilessly, or better said, fleeing disheveled and emaciated, dragging with them their little children through the dung heaps and cane fields, they suffered, they wept, and they begged for the liberty of Cuba. With some reason someone has called this the war of women!
>
> Something is taking place right now in the House of Representatives in the United States about the emancipation of women and about raising their social position to the same level as men's social position. In Cuba, women no longer need the intervention of men in the same sense. They have known how to equal men in their heroism and suffering. In the Cuban insurrection they have emancipated themselves, not from the tender and beautiful attributes of their sex, but from the slander that encouraged men to think vainly of themselves as heroic and of women as cowardly.[27]

But words such as these did not satisfy some of the mambisas, who preferred legal reform to flowery praise. During the final years of the war Edelmira Guerra de Dauval, a founder and later president of the Club Esperanza del Valle, helped formulate the revolutionary manifesto on March 19, 1897. Article 4 demanded equal rights for women, including limited suffrage:

> We want women to be able to exercise their natural rights through issuance of the vote for single or widowed women over the age of twenty-five, divorce for just cause, and the option for public employment in accordance with physiological and social laws.[28]

The War of 1895 ended in 1898 with the defeat of Spain by united U.S. and Cuban military forces. Cuba's sovereignty was in question until the signing of the Treaty of Paris, an agreement made between the United States and Spain and not involving any direct negotiations with Cubans. Unlike Guam, the Philippines, and Puerto Rico, which became protectorates of the United States, Cuba was promised sovereignty after achieving political and economic stability. In 1902, after Cuban delegates to a constitutional assembly signed the 1901 Constitution that made Cuba subject to U.S. intervention, U.S. troops withdrew.

Immediately, Cubans set about questioning the extent to which they were sovereign and putting an end to colonial structures of rule. Legal changes became the focus of attention both because it was appropriate to modernize laws and also because the law was one of the few areas of statecraft the Cubans could control. As a result, legal changes were directed at dismantling Spain's rules of governance but not at obstructing U.S. hegemonic power. Indeed, attempts were made in some areas of civil law to draw Cuba into line with North American standards. Proclivities to change the law and to consider women's rights because other modern nations were doing it influenced Cuban legislators and gave an emerging women's movement hope that it could win rights for women during the formative years of the republic.

Women's groups responded to the conditions of the constitution and women's legal status within the new republic in a variety of ways. Members of the Club Esperanza del Valle, for instance, publicly protested the 1901 Constitution because it ignored women's rights and because it included the hated Platt Amendment. For the most part, however, the female independence fighters returned to their homes, leaving their wartime contributions to legend. But the legend that recognized the mambisa as a warrior, a quick and wily contrabandista, a mother patriot, the moral center of national sovereignty, a loyal family member in the worst of circumstances, and a revolutionary spokesperson created a model for women in nationalist Cuba that would claim the rights for which the mambisas had died.

Statecraft and Women's Rights,
1902–1918

ᛦ

From the destruction of the colony in war, patriotic Cubans hoped to construct a nation in peace. Between 1902 and 1918, democratic principles, the separation of Church and state, secularized education, economic modernization, and Cuban nationalism seemed attainable. At the outset, mambisa war efforts dignified national independence and symbolized hope. But when legislators altered laws to conform to patriotic ideals, they rarely considered women's rights. Indeed, women's issues were little understood and peripheral to constructing a modern state. Nevertheless, dramatic reforms such as free public education, labor legislation, property rights, and no-fault divorce were passed by 1918 without much pressure from women.

Men changing these laws were concerned with matters of statehood and determining ruling order. They needed to exert their authority to provide stability. This was an era of transition from colony to modern nation, from patriarchy to calls for equality, and from nationalism to the adoption of foreign values. Lawmakers were not feminists, yet in their efforts to progress into the modern world of nations they passed laws that benefited women.

After four years of occupation the U.S. government agreed to withdraw troops only if the Cuban leadership accepted a copy of the U.S. Constitution as its charter and adopted the Platt Amendment, which granted the United States proprietorship over the island. In 1901 the Cuban constitution offered women few, if any, advantages over what they had as Spanish subjects. The mambisas did not passively accept the U.S.-imposed terms of Cuban sovereignty. In a March 1901 protest against that document, women participated in a demonstration in Havana, carrying flags and placards and bringing their children dressed as independence soldiers to remind Cuban officials that Cuban sovereignty had been won through Cuban, not U.S., efforts.[1]

In 1902, after a reluctant Cuban constitutional assembly accepted the constitution, the new leadership was faced with an unwieldy legal system with widely divergent canon. The new constitution declared that all citizens were created equal, but Spanish civil and penal codes rested upon the careful delineation of social roles and a graduated scale of political authority. Both systems were patriarchal, since neither allowed women political authority and both assumed varying degrees of men's legal authority over women. The elision of the two systems—one entirely foreign and the other familiar but anachronistic—confused legal procedures.

Education and Work Laws

An important order of business for Cuban leaders was educating a population capable of political participation and securing an economy devastated by war. Educating the young meant establishing a public school system and secularizing the teaching staff and curriculum, a process begun during the U.S. occupation. Securing the economy meant guaranteeing Cubans some control over their property and protecting families from the loss of land through marriage contracts.

The separation of Church and state was a standard reform that accompanied independence of Latin American nations. Drawing inspiration from Enlightenment thought, Cuban leaders, regardless of their political leanings, believed that just rule evolved out of democratic order and an educated populace. Nearly all agreed that rational thought had to replace mystical faith and that public schools should teach new positivistic values to young patriots.[2] Staffing a public school system required an immediate amassing of a teaching force. Political leaders called on women to become teachers and to nurture and educate the young. By this act, the leaders initiated women into the work force, the intelligentsia, and social responsibilities outside the home.

Little resistance formed against women teaching in public schools. Righteous women made appropriate replacements for the Religious who had been teachers. A precedent for moral purity in public schools was set during the U.S. occupation, when, by law, only unmarried women could teach in public schools. Thus, many leaders felt it wise for women to become teachers, since women had natural influence over children and being educators formally trained them in that vocation. Educated women would become the conveyors of a new knowledge and the principles of democracy. In a sense, mother nationalists replaced the Mother Church as the guardians of Cuba's morality and the teachers of the young.

Secular private education for girls began even before the War of 1895.

Dra. María Luisa Dolz, the founder of a modern girl's school in Havana during the independence struggle. Taken from Federación Nacional de Asociaciones Femeninas, *Memoria del Primer Congreso Nacional de Mujeres: April 1–7, 1923*, p. 165. The Stoner Collection, Roll 2.

Benefactresses subsidized schools for girls and devised new courses that introduced young women to science, modern technology, and physical exercise. As young women gained exposure to a modern curriculum, their accomplishments affected their personal experiences and predisposed many to more liberal points of view.

María Luisa Dolz, who was born in 1854 in Havana, was one of the early educators to challenge traditional values taught to women. She was the first woman to link educational reform with nationalism and feminism. Often described as the first modern Cuban feminist, Dolz attacked the concept of legal and intellectual inferiority of women and believed that education was the remedy for all social injustice and a fundamental necessity for national sovereignty. In 1879 Dolz became a professor of education at the Colegio Isabel la Católica (later renamed Colegio María Luisa Dolz), which produced generations of young female educators imbued with the doctrines of national independence and women's liberation. She worked to elevate the status of women to attain equality with men before the law and in the workplace. She believed that education was the key to women's liberation, and she disapproved of Catholic curricula that produced "incompetent and noncompetitive women unable to establish themselves in modern work outside the home."[3] Physical training for women was of special importance to Dolz; without physical stamina and coordination, women would not be able to sustain a modern lifestyle of work and public service.

María Luisa Dolz expanded her influence through public lectures, articles, and pamphlets.[4] Her message promised women improved social status along with educational achievements. She pointed out that education was no longer a privilege of the few but a responsibility of all. She exhorted women to become mothers of leaders in the nationalist cause. And, she promised, as educators and mothers, women would become full citizens of Cuba Libre.

But Dolz's school was not for the poor. Located at a prestigious address (64 Prado), the school had light and beautiful salons for classrooms, a gymnasium, a chemistry laboratory, a chapel, a schoolyard, and a cafeteria. Many girls from "good society" attended. One goal of their education was to become mothers and examples of virtue, much like women in 1848. But they were also trained as community and cultural activists.

Students studied for their baccalaureate in the humanities, business, and government. All programs included courses in art—principally piano and painting—and everyone enrolled in physical education, geography, history, physiology, botany, zoology, and bacteriology. Dolz adopted modern pedagogical techniques, and she traveled in Europe and the United States to stay current with teaching advances.[5] She had a faculty of about sixteen teachers for 108 students. The faculty dined with the students, during which time all were required to speak either French or English.

Dolz offered new identities for the daughters of the ruling class by challenging them to see themselves as full citizens of nationalist Cuba. Her school was in effect a private finishing school for the better classes, yet it contributed to women's liberation. It encouraged women who otherwise would have been educated by the clergy to reason rather than pray.

Not all Cuban citizens supported secular education for women. Devout Catholics feared a crisis in morality in the absence of Church teaching, but they were ridiculed by the independence heroes. Carlos de Velasco, a Cuban statesman of the independence and early republican periods, countered the conservative argument that education would produce masculine women by claiming that educated women would strengthen society. Educated women, he believed, were intelligent, cultured, courageous, principled, industrious, self-sacrificing, and loving mothers. Their duty was to humanize society by educating their own children, influencing their brothers and sisters, doing charitable acts, teaching, or writing in public journals and newspapers.[6]

Cuba was in some sense spared the strife over expelling the Church from schools because Cubans were less dogmatically Catholic than other Latin Americans and because the United States drew up the constitution separating Church and state and established the first secular schools. Under U.S. direction, public education began in earnest. The occupation forces under Governor-General Leonard Wood initiated a public education system designed to raise teaching standards by preparing manuals and program materials and requiring qualification examinations for elementary school teachers. The government also hoped to extend high-quality education (such as that found in Colegio María Luisa Dolz) to the public schools. In 1900 one thousand Cuban teachers, both male and female, attended a summer session at Harvard University to improve their preparation. Soon thereafter, Escuelas de Verano (summer schools) appeared in Cuba as summer refresher courses for educators. The Constitution of 1901, which contained the first educational reforms, created secular public schools under the control of the state. One of the first schools of higher education to graduate large numbers of women was the Escuela Normal de Kindergarten, established in 1906 during the second U.S. intervention (1906–9). By 1915 most of the normal schools had been founded, and in 1926 the Havana Normal School graduated 150 women. After that, other coeducational schools began to appear, specializing in business or secretarial skills and accounting. By 1930 normal schools, institutes of secondary education, the Escuela del Hogar (Home Economics School), the Kindergarten Normal School, the National Institute of Physical Education, the School of Arts and Business, the polytechnics, the Hogares Campesinos (Country schools), the schools of Journalism, Plastic Arts, and Business, the Industrial Technical School, the Aeronautical School, and the universities had women in their graduating classes.[7]

Thus, Cuban leadership, following its own directives and borrowing from North American public school models, created schools with a female enrollment in an effort to modernize women's knowledge and wean them from the catechism so central to early nineteenth-century education for women. While schools gave women professional training and encouraged scientific explanations for life's events, they still prescribed teaching, nursing, the arts, and social work as appropriate work for women. Women also entered the field of stenography—an occupation previously reserved for men—through the business schools. However closely public education held to acceptable norms for women's social roles, the effect of educating women was that they soon dominated new professional areas (see appendix). In time, these teachers, nurses, and office workers became dissidents who went to the streets to demand changes.

Labor Laws

The Cuban wars of independence marked the beginning of a cycle in which middle-class women took up work outside the home. During the wars women of all classes worked in munitions factories, hospitals, schools, and the army. After independence, while the country was attempting to rationalize an industrial base, women joined the expanding work force and contended for jobs as office clerks, teachers, nurses, and minor bureaucrats. Factories sprang up. Textile and tobacco enterprises, in particular, hired women in unskilled positions; in some instances, employers preferred female employees because they constituted the cheapest labor pool. About one-third of all women laborers, however, continued to be domestic servants. In 1899 women made up 10.66 percent of the total work force, a percentage that held constant until the early 1950s.[8] But the nature of work for women gradually came to include jobs other than agricultural work, domestic service, and street vending characteristic of the colonial period (see appendix).

Early labor legislation affecting women responded more to economic crisis than to a recognition of working women's rights. In the first decade of the republic, the depressed economy, sagging sugar prices, foreign ownership of land and refineries, and immigrant labor caused desperate Cuban workers to organize for job protection and minimum wage levels.

Foreign firms, particularly those based in the United States and Great Britain, demanded and received cheap, abundant, immigrant labor from Haiti, Jamaica, and Spain. Cuban politicians were caught between encouraging foreign investment through promises of cheap labor and obligations to Cubans for remunerative work. Nationalization of labor was an explosive issue among Cuban workers from the second decade of the republic until 1940.

Following independence, unemployment and underemployment were endemic. The patriot and Spanish armies discharged tens of thousands of soldiers to seek work outside the military. Many more freed civilians left fortressed camps to rebuild lives on destroyed properties without capital support. Overcrowded cities offered day labor to a fraction of the unemployed. Most women worked as domestic servants, laundresses, and laborers whose pay was not sufficient to maintain a family. The disruption of war left many women widowed and without a means of support. One of the earliest, and certainly the most ongoing, congressional duties was awarding pensions to war widows. Even in the 1930s Congress ruled on widows' pensions. As the drain on national resources increased, the government steered women toward employment and discouraged pensions. Specifically, the government guaranteed that certain work, such as sales clerking, would be preserved for Cuban women and would exclude foreign workers and Cuban men.

The proponents of favorable legislation for Cuban women workers were men. In the 1917 employment law, Leopoldo Cancio, the interim secretary of Agriculture, Commerce, and Labor, testified before Congress. Responding to his sense of nationalism and notions of a modern and just society, he objected to capitalist use of cheap foreign labor. Instead, in the employment law of August 3, 1917, he proposed that no immigrant man be hired for work that a native woman could do.[9] Considered to be the antecedent of nationwide labor legislation that passed in the 1930s, this law reduced the likelihood of immigrant men taking jobs from Cuban women. On May 18, 1922, Congress extended the above law to protect jobs for women from Cuban men as well as foreign men. Certain jobs, such as sales clerking in lingerie departments, were reserved for women only. This was a means of providing employment for many of the war widows, and it respected women's modesty in purchasing intimate apparel. The laws were not intended, however, to address issues of women's self-determination, and the guarantees aided only clerks in commerical stores, not factory or agricultural workers nor domestic servants.

Family and Property Law

After 1902 Cuban politicians turned their attention to matters of family law. They viewed the family as the basic social and economic unit of Cuban society. Property management and ownership, family responsibility, social status, and political influence all centered on family organization and regulation. Economic change and political instability intensified the importance of the family as an institution that acquired and transferred wealth and linked individuals to politically powerful groups. As standards of economic exchange evolved from small land-holders and local commerce to large landholders who produced for foreign markets to foreign ownership of the means of production, the Cuban family too had to adjust to new economic and social ethics. Hence, conventions of property rights, legal authority, and family relations were among the first civil reforms.

Marriage, property, and divorce laws changed in Cuba after 1917 and 1918 in ways that affected women. Men passed reforms as a means of separating Church and state and maintaining a family's wealth. Their sympathy with women's needs was superficial at best, even though protagonists in the debates used arguments about women's rights to support their positions. Only after the mobilization of women activists did property and civil law change specifically to accommodate women's functions within the family, thereby affecting gender relations.

During the early decades of the Republic, legislators responded to the pressures of property foreclosures and foreign incursion by writing laws designed to protect the holdings and power of propertied classes. Threatened property owners became interested in allowing their daughters to preserve their inheritances and maintain control over their earnings after marriage. Granting married women property rights challenged the husband's patria potestad, his complete legal authority over his wife's and family's person and property. Overturning the centuries-old custom reflected the concern of the propertied class with insuring its power and authority at a difficult economic juncture.

To find new means of securing the family estate, patriot legislators were required to alter the 1889 Spanish Civil Code, in which women forfeited their legal existence by marrying. The Spanish patria potestad ruled that, upon marriage, women lost control over dowries and para-phernalia property. Husbands assumed legal authority over women and children. The Civil Code treated women as helpless creatures in need of male protection to survive. Indeed, the code insured that women were legally bound to and dependent upon men after marriage.[10] By contrast, women had complete control over at least one-half of the conjugal estate after they were widowed.

While the Civil Code circumscribed women's financial authority, it also required husbands, as heads of household, to provide for the family. Article 57 determined that the husband had to protect the wife, and the wife had to obey the husband. Articles 188 and 221 stated that a married woman could acquire the rights and privileges of family management and corrective authority over her children in the husband's absence.

Article 63 allowed a woman who had children from a previous marriage, while under the authority of a second husband, to bequeath property, exercise rights, and contract debts from the first estate if this business were in support of the legitimate children of the first marriage. Otherwise, the second husband was the executor of the first husband's estate. Article 1360 established that a married woman conserved ownership but not usufruct of her dowry, while Article 1382 maintained a wife's ownership of her paraphernalia.[11]

According to the 1889 Civil Code, couples could divide their estates in a prenuptial agreement, thus authorizing a woman's control over the property she owned before marriage. This right was rarely pursued, however. Article 1436 ruled that property could be divided and responsibility for personal property could be conferred upon women with written agreements from prospective husbands. If a couple had agreed to separate personal property in a prenuptial vow, wives still had to turn over earnings from their property to their husbands. The article also ruled that, in cases of a husband's extended absence or in the case of annulment or separation where the wife was the innocent party, the dowry reverted to the wife along with the rest of her property, which served as subsistence income for the family. Article 1441 allowed for other types of legal arrangements whereby the wife gained control of conjugal property. The wife could administer joint property if she became the husband's guardian after the court judged him legally incompetent. The wife controlled joint property in the extended absence of the husband or in his lengthy incarceration.

Distilled to its primary elements, Spanish civil law presumed that, while a husband was healthy and in residence, he had complete control of the estate and the lives of people in the family. When husbands were absent or unable to manage the estate, wives had limited control. Only prenuptial agreements could overreach the Civil Code provisions.

The 1901 Constitution did not challenge these premises. While some legislators raised questions about shared ownership of conjugal estates, legal change had to wait until 1916 when members of Congress, without direction from women, first considered extending married women's rights. Motivation for changing the law had to do with the scramble to control private property and the adoption of progressive legal codes. Cuban congressmen were concerned with conserving wealth and promulgating laws that were free of colonial vestiges.

In May 1916, Senator Vidal Morales introduced a bill granting married women free administration of their dowries and paraphernalia, defending it as proof of the "high level of the spirit of justice and public opinion" in the new republic. He argued that the Spanish Civil Code reduced married women to chattel over which husbands had the authority of "*pater familae.*" According to Morales, Cuban women had proven in the Wars of Independence that they were not dependent upon men, for many had assumed responsibility for their own welfare and that of their children under the harshest of circumstances. Therefore, he concluded, it was natural that women have control of their own property.

Congress had to revise the Civil Code that clashed with the constitution since the former distinguished between women's and men's authority and the latter declared all citizens equal.[12] Interested in forcing agreement between the Civil Code and the constitution, Morales challenged the constitutionality of the old code. He believed that Cubans supported marriage free of male domination and that domination was an anachronism in a democratic system.[13] The opposition did not defeat the bill, but it did succeed in delaying action for a year while the Congress studied the possibility of changing the entire Civil Code to conform to the national constitution.

On April 30, 1917, Senator Morales and others reintroduced the bill. Again Morales argued that Cuba had not become a modern nation because old laws kept Cuba rooted in the past. By depicting Cuba as a fraudulent democracy with an insincere commitment to equality, he hoped to force the undecided senators to take his side. In his summary address, Morales said:

> In our Republic, democracy does not yet have life. It does not have the laws. The Republic is only dressed in the cloak of democracy without the shirt underneath. . . . The Republic as yet has no laws to uphold the Constitution. It has an outdated Penal Code [1870] that even Spain, a country that does not pretend to be a democracy, has updated.
>
> This bill is nothing more than a small reform, a pittance when compared to what Cuban women deserve. Cuban women ought to have equal civil and political rights with men because the Cuban people believe that equality is right. There is no reason for women's inferior legal status. Such status limits the rights of our mothers, our sisters, and our daughters. We are going slowly. We have been discussing this article for sixteen years and trying to decide if women need the permission of their husbands before disposing of their own property.[14]

Using the argument that the proposed bill agreed with early premises of the Civil Code, Morales demanded immediate passage of the law as an amendment of the old code.[15]

Senator Maza y Artola led the opposition to the bill. He rehashed the old argument that the new bill did not fit with the old Civil Code since it contradicted too many related laws.[16] He also pointed out that a new ruling threatened the very foundations of Cuban marriage because it questioned the chain of authority in married society, and he could not imagine how shared authority would function. Maza y Artola denied obstructing women's legal independence, but he turned his attention to protective legislation rather than equal rights, in effect begging the question. He thought that legal reform and social work should eliminate prostitution, a far more serious problem in his mind than a property law. He felt that women should have to prepare themselves for the responsibilities of legal and political self-determination, an argument often used by the Spanish against Cuban self-government, before they could execute their legal rights. Maza y Artola spoke condescendingly about equal rights:

> Neither women in other societies nor our own will gain complete liberation until they are well protected against the dangers of ignorance, poverty, or prostitution. They must attain outstanding education and superior instruction. Then they can open up all the office doors and enter the professions. Then they will obtain the necessary means, not just to subsist, but to enrich themselves without the help or support of men. That is when laws should guarantee against the tricks of men. Until then, equality will be a myth to which legitimacy only aspires.[17]

Reformists and propertied conservatives formed an alliance against this sexist position. Senator Ricardo Dolz, a political reformer and the nephew of María Luisa Dolz, believed that marriage, as defined by the Civil Code, was an inappropriate economic arrangement. The law, he argued, assumed that married women were incapable of managing their own estates, yet the Wars of Independence had rendered that assumption invalid. Since the law no longer reflected reality, it became a law of economic restriction. He insisted that only the law, not women's abilities, prevented the codirectorship of property.

Dolz acknowledged the historical momentum of the international feminist movement and admonished the senators for not taking it seriously enough to pass more general laws of equality between the sexes. He warned against resisting the movement and granting it only grudging concessions. "Women should have their rights," he said, "because the movement is acknowledged worldwide, it is just and moderate, and the women are not asking to dominate men. Resisting the woman's movement will encourage women activists to become socialists and fulfill everyone's greatest fear."[18] Dolz was no radical; he conceded women some rights to avoid revolution, socialism, free love, and the dissolution of the family. <u>Moderate reforms, he argued,</u> would divert social up-heaval.

From the conservative bench Senator Gonzalo Pérez argued the upper-class position in support of the bill. He offered the case of a father who had only daughters to inherit his wealth. His daughters' marriages would concern him not only for reasons of domestic felicity, but also for reasons of protection of family wealth. Under the Civil Code, a father's fortune, honor, and shame were bound to his daughters' capricious choice of mates. Therefore, Gonzalo Pérez argued, the laws had to protect a man's fortune as well as his daughter's honor by separating her wealth from her husband's holdings in order to avoid "making beggars of the wealthy."[19] <u>In a word, under a new law with women holding property rights, marriage would no longer pass property to another family line when a man's only heirs were his daughters.</u>

On May 11, 1917, Congress approved the initial bill to give married women the right to administer and dispose of their property. Married women could also make public and private property contracts. Shortly after the bill's approval, Senator Cosmé de la Torriente added to the document the resolution that a woman married for a second time should have patria potestad over her children born in the first marriage. His resolution passed by a simple voice majority.[20] A week later the Senate approved the final form of the law, which granted married women control over their dowries and family property, the right to sue and be sued, and authority over children from previous marriages.[21]

Granting women control over their paraphernalia property, dowry, and children by previous marriage with the necessary court privileges to protect their rights of control seemed an innocuous enough beginning to women's legal reform. After all, it merely granted women rights to property they had enjoyed prior to marriage and that they would regain upon the termination of marriage. The law legalized what many Cubans already accepted: that women could manage finances and estates. Yet these first laws reflected a transition in Cuban thinking regarding family organization, Catholic values, and modern notions of property control. Acrimony over their passage summarized the deep confusion about the nature and functioning of a modern Cuban family and how family organization could be used to consolidate wealth.

The 1917 property law had a revolutionary effect on at least one wealthy woman. In 1917 Elena Mederos, the seventeen-year-old daughter of a wealthy tobacco buyer, received a productive tobacco estate from her father, thereby enabling her to live in comfort, independent of any other support. Her father did the same for her sister. He saw to it that his daughters, his only children, would never have to live with men they did not love because they lacked the means to survive alone. It was a radical act in 1917, and it sidestepped the simple issue of property control and directly addressed the issue of women's rights through economic solvency.

Elena Mederos went on to earn a doctorate in pharmacology and became a leading feminist and social reformer who pursued cultural, social, and political interests because she did not have to earn a living or depend upon a husband for her financial well-being. She had free time to spend on the Cuban woman's movement and on issues surrounding the welfare of the poor.[22] She also married a young lawyer and by mutual agreement separated his property from hers. Mederos's husband built up his own law practice without using any of his wife's considerable resources.

Divorce

Whether to permit divorce or not provoked high-spirited debate from 1868 until 1959, despite the fact that no-fault divorce passed in 1918. Opinion hinged on religion, morality, finance, patria potestad, and the separation of Church and state. A divorce law was first suggested during the Ten Years War, and the insurgent government supported divorce as early as 1868 as a means of separating the Church and state, establishing secular law, and creating social equality. Insistence upon a divorce law had little to do with commitment to women's rights and everything to do with independence. For rebel leaders, establishing a nation meant replacing colonial, Catholic institutions with positivist ordering. A divorce law appeared in the Revolutionary Codes passed on September 14, 1896. Articles 30 and 40 of the Marriage Law said that Cubans could divorce and remarry, in clear defiance of Roman Catholic canon.

After independence, the divorce issue surfaced as a serious consideration in 1914 and carried with it not only challenges to family traditions but also the enactment of revolutionary promises. Before passing a divorce law, jurists and legislators reviewed Cuban customs and foreign laws. Prevailing sentiment in favor of a divorce law originated in revolutionary ideals, and rationalization of the law included women's rights. At stake was a resetting of marriage and family provisions and a restatement of moral values and customs.

When divorce debates began in 1914, women had not yet formed feminist groups, nor had they become effective, organized lobbyists, although individual feminists published arguments supporting divorce.[23] As a result, women had little influence on the initial law. What influence they had was wielded through informal family networks from which they focused attention on protecting the family after divorce.

The 1918 divorce law evolved out of a number of national political issues. First, divorce was only one issue in the more general project of separating the Church from government. The divorce law dramatized the struggle between conservative religious and progressive liberal forces over the authority of civil law. Divorce apologists such as Carlos de Velasco, editor of the liberal journal *Cuba Contemporánea,* and Francisco del Valle, a liberal thinker and writer, insisted that, in order to reduce the influence of the Church, the state had to assume legal control over public institutions such as marriage, birth, divorce, and death registration, thus relegating religious authority to the less public confines of the confessional box. Velasco and del Valle, in some of their stronger statements, demanded that the secular nature of the state be respected and that religious views be given no official weight.[24] Divorce antagonists led by Eliseo Giberga, an old Autonomist Party member and lawyer, did not argue for religious intervention in civil matters, but he believed that social morality was still essentially Catholic and should be retained because it was the predominant moral convention. Giberga accused divorce supporters of being advocates of socialist revolution and free love.[25]

Second, the divorce bill was a part of a larger question regarding the function of law. Distinguished lawyers such as Giberga maintained that the legal system should directly represent the moral preferences of the people. Although he was careful to disassociate himself from the Church faction, he was convinced that the majority of Cubans disapproved of divorce and opposed divorce legislation.[26] Velasco, del Valle, and Enrique José Varona, a man of considerable prestige, who was vice-president under Mario G. Menocal (1912–20) and professor of sociology at the University of Havana, countered Giberga. They argued that Congress should assume a progressive posture and draft laws to address social reality. They supported a liberal divorce law and argued that it did not threaten traditional morality, since those who did not want divorce did not have to obtain one, and it solved problems for the unhappily married. These men did not believe that Congress should ignore the will of the people, but they squarely faced the fact that this will was unknown and that Congress occasionally had to create solutions to social problems even if the solutions violated common moral preferences.[27]

Third, as Cuba entered the twentieth century, its leaders were committed to rapid modernization in all spheres of social development. For better or worse, the immediate model for a modern society was the United States, where divorce had roots in English Common Law. Many Cuban liberals believed the U.S. model to be a rational and progressive alternative for solving marriage problems, and some were comfortable emulating U.S. divorce legislation. Other pro-divorce Cubans cited France's divorce legislation promulgated in 1884 during the Third Republic and argued that the French model was more appropriate because Cuba and France shared the same Latin/Catholic heritage.

Fourth, the promulgation of a divorce law would equalize the accessibility of divorce for all classes of Cuban society. Divorce was already a reality for some Cubans with money. Couples from the middle and upper classes with the financial means to travel to Tampa, Florida, had been going to the United States to terminate their marriages. Separation was the more common means of resolving marital problems. Because colonial law allowed for separation of marriage partners and the 1917 property law provided for a fair separation of property, divorce advocates argued that the only remaining obstacle to total divorce was the legal pronouncement that would make divorce available to all Cubans at a low cost.

The fifth justification for a divorce law touched the political sensitivities of nationalists. Independence leaders Roberto Ignacio Agramonte and Salvador Cisneros Betancourt included the divorce law in their *Bases de la Revolución* published in 1896.[28] Since these leaders were mostly concerned with the separation of Church and state and the ultimate sovereignty of the Republic, the divorce issue was tied to the idea of independence and carried with it all the proud content of Cuban nationalism. For many Cubans the creation of state and society envisioned by the revolutionary leaders justified almost any reform. Patriotic rhetoric reinforced divorce debates, and opponents found themselves on the defensive, having to prove their patriotism and trying to find revolutionary heroes who had objected to divorce in Cuba.[29]

The sixth consideration in the divorce controversy was the law's moral consequences. Both advocates and opponents used moral arguments to support their positions and sought the approval of women. For cultural reasons women were perceived both by women and men as the guardians of morality, and it was only in this context that women participated in the otherwise male-dominated political and legal debate.

Divorce's central moral concern was the preservation of the family. Family unity and the relationship of Church and state were the most divisive points in the debate, with the Conservative Party representing traditional Catholic morality, and the Liberal and National parties siding with the proponents of divorce. Conservatives, led by Nicolas Rivera and Eliseo Giberga, believed that a renunciation of the permanence of marriage was a violation of Cuban morality. They worried that promiscuity, illegitimate children, immoral conduct, and the abuse of women might result. Conservatives warned against the irresponsible abandonment of women and insinuated that respectable women would resort to prostitution for their livelihood. When forced to defend marriages harmful to one or both parties, antireformers begged the question and argued that divorce insured the termination of the relationship while the impossibility of divorce provided the opportunity for reconciliation.[30]

Conservatives drew support from religious traditionalists and Church activists. Church supporters organized against the divorce law to protect their own interests as a policymaking institution and preserve Catholic morality. The clergy admonished its constituency, mostly women, as mortal sinners if they approved of a divorce law. Despite laws prohibiting priests from direct political activity, members of the clergy approached women on the streets and solicited their signatures on antidivorce petitions. Because compelling moral arguments surrounded divorce, women were reluctant to refuse the clergy's political solicitation. Women were particularly susceptible to this kind of manipulation since they formed the largest religious audience in Cuba.[31] Consequently, reform and conservative politicians addressed family issues in order to reduce Church influence among women. As a pivotal political constituency for the pro- and antidivorce lobbyists, women had a presence in the national political debate.

Initially, two factors encouraged many women to oppose the divorce law: many women viewed divorce as an irreligious act and divorce offered the real possibility that women would be turned out of the house, legally. Since in those early days no one knew how a divorce law might be used, many women saw it as a threat to their domestic security rather than an advantage to their personal happiness and prosperity. As a result, women formed a significant proportion of the conservative faction.

Some women supported divorce, of course. Outspoken individuals such as Dulce María Borrero de Luján, poet laureate, and Aurelia Castillo de González, also a poet, testified before Congress and wrote in support of the divorce bill.[32] Borrero de Luján and Castillo de González also argued that the family was most secure when women could rid themselves and their children of philandering, abusive, and nonproductive husbands.

Divorce advocates, both men and women, attacked Church supporters who claimed to be the only representatives of morality. They
maintained that divorce would not promote moral degeneration and
instead blamed human misery and social and economic difficulties for
destroying family relationships. Rather than promoting marital dissolution, divorce would terminate failed marriages. They insisted the law
should not impose a rigid morality that was irrelevant for significant
numbers of Cubans. The law should provide the greatest latitude for the
resolution of individual need while acknowledging that happy marriages
were the highest good.[33] If anything were immoral, advocates insisted, it
was the separation convention that, in practice, condoned promiscuity
among men and condemned it among women. The Civil Code provided
for separations in the case of adultery, but men could commit adultery
without fear of separation if they did not create a scandal and if there was
no financial hardship for the wives. Wives absolutely could not commit
adultery, any sexual indiscretion on their part was incontestable grounds
for annulment. Further, under the Penal Code, a wife caught in the act of
commiting adultery could be murdered by her enraged husband, and the
husband would receive little, if any, penalty. In this way the traditional
system facilitated men's rights to extramarital relationships, rights that
were denied to women.[34]

Social injustice issues supported other pro-divorce arguments. According to the existing laws for separation, married women remained
under the authority of husbands, even after years of separation. Divorce
advocates insisted that a new law should liberate separated women from
the authority of estranged husbands.[35]

Liberals directly attacked the notion that divorce jeopardized the
family. They believed that children exposed to separation and adultery
suffered more than children whose parents were divorced and remarried.
Nonrecognition of divorce resulted in couples having adulterous relationships if they were not celibate for the rest of their lives, and children
issuing from new unions were illegitimate. Such children had no inheritance rights and suffered social contempt. Bigamy, adultery, and illegitimacy were held to be more serious threats to family morality and
stability than divorce. Therefore, according to the liberals, divorce was a
healthier resolution to marital disharmony than the recourse offered by
existing law.[36]

Women's mobilization around the divorce issue was often orchestrated by men. It was the unusual woman who took a public stand either
for or against the controversial legislation. But not all women were silent.
Men often reported family pressure to act on the divorce issue one way

or another. Mariana Seva de Menocal, the wife of the Cuban president, opposed divorce legislation. In a letter addressed to Pope Pius X in September 1913 she assured the Pope that, while her husband was president, the divorce law would not pass Congress, and she promised to use her influence among the congressmen to block legislation.[37]

All the protagonists in the divorce issue were not Cubans or officials of the Catholic Church. Politicians in the United States stood on the authority of the Platt Amendment and attempted to impose Catholic morality on the newly secular state. In 1915 Secretary of State William Jennings Bryan directed the U.S. minister in Havana:

> I write to suggest that you unofficially and confidentially confer with the President and *advise against any change in the marriage law*. Marriage should be allowed before religious and civil authorities. To deny either kind of marriage would be a backward step. . . . Earnestly advise against any change of the law in this respect. In the matter of divorce consideration should be given to the fact that Cuba is a Catholic country, and causes should be as few as public opinion will permit. While insisting on religious freedom in every respect the Cuban government should be careful not to undermine that respect for religion which is essential for moral progress.[38]

The ultimate passage of the 1918 divorce law proved difficult. A divorce bill passed the House of Representatives in 1915 but was blocked in committee by senators loyal to the Church lobby. Church leaders and U.S. Minister Gonzales attempted to secure a presidential veto of the divorce bill by directly petitioning Mario Menocal. The president's answer was "Procederé de acuerdo con los deseos expresos de la sociedad cubana" (I will proceed according to the wishes of the Cuban people).

When the Senate finally passed the divorce bill in 1918 by an almost unanimous vote, President Menocal did not veto it. He did not sign it, however. Instead, he allowed the time limitation for the presidential veto to expire, and the bill became law without presidential signature. It would have been difficult for the president to block the law outright, despite his wife's efforts, since he considered himself part of the revolutionary leadership and revolutionaries supported the bill.

The first Cuban divorce law was spectacular for one reason: it provided for no-fault divorce. Beyond that, it had narrow provisions for cause of divorce and family support. It called for a separation of property and the liquidation of estates in order to arrive at a fair settlement. When a guilty party existed, her/his property rights could be forfeited. Guiltless wives could be awarded alimony, and pensions were awarded to children. Guiltless mothers had authority over children.[39]

In principle, the no-fault clause threatened to destroy the foundations of Catholic marriage and family. In practice, however, few people availed themselves of the option. Between 1918 and 1927 there were a total of 2,374 divorces, 43 percent of which were filed by women, 47 percent by men, and 10 percent mutually.[40] The habit of separation remained the preferred means of ending a failed marriage. The law did what it was intended to do: it demoted the Church to inconsequential political status; it gave a minority the chance to dissolve marriage; it eulogized revolutionary objectives; and it left the Cuban family intact. It also left problems of mother's rights and enforcement of alimony payments unresolved. These issues would become concerns for the feminists in 1930 and 1934.

Conclusion

The first twenty years of the republic established a new ruling order and a modicum of social reform. Schools that previously were reserved for the wealthy now educated members of the middle class, but they were beyond the reach of the poor. As parochial schools became public, the new curriculum eliminated catechism and included science. Women of the middle and upper classes benefited from the reforms and soon became teachers and reformers within school systems.

Politicians had to protect jobs for Cubans in order to appear concerned about economic catastrophes that were crippling commerce. It was the least they could do to disguise their helplessness in the face of U.S. dollar diplomacy, foreign investment strategies, disadvantageous trade agreements, and the lack of financial aid. Contention over property became increasingly vicious, and laws changed to broaden the rules for acquiring and controlling wealth. As a result, propertied women gained control over their dowries and estates.

Divorce, long a Catholic anathema, passed into law as a way to separate Church and state, respect revolutionary principles, and regulate authority. Women's issues were used to defend and attack the proposed legislation, but women seldom directly participated in the debates.

Despite the secondary importance of women's rights in legislative deliberations, early legal reforms directly affected women as citizens and prepared them to act in their own behalf. Male legislators advanced women's rights in their desperate effort to consolidate their own power and modernize Cuba. The effects of legal change, whether intended or not, evoked a woman's movement that would take charge of women's issues in the following decades.

Feminist Congresses and Organizations

⌇

Neither national independence nor early legal reforms directly ad-dressed women's aspirations for self-determination. New laws granting property rights, minimal labor provisions, and divorce did not result entirely from an appreciation of women's rights, nor did they relate to issues such as respect for women's contributions to family and community, demands for political power, and labor reforms. Gaining respect and authority required changing social attitudes, an almost impossible task under the circumstances. In 1918 Cuban women were in no position to promote that change. They lacked power, they were without organization, and their cause interested few people. Building a viable economy and rules of government took precedence over promot-ing social reform. For the first two decades following the Treaty of Paris (1898), only a small group of women identified women's rights as their central concern.

The only hope for an effective woman's movement came out of the general chaos that erupted between 1923 and 1940, resulting from Cuban frustration with political corruption, politicians' disregard for democ-racy, U.S. interventions, economic collapse, and a breakdown of the social order. By the late 1910s the crisis in Cuban leadership was unmistakable. Dissident groups formed to alter the mechanisms of control so that they might present alternatives to failed policies. In the turmoil that ensued, feminist groups influenced vulnerable political forces to support women's rights legislation.

Winning the attention and support of politicians depended upon impressing them that feminist organizations held power and established political positions. Feminists formed small organizations, and they identified leaders whom they lobbied to support their feminist agenda. As feminist groups differed on important issues, it soon became apparent that the movement was not unified and that feminist appeals would be directed at conservative, moderate, and radical politicians.

Moderate feminists appealed to members of the National and Liberal parties primarily for the vote. Progressive feminists appealed to active reformers such as Authentic and Liberal Party leaders for extensive welfare and labor reforms. Radical feminists worked with revolutionary organizations outside the government for a Marxist political and economic order. The various alliances, rather than weakening the feminist effort, guaranteed that feminist demands appeared before a variety of political groups, and, thus, women's issues could not be ignored. The Cuban feminist movement was divided and contentious, to be sure, but it also held broad appeal, as feminists attached their issues to questions of social justice and independence raised by José Martí and pursued by most political factions.

Independence and Early Feminism

Feminists took the model of the mambisa to dramatize their own efforts as women constructing a new nation. The mambisa, who fought for independence as bravely as men, often assuming men's duties, was recognized by everyone as a heroine of Cuban independence. Being both a warrior and a mother she was seen as both brave and vulnerable, and her sacrifice consecrated the Cuban struggle. Feminists also adopted the image of motherhood to stand for morality and social justice, values the new nation sought to define for itself. The women attempted to fuse concepts of feminism, motherhood, and nationalism, thus creating a place for themselves as Cuba's moral political leaders.

From the first moments of nationhood, women voiced their political and moral opinions. During the War of 1895 the Club Esperanza del Valle, one of the revolutionary clubs mentioned earlier, lashed out at the cruel policies of General Valeriano Weyler and established a program of government that the membership unveiled after the patriots had won independence. Article 4 of their program declared:

> We want women to exercise their natural rights. Single women and widows over the age of 25 should have the right to vote. There should be divorce for just cause. Women should have the right to public employment limited only by their physiological and sociological makeup.[1]

Club members signed the program on March 19, 1897, and presented it to the 1901 Constitutional Assembly, which deliberated Cuba's first constitution. The assembly did consider suffrage, but only ten delegates supported the then radical departure from exclusively male democracies. When the delegates approved the constitution and the Platt Amendment that made Cuba a protectorate of the United States and denied suffrage, the Club Esperanza del Valle protested. Edelmira Guerra, its founder, said that the 1901 constitution left Cuba a virtual colony and made noncitizens of its women.[2]

Disappointed by their circumscribed freedoms, mambisas and younger generations of women activists began forming clubs to raise women's issues for public consideration. Some of these organizations published journals that both projected feminist views and invited popular comment. *Aspiraciones* was established in 1912 as a patriotic civic journal to defend women's interests. The *Revista de la Asociación Femenina de Camagüey*, first published in 1921 as a literary journal, contained feminist commentary about the Asociación's activities. Embellished by the romantic, Victorian vernacular, these journals used photographs and drawings to portray women as beautiful, thoughtful members of society wishing for serious considerations of their rights. They initiated a national discussion about the precise meaning of Cuban feminism. Impassioned articles claimed that femininity was central to Cuban feminism; other articles detailed the condition of working women, and especially tobacco stemmers, whose work conditions were among the harshest. The journals included contemporary literature, music, and poetry written by women. Readers' responses to journal articles amplified opinions about feminism, women's responsibilities in the community, and home problems. Feminist campaigns in other countries were also covered. As early as 1912, literate Cuban women and the reading public stayed abreast of Cuban and foreign feminist ideals, and some presented their own views. Despite the intellectual efforts of these early feminist writers, however, the public only mildly shared their concerns.

For women to attain any degree of self-determination required organization. Feminist movements elsewhere had become effective only after women formed associations that linked gender issues with larger national concerns. Cuban feminists came to understand the importance of these linkages. Moreover, growing national unrest required feminist alignment with established political movements and leaders as a means of survival.

Beginning in the early 1910s, a number of new women's organizations formed for the purpose of bringing feminist issues to national attention. In 1912 the Comité de Sufragio Femenino organized to advocate women's participation in electoral politics. The Asociación Femenina de Camagüey was an intellectual and feminist club that published the island's first feminist journal. The Asociación de Damas Isabelinas emphasized charity work, with a special interest in tubercular children. The Damas Isabelinas also advocated women's political rights and insisted that care for chronically ill children should be subsidized by public and not private funds.

Perhaps the most important organization of these early years was the Club Femenino de Cuba that formed in 1917 around a number of social issues, including ending prostitution, establishing women's prisons and juvenile courts, and winning women's rights. Inspired by feminist movements elsewhere, the membership of the Club Femenino organized the First National Women's Congress in Havana in April 1923. They sought to coordinate political action that would achieve popular reforms benefiting women. Planners of the congress combined patriotic nationalism, commitment to motherhood and the family, and women's rights as the motivating factors of the Cuban woman's movement.

The Background of Unrest

The year 1923 was propitious for massive challenges to the administration of President Alfredo Zayas. A political elite had emerged after independence that depended upon U.S. support to maintain its political dominance. These politicians benefited financially from monies illegally attained from the national lottery and political kickbacks.[3] Corruption, the betrayal of the nineteenth-century ideals of national independence, and U.S. imperialism were linked in the public mind as the causes of the failure of the Republic. Because the United States controlled Cuba's economic and political operations, the only means any president had to maintain himself in power was to pay off opponents and supporters alike with public funds. Any insistence by the U.S. government that corruption stop, as with the moralization program introduced by the Crowder Commission in 1920, threatened to destroy the incumbent regime and U.S. influence in Cuba. Therefore, the United States tolerated corruption as a means to political stability, and by 1923 it became a stable feature of Cuban government.

A number of opposition parties and radical organizations formed to denounce both corruption in the national government and North American intermeddling in the internal affairs of the republic. A new generation of Cuban professionals and an older generation of patriots challenged the political elite. Doctors, lawyers, small investors, teachers, students, and the old veterans of the nineteenth-century wars of independence wished to break the chains of patronage and corruption. They sought to restrain arbitrary political authority and enhance Cuban national interests over North American ones.[4] Their watchword was *regeneración*, implying a return to Cuban nationalist ideals, honest rule, and economic development.

Rebellion was in the air. Cubans took sides in a spirited political debate and activists stirred the consciences of the previously apathetic citizenry. In January 1923 students at the University of Havana denounced corruption in government, seized part of the campus, and demanded the dismissal of incompetent faculty. They petitioned for free higher education and university autonomy. Out of this student activism developed the first militant student organization, the Federación Estudiantil Universitario (FEU). At the First National Student Congress in 1923 students from all parts of Cuba repeated the university's demands for participation in school governance, high professional standards for faculty, and increased public support for education.

In the same year the Veterans and Patriots Association, a distinguished group of independence war veterans and highly regarded patriots, organized to oppose reduction of the veterans' pensions and combat corruption in the Zayas government. The association was one of the first to speak of "regenerating" Cuba. It demanded an end to corruption and protested nondemocratic practices that consolidated power and wealth in the hands of political elites.[5] Among the signatories of the veterans' resolution were some of Cuba's leading feminists: Pilar Jorge de Tella, Emma López Seña, Hortensia Lamar, Serafina R. de Rosado, Mariblanca Sabas Alomá, Loló de la Torriente, Rafaela Mederos de Fernández, Bertha Neckerman, Rosario Guillaume, and Pilar Morlon de Menéndez—all leaders of the Club Femenino de Cuba.[6]

Difficult economic times during the early 1920s roused national tensions. Agricultural and industrial workers grew desperate for work, decent salaries, and humane working conditions. Workers had only limited representation through their guilds and syndicates. Rural laborers, without work during the "dead season," moved to the cities in search of employment. Trade unions increased in number and size, and, by the mid-1920s labor organizations assumed formidable proportions as they formed coalitions and expanded the use of strikes.

In 1923 workers mobilized and convened the Second National Labor Congress. Workers demanded public housing, an eight-hour workday, price controls on basic staples, equal pay for men and women, the abolition of piecework in homes, and a denunciation of U.S. imperialism. In 1923 many workers threw their support behind a new militant group, the Agrupación Comunista de la Habana, a loose confederation of labor organizations. In 1925, at the Third National Labor Conference, unions formed the Confederación Nacional Obrera de Cuba (CNOC) to lend more power to labor demands. The Stemmers' Guild, predominantly a women's group, belonged to the CNOC. In the same year many unionized workers were attracted to a leftist ideology and joined the newly formed Partido Comunista de Cuba (PCC).

The National Women's Congress of 1923

The women's movement held its first national congress in 1923 amid an atmosphere of national unrest and in a moment when new social attitudes about women's public roles were forming. Women had become effective advocates for social reform through membership in philanthropic organizations and clubs. They worked as stenographers, teachers, and nurses, new areas of work that commanded a living wage and made possible an independent life-style. Most organized women and professionals came from the middle and upper classes, so their demands centered on reformist and not revolutionary change.

In 1923 the Club Femenino de Cuba formed the umbrella organization, the Federación Nacional de Asociaciones Femeninas, that planned the First National Women's Congress. Under the leadership of Pilar Morlon de Menéndez, the Federación set an agenda and invited participants from every women's organization, feminist or not. The idea was to have an accurate balance of women's views and not a predominance of feminist representatives.

On April 1, 1923, Pilar Morlon de Menéndez opened the congress in the National Theatre in Old Havana. Until the closing session on the evening of April 7, women debated and passed resolutions that would give general direction to a movement they hoped to form. They visited nursery schools, orphanages, the Maternity and Charity Home, and other institutions dealing with women, mothers, and children. They invited public officials and politicians to champagne receptions to discuss women's political rights. The congress was designed to be a gala affair, for which the Cuban women dressed in elegant attire and invited the president of the republic and other ruling dignitaries. From the start, the Congress's activities were directed at influencing national reform policy. Its strategy was to work with, not against, men in public office by associating with those in power and supporting politicians who advocated women's issues.

Thirty-one women's organizations representing the full range of political orientations attended the congress. Nonpolitical groups such as the American Red Cross and the Academy of Painting and Sculpture sent delegates, as did the more militant Club Femenino de Cuba. Forty-three women spoke on themes ranging from women's participation in govern-

Opening session of the First National Women's Congress. Pilar Morlon de Menéndez is seated (right of table) and President Zayas is behind the table. Taken from *Memoria del Primer Congreso,* p. 33. The Stoner Collection, Roll 2.

A group of delegates attending the First National Women's Congress, 1923. Taken from *Memoria del Primer Congreso,* p. 22. The Stoner Collection, Roll 2.

ment to the beautification of Havana. Other topics included the rights of illegitimate children, the abolition of the adultery law, women's jurisdiction over public welfare, the elimination of prostitution, white slave trade, drugs and alcohol, a fair working wage for women, home economics curricula in schools, reforms in women's education, feminism,

Sra. Pilar Morlon de Menéndez, president of the First and Second National Women's Congresses. Taken from *Memoria del Primer Congreso,* p. 17. The Stoner Collection, Roll 2.

and historical and nationalistic pronouncements. The agenda reflected the diversity of causes and the differences in opinion about women's political mission, setting the scene for conflict.[7]

Pilar Morlon de Menéndez established two objectives for the conference: (1) the creation of new options for women in twentieth-century Cuban society, and (2) the articulation of women's views regarding problems that affected individual, family, social, and national matters. She called for women's "moralization" of the streets, the home, schools, factories, public administration, and the highest office of the state. She invited detractors of feminist causes to "come and judge" women's work in public affairs.[8]

Throughout the week of the conference, delegates offered resolutions outlining a range of feminist objectives. Most speeches were patriotic and passionate. Resolutions that reinforced traditional family values were approved and served to give the impression of unity and consensus. Reforms that challenged family relationships and traditional mores, however, divided the congress into hostile factions.

There was no lack of talent among the radical feminists, who introduced the most controversial resolutions. Many were highly regarded members of the intelligentsia, and their proposals generally attacked women's social isolation and inferior status. Dulce María Borrero de Luján, a well-known poet and feminist, suggested that women were responsible for the degeneration of the Cuban spirit because of their insulation from public life. From the home, they were unable to contribute knowledgeably or constructively to the building of a nation. Women's isolation was a result of Hispanic, Catholic tradition.[9] Hortensia Lamar, one of the key leaders of the feminist movement and a woman of considerable wealth, attacked sensitive topics about crime. She demanded solutions for drug trafficking and prostitution.[10] Loló de la Torriente, art critic and writer, insisted that the salvation of Cuba's youth required the rejection of U.S. models for culture and education.[11] Dra. Rosa Anders, one of Cuba's first female lawyers, demanded a change in the adultery law that allowed husbands to murder their unfaithful wives while permitting philandering husbands to commit adultery with only minor, if any, sanctions.[12] Antonia Prieto de Calvo called for sex education in the schools.[13] In sum, this minority rejected conservative values deemed detrimental to a progressive woman's movement, and in the process they clashed with conservative women interested in beautifying the city, showing kindness to animals, and contributing to charitable organizations.

The majority of delegates adopted a more conservative stance. Women's suffrage drew support from most women who believed that the vote would influence the course of electoral politics. Benign resolutions, such as beautifying Havana and being kind to animals, passed without comment. Changing existing adultery laws met with shy approval, as did the commitment to abolish prostitution and end the drug trade. But the harmony of the congress was broken by the proposal to grant illegitimate children the same rights to recognition, inheritance, and protection as legitimate children. Such a change, conservatives believed, would threaten family cohesion and legitimacy.

Ofelia Domínguez Navarro, a young and outspoken lawyer from Santa Clara in Las Villas, introduced the resolution on illegitimate children. She argued for the incorporation of these children into the financial, if not the emotional, family circle, thereby increasing an illegitimate child's economic resources.[14] Domínguez argued passionately that illegitimate children should not be punished or humiliated because of their parents' indiscretions. If anyone should be punished, she thought it should be the parents. (When a child without a father was born, the Church and civil records put the initials s.a. after her/his name that stood for *sin apellido*, or "without surname." Anyone's legitimacy was, therefore, a matter of public record.) Because illegitimate children were loved by their mothers and because women should not be afraid to bear and raise these children, Domínguez asked for their equality with legitimate children:

> Marriage as a contract and as a sacrament is purely artificial and responds to a sacred convention of habit, custom, and law.
>
> Reproduction is not artificial and it is one of many natural phenomena put before us. If someone were to do a study, a statistical analysis of parental love, we would see that there is little detectable difference between paternal (or maternal) love in the instances of legitimate and illegitimate births. And we perhaps might add that love is intensified in cases of illegitimacy, owing to the consideration or pity that inspires parents because of the infamous status of their illegitimate children.[15]

Reverence for motherhood and family girded Domínguez's radical position. She appealed to the delegates as women and mothers to nurture all children, regardless of their civil status. She wanted to dignify motherhood and to shield women and their children from shame and destitution. She argued that women had the right to be mothers, whether married or not. Domínguez's passion for her cause went beyond an intellectual commitment to fatherless children; it was a personal obsession.

The problem of illegitimate children was not a hypothetical digression from feminist matters. In the 1919 census illegitimate persons comprised 24 percent of the total population. Tables 2 and 3, taken from the 1919 census only four years before the women's congress, demonstrate the regional and racial incidences of illegitimacy. The tables show high illegitimacy rates, especially among the rural population of color. Since a significant portion of the population was illegitimate and colored (Chinese, Mulatto, and Black), to grant rights to these people threatened the ideal of sanctioned marriage and formal family, and it meant dealing with illegitimate children of mixed blood. Allowing unwed mothers and their offspring access to legal recognition and provisions from the father threatened to diminish the married woman's claim to respectability and financial security and promised to challenge the elevated status of people with "pure blood" (white heritage).

Domínguez's pronouncements pushed well-intended but conserva-

Table 2   Proportion of Illegitimacy by Region and Age, 1919

Province or City	Percentages of illegitimacy in total population	Percentages of illegitimacy among children under ten
Cuba	24.0	—
Pinar del Río	27.0	25.7
Havana	17.1	16.0
City of Havana	20.3	21.5
Matanzas	25.9	19.9
Santa Clara	19.5	15.5
Camagüey	17.1	16.7
Oriente	35.0	37.0

Source: Cuba, Dirección General del Censo, *Census of the Republic of Cuba* (Havana: Maza, Arroyo, 1921), 365 and 367.

Table 3   Proportion of Illegitimacy by Age and Race, 1919

Age	Percentages of illegitimacy		
	All Races	Native White	Colored
Under 5 years	23.2	13.6	49.9
5 to 9 years	23.5	13.5	52.0
10 to 14 years	24.1	13.5	53.9
15 to 19 years	25.3	14.0	55.2
20 to 24 years	25.0	12.8	54.8
25 and over	23.9	11.0	56.8

Source: Cuba, Dirección del Censo, *Census of the Republic of Cuba* (Havana: Maza, Arroyo, 1921), 366.

tive delegates beyond their tolerance for reform. These feminists felt more comfortable discussing the protection of animals and plants, the advances women had made in education, and plans for advancing women's political participation. Marriage, the traditional family, and female chastity were sacrosanct. Any resolution threatening old versions of moral purity and social stability, such as aiding single mothers or granting recognition and inheritance rights to illegitimate children, was condemned by the majority. Where Domínguez believed in the sanctity of motherhood, the conservatives believed in the sacrament of marriage and the legitimacy of the formal family.

The division between radical and conservative feminists deepened. To avoid an unfortunate confrontation, president of the congress, Pilar Morlon de Menéndez obtained a delay on voting on the illegitimate children's rights resolution until the second congress.

The final resolutions of the First National Women's Congress declared that women would develop political campaigns to establish women's and children's courts, a welfare system, moral and material aid to working women, the equalization of women's legal status, civic activities, action against social vice and crime, an end to the adultery law, and most importantly, the vote.[16] Despite the consensus on general issues, considerable disagreement existed between radicals and conservatives over the responsibilities of state welfare programs, the use of class and gender analysis to describe oppression, and the moral responsibilities of individuals for their children. Though apparent in 1923, these differences were intentionally downplayed until the 1925 congress when they could no longer be ignored.

The Women's Congress of 1925

Events between the 1923 and 1925 women's congresses gave some Cubans reason to hope for an improved national leadership. The popular call for regeneration that had resounded in the last years of the Zayas administration became the campaign slogan for General Gerardo Machado, the Liberal Party's candidate for president. He promised an end to corruption and presidential reelection. To stimulate the economy and incorporate more Cubans into capital enterprise, he advocated public works programs, new schools, and social services. Education and social service programs complemented feminist objectives, giving feminists a means to advance women's employment and aid strategies at the level of federal government. To deter further U.S. economic expansion into the Cuban economy, General Machado vowed to protect local industry and to diversify the economy by relying upon Cuban enterprises. The brash presidential hopeful appealed to Cuban nationalist sentiments by promising to abrogate the Platt Amendment. Gerardo Machado won the 1924 election and restored hope that "Cuba was for Cubans."

Amidst the optimism, the Club Femenino held the Second National Women's Congress in April 1925. President Gerardo Machado and Vice-President Carlos de la Rosa spoke briefly at the opening ceremony

Opening session of the Second National Women's Congress, 1925. Speaking is Pilar Morlon de Menéndez and seated are President Gerardo Machado (left rear) and Vice President Carlos de la Rosa (right rear). Taken from the Federación Nacional de Asociaciones Femeninas, *Memoria del Segundo Congreso Nacional de Mujeres: April 12–18, 1925* (Havana: n.p., 1925), p. 57. The Stoner Collection, Roll 3.

and received the final resolutions. As before, each provincial representative of the Club Femenino attended, as did members of other women's clubs. This time, however, the conservative delegates were prepared to oppose inclusion of radical reforms in the final resolutions. Only days before the registration date, they organized a number of front organizations, including the Hijas de María y Santa Teresa de Jesús and the Asociación de Hijas de María del Sagrado Corazón, both of which espoused Catholic and religious views. By stacking the congress with conservative representatives, the groups planned to control the meetings and pass acceptable resolutions. Before the meeting convened, the progressives protested the seating of "organizaciones fantasmas" (phantom organizations), but no group was disqualified. Seventy-one organizations registered, forty more than in 1923.

As in the first congress, each delegate gave a speech designed to gain support for social welfare causes. The Red Cross, the Band of Mercy (an animal humane society), Catholic charity organizations, music and arts associations, the journalist guild, and public health experts testified about how women should undertake social welfare campaigns. Although most delegates supported suffrage, many opposed restructuring the family or the class system, and they had rigid moral standards. The delegates could more or less agree on measures giving women improved legal and civil status. There were no objections to civic projects or to asking the state to assume greater responsibility for education, welfare, and health—traditional charity projects. The battle lines were again drawn over the rights of illegitimate children and public responsibility for unwed mothers.

Progressive feminists challenged Church and family morality, calling religious standards for women's behavior "false divinity" and insisting that social justice required economic, political, and social freedom for all people. These feminists proposed to redefine family to include illegitimate children—not to penalize women for having children out of wedlock but to empower them by paying homage to their life-giving power—to end prostitution, and to provide jobs and respectability to former prostitutes. Adherents to these views included Ofelia Domínguez Navarro, Hortensia Lamar, Emma López Seña, Mariblanca Sabas Alomá, Dulce María Borrero de Luján, and Ofelia Rodríguez Acosta.

Given the ideological composition of the delegates, Domínguez knew she was courting defeat when she offered her resolution. Domínguez reiterated her proposal that civil law guarantee illegitimate children legal recognition, protection and shelter, and inheritance. She appealed to women to rise above the petty notions of the past in ways that men could not. Women, she argued, could decide issues on moral grounds. She noted that most of Cuba's able women were attending the congress and that it was up to them to provide justice for innocent children. She sought to arouse their national consciousness by challenging the delegates to help move the country from its colonial origins to a "liberal, ultra-democratic republic." In such a nation, she maintained, every woman could "preside over the moral life of the Republic," which included modern concepts of family, society, and politics.[17]

Domínguez clearly saw women as providing moral guidance, a view congruent with that of conservative feminists. But the two groups disagreed over the nature of morality. Domínguez Navarro proposed to modify articles 807, 808, 834, and 840 of the Civil Code. Her proposed law read:

> Natural children who are recognized by their mothers and fathers are heirs to their parents' property in the same proportion as legitimate children.[18]

Domínguez's lengthy and emotional speech failed to convince conservative and religious delegates. They had formed a voting block to defeat progressive causes and condemn free thinkers for violating the religious sanctity of the home and family. Because Domínguez had relied on moral

Srta. Hortensia Lamar, president of the Club Femenino de Cuba and also of the Federación Nacional de Asociaciones Femeninas. Taken from *Memoria del Primer Congreso,* p. 58. The Stoner Collection, Roll 2.

arguments claiming that women were entitled to the dignity of motherhood and protection, she gave the conservatives an opening to counter with their own moral invectives. They went on the offensive and impugned the moral character of the radical feminists. The heated and personal debate incited irate conservatives to clamber onto chairs, stamp their heels, and shout down Domínguez's pleas for support. Hortensia Lamar, a highly respected spinster who sided with Domínguez, was even accused by one delegate of supporting free love. Domínguez's argument was sullied with insinuations that she was not rational but weak and given to self-pity. (It was rumored that Domínguez had an illegitimate child, and letters from Hortensia Lamar in 1927 refer to a child, although there is no other evidence for this rumor.)[19] Compromise was impossible as emotions on both sides ran high. The president, Pilar Morlon de Menéndez, had to gavel the meeting to order and terminate the unruly confrontation.

To dilute intense feelings about the rights of illegitimate children, Dr. Margot López of the Creche "Habana Nueva," proposed a compromise. She emphasized proving the paternity of the illegitimate child and

Dra. Ofelia Domínguez Navarro, member of the Club Femenino, founder of the Alianza Nacional Feminista, and founder of the Unión Laborista de Mujeres. Taken from *Memoria del Primer Congreso,* p. 45. The Stoner Collection, Roll 2.

requiring both parents to give the child a surname and food to survive. López thus circumvented Domínguez's demand that the illegitimate child have rights to shelter and inheritance and that mothers be protected regardless of their civil status. But even López's resolution upset the conservative delegates, and it was rejected.

Because the majority of delegates refused to pass the resolution giving illegitimate and legitimate children equal rights, Ofelia Domínguez, Hortensia Lamar, Dulce María Borrero de Luján, María Luisa Dolz, Pilar Jorge de Tella, Mariblanca Sabas Alomá, Consuelo Miranda, Emma López Seña, and Loló de la Torriente walked out.[20] The delegates knew that the women's congresses were definitive events in the feminist movement because they established an agenda and leaders. The inability of the radicals to broaden concepts of family and morality and to include lower-class issues among their resolutions for change meant that they would be marginalized. The radical cause was lost, and its leaders were disgusted.

Cuba's Second National Women's Congress ended with a break

between conservative and radical feminists. Conservative and religious feminists who supported some reformist policies authored the congress's resolutions. By claiming social welfare and women's suffrage as their political territory, the conservatives, moderates, and progressives established their authority over such national interests as education, maternity hospitals, cultural events, charity, research on childhood diseases, welfare, and moral justification for political movements. More importantly, they made themselves the leaders of a feminist movement. A reverence for traditional motherhood girded every debate. Their programs aimed at protecting the traditional family and a class society, and they applied middle-class solutions (education and social welfare) to lower-class problems of unemployment, prostitution, drugs, illegitimacy, and poverty. The patriarchy and class structure rarely became targets of attack. Instead, the feminists established themselves as the matriarchs of a new state who sought to preserve and protect traditional institutions of the family while enhancing women's power within the democratic context.[21]

When the congress concluded, President Gerardo Machado promised the delegates the vote during his presidential term. His promise won loyalty from the suffrage organizations but only temporary support from the other feminist groups.

Repression and Division

As 1925 drew to a close and criticism of Machado increased, he made it clear that he would brook no opposition to his policies. The newly formed Communist Party and the CNOC became targets of political repression. Students, campesinos, workers, and intellectuals were arrested and imprisoned without trial. Assassinations increased. In response to the arrests of labor leaders, workers called strikes, and a period of severe political instability began. The feminists, too, were swept into the political turmoil. Where moral issues had divided women activists in April 1925, explosive political events drove them even further apart as the year progressed.

In November 1925 Julio Antonio Mella, the founder of the Cuban Communist Party, was jailed in Havana and held without bond for allegedly inciting a riot. In protest of this arbitrary arrest, Mella went on a hunger strike that lasted fifteen days and swayed popular opinion against the government. The Club Femenino de Cuba, the only women's organization to oppose Mella's arrest, appealed directly to President Machado to revoke the charge but got no response. On December 16,

1925, the Club decided to join labor unions and students in a public protest over the handling of the Mella case. Members demonstrated in Havana, and activated the provincial chapters in public resistance to Machado's tactics. Perhaps the most effective feminist dissident was Ofelia Domínguez Navarro.

Domínguez responded promptly to the Club's request to mobilize the Santa Clara membership. She was motivated by her commitment to due process before the law, but especially by her friendship with Julio Antonio Mella. Both of them had an earnest commitment to the rights of illegitimate children, and Mella had invited Domínguez to the University of Havana to speak to the Federación Estudiantil Universitario about her proposed reform. Domínguez and Rosario (Charita) Guillaume, from the Club Femenino, and Aureliano Sánchez Arango and Domingo Gómez Guimeranes, from the FEU, organized workers and students and marched on the provincial capital. They held a protest vigil in the city's central park and then peacefully dispersed.

But the leaders were not through. In a stroke of genius, they took a small contingent of demonstrators to the home of President Machado's parents, who lived in Santa Clara. Domínguez spoke for the delegation and urged Lutgarda Morales, Machado's mother, to ask her son to release Mella. According to Ofelia Domínguez's autobiography, Morales was visibly moved by the description of Mella's desperate physical condition, and she immediately sent a telegram to her son imploring Mella's release.[22] Due to popular opposition to Mella's arrest, and perhaps to the telegram, Julio Antonio Mella was released from prison on December 29, 1925, and charges against him were dropped.

Increased selective repression alarmed feminists, but each group responded to political unrest differently. Moderates believed that if women had the vote and participated in politics, corruption and repression would cease. Radicals countered that only structural change and revolution could wrest power from the privileged classes and distribute wealth without preference for race, creed, gender, and class. Divisions within the feminist movement reflected political, social, and economic stresses that underlay Cuba's national crisis.

Women's Organizations and Political Activity

The failure of national women's congresses to organize a centralized women's movement in the context of political instability motivated activists to form new feminist organizations. Although feminist consti-

activists to form new feminist organizations. Although feminist constitutions and objectives shared common concerns, the organizations could not form a unified front, mostly because egocentric leaders would not relinquish their powerful roles within the organizations. One might conclude that the feminist movement should have been seriously weakened by disunity and personal jealousies. In fact, diversity enhanced its effectiveness. Each feminist organization established links with sympathetic national political organizations, thus ensuring that women's rights would appear in most political manifestos and official promises, regardless of the ideology of the national organization.

By 1923 divisions had formed in the feminist movement over morality issues, political direction, and ideology. In 1927 these divisions were exacerbated by national political events that produced irreparable rifts among feminists manifested by the splintering of old organizations and the formation of new ones. In May President Machado called a constitutional assembly to extend the presidential term from four to six years and allow him to seek another term in office under the new constitution. Many Cubans were outraged by Machado's political maneuvering and charged that the changes foretold dictatorship. Political unrest began and continued to increase in the years that followed. In response to political opposition, Machado terrorized his opponents and used women's suffrage to demonstrate that he would not become a dictator. To these ends, he banned the Partido Comunista Cubana (the Cuban Communist Party) in 1927. Members of other opposition groups soon found themselves threatened with arbitrary arrests, deportations and exile, and assassination.[23] But women's suffrage was touted as evidence that Machado would hold elections in 1934 in which all Cubans could participate.

Machado's pretensions for democratic order thinly veiled the brutality he was prepared to use to maintain himself in power. His violation of democratic process and his resort to repression and terror forced students and workers to side with the militant opposition. Cuban politics moved to the streets, and public violence made it impossible for citizens to stay out of political disputes. In this highly charged atmosphere, feminists could no longer adhere strictly to gender arguments. They sided with political groups because Cuban democracy was at stake. For feminists, the importance of this issue had special significance, since it meant the suffrage campaign would be pointless under a dictatorship. Regardless of their political views, feminists left the polite society of their club meetings and became activists in the streets, where they held vigils outside the capitol building and aired their views in public newspapers.

In taking militant public positions, they forsook their earlier promises to act as political healers.

When political discontent exploded into civil unrest after 1928, feminist organizations reformed along more political lines. After a visit from a delegation of the National Women's Party of the United States in 1927, Pilar Jorge de Tella, a founding member of the Club Femenino, and Ofelia Domínguez Navarro merged two smaller associations, the Comité de Acción Cívico and the Comité de Sufragio Femenino, to form the Alianza Nacional Feminista (ANF). By the end of 1928 the Alianza was among the more active and influential of the feminist organizations. Its leaders were decidedly middle- and upper-class, most of whom had been delegates to the women's congresses.[24]

In the early years the Alianza represented a diversity of commitments and strategies for improving women's status. Pilar Jorge de Tella petitioned Congress to grant suffrage. Ofelia Domínguez Navarro worked directly with the Socialist Party and the cigar and sugar workers to improve working conditions. Leticia de Arriba appealed to upper-class women as she spoke over the radio and in fashionable homes about the importance of women's unique social contributions. Celia Sarra de Averhoff, the heiress to the fortune of the family's drugstore chain, urged business and factory women to join the feminist movement. Hortensia Lamar became a noted public orator in opposition to prostitution and drugs.

While the Alianza's charter asserted that working women could be members, only a few workers joined, and these had little voice and no officers within the ANF. Eudosia Lara, president of the Tobacco Deveiners' Guild, was perhaps the most prestigious working-class member, but she was not an ANF officer. That the Alianza often held its meetings at the Havana Yacht Club might have signaled to working women the class preferences of the leadership. Elite officers set an agenda that reflected their concern for poor and working women, but their solutions relied on charity, social welfare, and legal change. Though militant in some of their demands, Aliancistas were opposed to giving working women power. The Aliancistas joined revolutionary factions after 1930 to oust Machado, but their insurgency did not extend beyond the post-Machado era. Their concern was democracy and political participation, not social revolution.

The tentative ties that bound the Alianza in 1928 unraveled in May 1930 with the election of new officers. Domínguez Navarro hoped to become president, but her alliance with socialist groups offended the majority of the membership. Rumors of a rivalry between Domínguez

Navarro and de Tella did not reinforce the fragile association.[25] De Tella thought that the Alianza should be a political pressure group as well as a cultural and recreational organization. Domínguez Navarro believed that the Alianza should advocate political and economic change in the direction of socialism.

At the core of the dispute were class issues. Most members did not have to work for a living, and they resisted a total commitment to political and social issues. Many lacked a deep sympathy for the working woman. Some were also loathe to defy the opinions of the Church and their husbands. Domínguez Navarro challenged traditional values and therefore received only weak support. When the balloting was completed, the moderate María Montalvo de Soto Navarro was elected president. Ofelia Domínguez cried foul and accused the association of corrupt electoral practices, but the results stood. Ofelia Domínguez withdrew, taking with her the faction that supported her views.

Two new women's organizations were formed out of the disputed elections: the Lyceum and the Unión Laborista de Mujeres. The Lyceum, later called the Lyceum Lawn and Tennis Club, was the most cultural and intellectual of the feminist associations. Its founders included Berta Arocena de Martínez Márquez and Renée Méndez Capote, both of whom were members of old propertied families. The group argued that intellectual approaches to reform were the best means to enhance national and women's interests. The Lyceum's objectives were "to foment a collective spirit among women, to facilitate an interchange of ideas and to generate beneficiary activities." Women of the Lyceum believed that radical change was impossible without exposure to education and culture. Rather than specify what change should be, the Lyceum emphasized women's education and political participation so that the collection of women could decide future issues and not a select group such as themselves. The Lyceum favored votes for women, lobbied Congress, and funded feminist and socialist lectures in Havana. Many of the women in the Lyceum belonged to more politically active organizations as well. Although the Lyceum represented an aristocratic approach to change, by definition it had to entertain revolutionary as well as reformist ideas. As a result, the lecture schedule included Raul Roa, Juan Marinello, Fernando Ortiz, Ofelia Domínguez, Mariblanca Sabas Alomá, and Ofelia Rodríguez Acosta on the left and President Gerardo Machado, Carlos Márquez Sterling, María Collado, and María Gómez Carbonell on the right. Beyond establishing schools for the poor, the Lyceum also supplied a forum where political advocates could air their beliefs.

After her resignation from the Alianza, Ofelia Domínguez formed the Unión Laborista de Mujeres, the most radical women's organization. The Unión's devotion to class issues almost surpassed its support for the liberation of women, yet its leadership was bourgeois.[26] Initially, the Unión declared itself in favor of education and social reforms, including the vote and the abolition of capital punishment. More importantly, it emphasized issues of working-class women over the right to vote. By 1931, when opposition to Machado was openly defiant and the socialists had gained strength, the Unión broke with the other feminist organizations and denounced women's suffrage as an accommodation with the Machado government. Domínguez did not oppose women's suffrage outright, but she was against suffrage as the organizing principle, the summum bonum, of the woman's movement. The reversal resulted from Domínguez's conversion to Marxism and her consequent demands that Cubans expel U.S. political and economic interests and transform the capitalist-based society into a nationalist version of socialism.[27]

But even the Unión could not escape a middle-class orientation. The Unión was governed by a meritocracy that carried out revolutionary activities in the name of the proletariat. While workers made up part of the membership, they were more seen than heard. The Unión's activities consisted of providing legal defense for jailed students, campesinos, workers, and political radicals, and this task required lawyers and not workers. Domínguez, Bertha Darder Bebé, and Rosa Laclerc addressed political gatherings about radical resistance and not narrowly defined women's issues. But the Unión never forsook the women's cause, nor did it accept the Marxist tenet that women could be liberated as part of the proletariat. The Unión produced a socialist-feminist manifesto and incorporated it in the Communist Party manifesto of 1928.

The Unión's most steadfast opponent, the Partido Demócrata Sufragista, was established just before President Gerardo Machado's constitutional assembly met in 1927.[28] The Partido pledged support for President Machado's administration and constitutional reforms, and they generally approved of his *regeneración* program to stop corruption and build Cuban enterprises that benefited Cubans. For their loyalty they expected that the president would fulfill his promise to the Second National Women's Congress by enacting suffrage legislation during his administration. Members of the Partido believed that Machado offered the surest route to political participation, and the membership also believed that democracy would lead Cubans to self-governance and, in time, social justice. They were not as impatient as the more radical feminist groups over the miscarriage of democracy, fraudulent elections, U.S. meddling in the Cuban economy and politics, and the conditions of the working class. Partido president María Collado, an upper-class poet with reformist ideas, focused the party's attention on the vote. But even as she made suffrage her major objective, she was not fully convinced that women in general had the necessary public experience to vote. She believed that women should prepare themselves for their new duties by attending school and looking beyond the home for employment.

Though the Partido Demócrata Sufragista concentrated on the vote, it also worked for fair employment practices. One of its first campaigns, carried out primarily in newspapers and in meetings with politicians, was to convince the Department of Transportation to hire women as bus and streetcar drivers. María Collado took her commitment to working women seriously, albeit from an upper-class perspective. Although she did not need to work, she was an investigator for the Department of Agriculture, Industry, and Commerce, in charge of evaluating the treatment of women in private enterprise. Her reports provided information the government needed to prosecute violators of protective work legislation. Collado believed that through cooperation and not revolution, the Partido could improve working conditions for women. Her strategy was to support President Machado's labor regulations and oppose work action.[29]

María Collado and the Partido's affiliation with Machado began as an alliance of convenience, but it ended in guilt by association. Machado did not deliver on votes for women nor guide his administration through the mine field of political opposition or the disaster of the world depression. As Machado's popularity declined, so did the fortunes of the Partido Demócrata Sufragista.

Despite all their differences, the feminists occasionally found common cause. Bound by class and personal association, women sometimes united to protect their associates. Ofelia Domínguez tested her friendship with moderate feminists by breaking with them over ideology, yet, when she was arrested in 1931 and incarcerated despite a pulmonary illness, many former antagonists went to police headquarters to protest her arrest. Years later, in 1948, when Domínguez was being considered by the Batista administration as a member of Cuba's United Nations delegation, Elena Mederos de González, a respected leader of the Lyceum and a member of the Cuban UN mission, defended her candidacy on the grounds that Cuba was a democratic nation that recognized all political ideologies and that Domínguez Ofelia was eminently qualified to serve. Personal bonds held these women together even as politics drew them apart.

Influenced by the resolutions at the national women's congresses, feminist organizations projected a reformist, but not radical, agenda. Through their hortatory directives and adherence to noble motives, feminists established themselves as political leaders who by 1925 had three mandates: political equality for women, social reform, and institutionalizing their programs to aid and represent women. Political equality meant women's incorporation into the national leadership through an electoral process. Social reform referred to state responsibility for welfare programs, with special attention to services for women and children. Institutionalized feminist programs established centers of power to affect change, which gave respectability and authority to those designated to lead. A hierarchical system of command within the feminist movement took hold. Indeed, feminists presided as matriarchs over the female population, promising help and assistance where it was needed.

4

A Prosopography of
the Feminist Leadership

⌖

Wealth and privileged status gave feminist leaders access to power and created a context for their ideology. The leaders were middle- and upper-class women with college degrees, financial resources, and political connections, and thus they were in positions to advance their causes. But beyond having influence, the leaders' privileged positions molded their prescriptions for women's liberation. Servant help, for instance, allowed leaders and writers to be pro family, pro women, and pro liberation without resolving contradictions between caring for the home and competing with men for jobs. Feminists could describe the liberated woman as one who was feminine, in possession of equal civil rights, and protected by the law and men when she was a mother. Given this orientation, the leaders never identified family responsibilities as impediments to women's liberation. Only women who were accustomed to a comfortable life-style could have supported these objectives and advocated them for all women.

Biographical information on the leaders informs us of their commitments to family and public interests. My survey of people who knew the feminists illustrates that approximately 40 percent of the leaders were mothers, 60 percent had been employed at some time, 75 percent graduated from a university, 33 percent had postgraduate degrees, and all had at least one servant. By these standards, feminists were not representative of the majority of Cuban women, but they were in positions to define women's rights and put resolutions before the public and law-makers.[1]

The feminists were white, middle- and upper-class, and a numerical minority. Indeed, the total number of feminists probably never came to more than one thousand women at any given time between 1927 and 1940.[2] Photographs of organizational activities show an all-white mem-

I would like to thank Dr. Robert Levine, chairman of the History Department at the University of Miami, Coral Gables, and Dr. Paul Siegel, chief of the Education Branch of the Bureau of the Census, Washington, D.C., for their valuable suggestions regarding the structure of my survey in chapter 4.

bership. Of the leaders for whom I have information, all were white, one-third had independent wealth, and two-thirds came from the professional class. The rank and file of the feminist associations included teachers, nurses, stenographers, and salaried professionals. Each organization claimed to have had women who worked in factories for minimum wage among its membership, but their numbers were admittedly few.

The leadership was distinct from the average Cuban woman in a number of ways. The leaders enjoyed comfortable living circumstances; their house addresses indicated social and economic status. Though the leaders might have had several homes, the sixteen homes in Havana were located in well-appointed neighborhoods, such as Miramar, Vedado, Nuevo Vedado, La Víbora, or in an apartment or hotel along the Prado in Old Havana. Only 37 percent of the addresses were mansions or rich estates, but 44 percent were large, newly built homes with multiple bedrooms, modern appliances, gardens, and garages, and only 19 percent were simple accommodations in apartment buildings or hotels.

Marital status is an approximate indicator of the leaders' commitment to the traditional home, marriage, and motherhood. Forty-two percent of feminist leaders followed social prescriptions for women and married. Fifty-eight percent of the leaders remained single, ignoring social expectations and pursuing independent and solitary goals. While it might be incorrect to assume that each feminist voluntarily chose her matrimonial status based upon a feminist ideal of womanhood, it is fair to assume that marital status did influence feminist attitudes about dignifying motherhood and attaining respect and legal guarantees outside of the home. Interestingly, single feminists tended to idealize motherhood to the extent that they demanded respect and state support for mothers despite their civil status. Married feminists, all of whom were mothers, translated mothering into social welfare programs focusing on financial and educational aid to the poor. Both groups centered their attention on maternity and argued for reforms in the name of motherhood.

The marital status of feminist leaders deviated from the national average for women of their race and class. Table 4 compares the marital status of feminists with other white women in Havana and white women throughout Cuba in 1943. (By this time all of the feminists in the survey were forty years old or more and had settled on their marital status.) No data are available to compare the marital status of feminist leaders with women in their age group. Such a statistic would certainly have increased the differentiation between the percentage of married feminists and the percentage of married white women in Havana and throughout the island, since the percentage of ever-married women increases with age.

Table 4   Comparison of Marital Status of Feminists with that of White
Women in Havana and throughout Cuba, 1943[a]

Women	Single	Consensual Union	Married	Widowed	Divorced
Feminists[a]	57.8	0	37.8	2.2	2.2
Habaneras[b]	47.73	?	41.53	8.99	1.74
Cubanas[b]	53.23	?	38.64	7.1	1.02

Note: 1943 was chosen as a date to compare the feminists with other populations of women because all feminists, except one, were between the ages of thirty and fifty and had determined whether they would marry. Of course, many became widows later on. The 1943 census is generally believed to be more complete than the 1931 census and more reliable than the 1953 census.
[a] Numbers come from my survey of forty-five out of one thousand Cuban feminists.
[b] República de Cuba, Dirección General del Censo, *Informe general del censo de 1943* (Havana: P. Fernández, 1945), 947.

Even though the feminists were more often single than the national average by at least ten percentage points, it is still true that a significant proportion were married (38 percent), 2 percent were divorced, and 2 percent were widowed.

Table 5 compares the marital status of feminist leaders with all Cuban women, regardless of race and region, who belonged to the feminists' age group. The tendency of feminists to be single is even more striking here than in the previous comparison, since feminists between thirty and thirty-nine years of age were single more often than the national average by 20 percentage points, and feminists between forty and forty-nine years of age were single more often than the national average by 15 percentage points. Only one feminist divorced, but less than 1 percent of married Cubans divorced. Unfortunately, the 1943 Cuban census did not record the numbers of Cubans who were joined in consensual unions—that is, unions not sanctioned by the Church or state.[3] In the 1909 and 1919 censuses about 6 percent of all Cuban marriages were marriages by consensual agreement. None of the feminists had this kind of arrangement by 1943, or even before, although at least four of the single feminists had had lovers.

That feminist leaders married less often than most other Cuban women suggests that single feminist leaders believed they could not manage a marriage, a career, and political activism. Perhaps marriage and the social/psychological expectations of being a wife and mother impeded feminist activism for some but not for all leaders.

Radical politics and marital status did seem to be related. Radical

Table 5   Comparison of the Marital Status of Feminist Leaders with that
of All Cuban Women by Age Group, 1943

Women by Age	Single	Consensual Union	Married	Widowed	Divorced
Age 30–39					
Feminists[a]	63.4	0	34.3	0	2.2
All[b]	41.0	?	54.6	2.8	1.6
Age 40–49					
Feminists	54.2	0	43.6	2	0
All	29.8	?	59.3	9.3	1.7

[a] Numbers come from my survey of forty-five of one thousand feminists.
[b] República de Cuba. Dirección General del Censo, *Informe general del censo de 1943* (Havana: P. Fernández, 1945), 773.

thought here means a sharp departure from traditional customs via revolution or the destruction of patriarchy. The leadership is seen as radical by its affiliation with Marxist or revolutionary groups, the severity of its attack on the patriarchy, and its disparagement of social reforms. The moderates, who tended to be married, sought to correct women's oppression through legal reforms, education, and labor reforms. The nine single leaders were more strident than the seven married ones. Most of the radical thinkers adhered to Marxist analysis, but two of them, María Collado and Dr. Rosa Anders, who were radical conservatives, advocated the destruction of patriarchal authority and equality between women and men. Both married and single leaders remained active in the feminist movement about the same lengths of time, which implies that marriage and family did not reduce the married leaders' commitment to the movement.

Family size also indicates whether the leaders were mothers and the number of years of their lives they devoted to caring for young children. The feminist mothers had an average of 1.7 children between 1920 and 1940, which was far below the average family size. In the city of Havana in 1919 the average size of a white family was 8.2 people, meaning that the average white woman might have had 6.2 children, although the number is probably smaller, since the extended family and servants often resided in the family compound.[4] The 1931 and 1943 censuses did not correct for race for the city of Havana, but they did indicate that for all women living in Havana in 1931 and 1943 the average family size was 5.3 and 5.2 people, respectively.[5] These indicators suggest that feminist leaders tended to have fewer children than their same-age cohorts in Havana by at least one

Doctors of Pharmacology, ca. 1919. Some Cuban women attained high levels of education, and nearly all the feminists received postgraduate degrees, one of which was in pharmacology. Taken from *Aspiraciones* (Año 5, No. 8): 5.

child. Feminist leaders who were mothers spent fewer years caring for children than most Cuban mothers. Over two-fifths of the leaders experienced motherhood, but by limiting the sizes of their families, they reduced the number of years they were committed to child care and increased the time they had for additional interests.

Levels of education indicated class as well as membership in another select social category: the ruling intelligentsia. In 1919, a year when all leaders in the survey had graduated from high school, only 23 percent of all Cuban women had entered public school, and of that population 73 percent were white women. By the time the sixteen leaders had completed their educations, their accomplishments were as follows:

Secondary school:
    Fifteen finished high school.
    One graduated from a finishing school for girls in the United States.
University education:

Twelve earned bachelor's degrees from the University of Havana.
Postgraduate degrees:
Two received law degrees.
Four graduated from graduate school with doctorates in pharmacology or the humanities.

With instruction and time to reflect on women's moral and political causes, feminists devised their own versions of feminism and contemplated appropriate action to win their objectives. They had been exposed to political theories of governance, which included theories about democracy and the philosophies of José Martí, John Locke, and Karl Marx. They had also read feminist treatises from other countries. The vast majority believed that democratic principles pertained to women as well as to men, and they were capable of presenting the arguments that defended that view.

Most of the leaders were proficient writers and orators, and they communicated their ideas to political officials and the Cuban public. Their appeals were transmitted via radio and newspapers, which meant that their messages traveled beyond the Havana intelligentsia and set a national agenda that was carried to the presidential palace, the Congress, the courts, and to the people.

The movement's effectiveness was enhanced by the leader's connections with powerful, elite men. In some of their professions feminist leaders associated with influential men. Many feminists practiced a profession for at least a brief period of their lives. Thirteen of the sixteen leaders worked for at least two years, and five supported themselves. Several of the women had more than one career during their lifetimes. The professional affiliations of the feminist leadership were as follows:

Seven writers (usually journalists, but also poets and novelists)
Two lawyers
Five educators (taught at the Havana Normal School and the University of Havana, the School of Social Welfare at the University of Havana)
One architect
Three politicians (one elected; two appointed as delegates to the UN).[6]

No feminist leader was a domestic servant, a sales clerk, a deveiner in a tobacco factory, a textile worker, a farmer, or a worker in the trades.

Husbands and fathers were of the middle and upper classes. The seven husbands for whom there is reliable information were:

two lawyers (one was also chairman of the University of Havana School of Law, and rector of the University of Havana)
a journalist

a wealthy businessman
the owner of a prosperous tobacco business
a professor at the University of Havana
a writer

The fathers too were predominantly privileged or professional gentle-men. The ten fathers for which there is information were:

a pharmacologist and owner of the best-known Cuban drugstore chain
    (therefore, he was a very wealthy businessman)
a banker
a lawyer and businessman
four businessmen
a landowner
a tobacco wholesaler
a farmer

Family connections brought feminist leaders into contact with na-tional public officials. Several husbands and fathers also held public offices. One of them was the secretary of Public Education and the Arts; another was the secretary of Finance and secretary of State; and another was the mayor of Havana.[7] Position and power were important to feminist leaders. Their selection of husbands indicated a cultural and financial preference for successful men. Husbands averaged between six and seven years older than the wives and were already established in a profession at the time of marriage. Feminists, therefore, had some indication about their fiancés' economic and social status before marry-ing. There were counterexamples to this model. Elena Mederos married a man who was a young lawyer and beneath her economic status. The couple agreed to separate its assets, and Mederos's husband built his own prestigious law firm without his wife's financial backing.

Many feminist leaders preserved the social and economic statuses of their fathers by not marrying poor men. Of the sixteen feminist leaders, only five had to work for a living, and those five were either well-paid professional writers or lawyers. Feminist leaders were economically secure, and many could depend upon husbands and fathers for economic support and political contacts.

Feminist leaders also lived with sufficient wealth to afford domestic service, which freed them to pursue careers and volunteer activities. All sixteen women hired servants to wash their clothes, cook, and shop. The mothers had governesses to care for their children. Ten of the sixteen had chauffeurs and gardeners. With this domestic help, the leaders were free to integrate their diverse activities and be mothers, professionals, and activists.

Leisure time also allowed feminist leaders to participate in political and community activities beyond feminist associations. These women belonged to philanthropic, educational, and political organizations. In addition to their feminist affiliations, the sixteen feminists collectively belonged to thirty-three different organizations, ranging from the Communist Party, the Grupo Minorista, the Women's Journalist Union, and Women in Opposition to the Damas Isabelinas (a charity society that cared for tubercular and ill children), the American Cancer League, and the Humane Society. All belonged to at least one educational organization or honor society. Only four of the sixteen expressed any interest in religious associations. Their diverse affiliations outside the feminist movement mirrored their commitments to welfare causes and political ideology.

Culture of Privilege

There is nothing startling in the fact that the feminist leaders were educated, financially secure, and associates of influential men. The real significance of the feminists' social and economic status is in the culture of privilege—that is, an assumption that these women would empower themselves in their relations with men and to lead powerless women to self-determination.

Feminists differed from the majority of Cuban women because they had the luxury to reflect upon women's inferior gender status. They had the sense that they could reject subordination and that they could encourage all women to follow their examples. They could articulate new visions for social relations that gave women more authority and respect, and they could project an image of the liberated women. They were in a position to organize and fund campaigns to change political and legal institutions that had traditionally placed women under the tutelege of men. They were able to communicate broadly to alter the consciousness that shaped male and female identities. In a word, the success of Cuban feminism depended upon the social position of the leadership.

Wealth and privileged status raised the possibility that feminist leaders could manage motherhood, a profession, and political activism. The amalgam of these life endeavors might have encouraged a vision that emphasized the virtures of motherhood while empowering women as Cuban citizens. The centrality of motherhood restrained an attack on patriarchy, marriage, and the family for conflicting with women's liberation. Without a servant class, Cuban feminists would have been forced to choose between motherhood, careers, and political authority. As it was, Cuban feminist leaders could carry out all three roles, which helps explain why motherhood was not perceived as a debilitating vocation and why Cuban feminism could only apply to privileged women.

Combining motherhood with respectable professions and political activism was impractical for most women, but for feminists it had explicit advantages: it enabled the leaders to become politicians and community leaders. Indeed, Cuban feminism created a new facet of the ruling class: select women authorized to oversee national educational, welfare, and women's interests and to dream of a world in which all women could partake of the luxury of leisure time, financial security, and a sense of personal independence. It also helped to produce a feminism centered on motherhood, cooperative with the patriarchy, and respectful of class ordering.

5

The Feminist Journalists

The intellectual activism of feminist writers contrasted with the organized campaigns of feminist political leaders. Writers drew together the symbols of the struggle while remaining aloof from political involvement. While the activists formed policy and instigated action, the writers created ideals and icons. Leftist writers expanded Hispanic notions of revered motherhood to establish social morality, and conservative feminists exalted the *mambisa* to argue for civic equality. Taken together, these writers articulated Cuban images of self-actualization for women.

Feminist journalists followed a Cuban colonial tradition of political debate in newspapers. In important instances, Cuban women founded and ran revolutionary newspapers during the Wars of Independence.[1] After independence women continued as journalists and editors, in some cases becoming advocates for political causes.[2] It was normal for feminist writers to emerge and present their views to the public through popular newspapers and journals as well as through feminist publications.[3]

Feminist writers not only disagreed with traditional attitudes, they also disagreed with one another. Following the literary and political impulses of the day, feminist intellectuals viewed it their duty to enlighten literate society and advocate their positions. In their haste to mold values, writers vied with each other over the definition of *feminism*, who should lead, and the campaigns they should wage. More than the activists, the writers developed the rationale and essence of Cuban feminism.

The Emergence of Cuban Intellectual Activism

Cuban feminist writers were part of a larger political and intellectual ferment. During the 1920s, the decade that Juan Marinello Vidaurreta called the "critical decade," Cuba's intellectuals wrote lyrically and critically about the national crises. They published effusive manifestos in popular journals, criticizing the failures of the political leadership.

Novelists, poets, playwrights, essayists, and journalists challenged readers to think about fundamental values. These author/activists believed that they could lead the republican generation of Cubans to effective and honest self-rule.

By 1923 intellectuals such as José Enrique Varona and Carlos de Velasco denounced political corruption and the "rebirth of the colony in republican Cuba." The new republican generation raised objections to the poor standards of education, U.S. imperialism, the exploitation of workers, and political corruption. In 1923 a group of young academics voiced its outrage at governmental corruption during a meeting in the Academy of Sciences. After that protest, thirteen of the original group moved their demonstration to the Club Femenino, where Erasmo Reguiferos Boudet, President Zayas's minister of justice and a known participant in awarding *botellas* (payoffs and kickbacks), lottery scams, and the arbitrary enforcement of the law, was an invited guest. This was an opportunity to criticize the rampant corruption in the Zayas government. Ruben Martinez Villena interrupted the *homenaje* to Paulina Luisi, a Uruguayan feminist and writer, to rail against the government's irregular purchase of a convent as an example of political corruption. Thereupon, he and twelve of his colleagues walked out of the hall. This act in the Club Femenino, subsequently known as the Protesta de los Trece, set the stage for the formation of the Grupo Minorista, a literary vanguard for social change that was active between 1923 and 1927.[4]

The Grupo Minorista met on Saturday afternoons at either the Lafayette Hotel on the Prado or the Café Martí in Old Havana. Young intellectuals formed their own thinking from strains of vanguardism in Europe and the Americas. The majority of Minoristas were men, with only two women in the original membership. But one of those women was Mariblanca Sabas Alomá, a leading feminist writer. The Minoristas took Marxism as the group's ideological center and expressed their ideas through collective acts, declarations, and manifestos. Yet the ideology of each person diverged from the collective position of the group. Feminists, for example, insisted that women's issues receive more prominence in political debate than Marx or Lenin had prescribed. The Grupo Minorista was, in fact, a heterogeneous group of intellectuals with a preference for leftist, but not necessarily revolutionary, solutions to national problems.

The Minoristas were most active during the first years of the Machado administration. They coined the term "the tropical Mussolini" for Cuba's president and proclaimed themselves "for the freedom of all people in our America and against North American imperialism."[5] A comparatively small group, never exceeding forty members, the Minoristas pointed the way for cultural and political regeneration by outlining a range of solutions to Cuba's problems. Minorismo continued a century-old tradition of club organization and popular influence through newspapers and journals and expanded into an art form of social criticism in popular tabloids.[6]

By 1925 the most outstanding journals routinely published Minorista articles.[7] Minorista articles also appeared in leftist journals such as *América Libre* and *Revista de Avance* as well as in leading newspapers. While Jorge Mañach might have coined the term *Grupo Minorista*, referring to the group's minority position, Juan Ramon Jiménez, the Spanish poet, referred to the group as the "inmensa minoria" because of its impact on Cuban political views and international opinion.[8]

The Feminist Writers

Like the vanguardists in the Grupo Minorista, feminist writers emerged as intellectual leaders of social justice campaigns with an emphasis on women's issues. Their published works challenged Catholic notions of motherhood, religion, family relations, morality, and women's place in Cuba's social order. They invited readers to respond and publish their correspondence, thus placing a serious exchange of ideas before the Cuban readership. Their dialogue and acrimony consolidated views and gave a forum for serious debate on feminism.

Mariblanca Sabas Alomá, Ofelia Rodríguez Acosta, and María Collado were among the most prominent writers.[9] Sabas Alomá, referred to by some as the "Red Feminist," and Rodríguez shared a leftist orientation, and they published regularly in *Carteles* and *Bohemia,* respectively. Collado was a conservative feminist who supported Machado and advocated limited reforms and the preservation of property and capitalist interests. She was the president of the Partido Demócrata Sufragista and served as the editor of *La Mujer,* the official publication of the party. Taken together, these three women framed a broad interpretation of Cuban feminism.

MARIBLANCA SABAS ALOMÁ

Mariblanca Sabas Alomá was a founding member of the Grupo Minorista, though her male colleagues only begrudgingly acknowledged her attendance at weekly meetings.[10] Jorge Mañach, a fellow Minorista,

Srta. Mariblanca Sabas Alomá, outspoken feminist and one of two women writers in the Grupo Minorista. Taken from *Memoria del Primer Congreso*. The Stoner Collection, Roll 2.

having to account for the faithful attendance of Sabas Alomá and Graziela Garbalosa at the weekly meetings, said of them: "[They were] women of inspiration and fluff who joined the young men and teased them about their gallantry. I wonder why these congenial women are allowed to come. Perhaps because they have illusions of high culture, and they want to give some spiritual flavor to their lives."[11] Fortunately, his was not the last word on either of the writers.

Born in Santiago de Cuba in 1901, Sabas Alomá won two gold medals for her poetry in the Juegos Florales in Santiago in 1923. In that same year she moved to Havana, attended the First National Women's Congress, and began participating in the regular Saturday *tertulias* (meetings) of the Grupo Minorista. Between 1924 and 1927 Sabas Alomá worked for various Cuban newpapers and journals, and she took leaves of absence from Cuba to study art and literature in Mexico, the United States at Columbia University, and Puerto Rico at the University of Puerto Rico with Pedro Salinas.

Permanently located in Havana in 1927, Sabas Alomá accepted a full-time position with *Carteles*. Her weekly column more often outraged than satisfied the readership. Adopting the Minorista preference for leftist solutions, Sabas Alomá undertook the intellectual leadership of the woman's movement. The tone of her essays was arrogant, combative, and uncompromising. She was self-righteous and at times shrill. She took on her detractors with reasoned argument, but she could be sarcastic. She exaggerated the errors in her opponents' positions and asserted that hers were morally correct. When her audience applauded her views, her tone became apologetic and humble. When she was criticized, she went on the offensive, often using sarcasm and emotional persuasion for reasoned logic. Brilliant, egocentric, and manipulative, she demanded complete devotion from her followers.

Marxist analysis drove Sabas Alomá's reasoning, but so did her own assessments of Cuban culture. She assumed that economic status and legal structures prevented women from taking control of their lives. She also asserted that cultural and attitudinal reforms were prerequisites to women's independence, and here she differed with Marxist canon. She criticized revolutionaries and elites alike for neglecting the intimate and psychological roots of repression in their plans for change.[12] She also held women responsible for not pursuing more radical solutions to their own and their families' inabilities to free themselves from conventions of subordination that repressed a gender, a people, and a nation.

Sabas Alomá believed that women of the *gran mundo social* (social elite) contributed to the suffering of the majority of women. She claimed that most wealthy women were preoccupied with their own social status and were happy to get ahead at the expense of other women. An obsession with social appearances prohibited women from carrying out their natural functions, which, in Sabas Alomá's opinion, was sensitivity to the needs of others. Instead, privileged women developed cultural habits such as gossiping and ostracizing other women that were particularly cruel and certainly unproductive. According to Mariblanca's use of the term, these women could never be feminists.[13] Sabas Alomá blamed the mean-spiritedness of women on poor education, unenlightened philosophical ethics, and a lack of humanist values.[14]

According to her feminist philosophy, women should be productive. Sabas Alomá detested the destructive effects of gossip and whispers but hated even more the hypocrisy of women who attempted to appear charitable. She believed that those women were "exhibitionists" more interested in being seen helping the poor than in achieving an equitable distribution of wealth.

If Sabas Alomá was critical of women's tendency to betray one another, she was also intolerant of the same tendency in Cuban society. It was impossible to achieve social justice, because Cubans were taught from birth not to trust one another. At the bottom of it all, she said, were mothers, who preserved and taught conventions of mistrust and betrayal to their children.

For Sabas Alomá, feminism was not merely a sentimental humanitarian response to poverty and misfortune, it was a revolution that sought to correct class and gender exploitation. The origins of that revolution stemmed from a profound belief in the dignity and strength of motherhood. She made women responsible for much of society's failures, even as she admitted women's political and economic powerlessness. She insisted that, as mothers, women created men capable of monstrous social practices. While formally they were disenfranchised, women in fact held the power to remake society.

> Women create men and make them as women wish them to be. The mother in the home is the one who forges the character and spiritual models for her children. Mothers can produce the man/friend, the man/compañero, and the useful woman with a mind, heart, and dignity. If men are bad, then a great part of the responsibility belongs to women.
>   . . . Our mission of creating human love is higher, more noble, more transcendental than men's. We destroy the cowardly hypocrisy that makes economic aspects of marriage more important than human ones. We can bravely destroy the chains of ignorance and fanaticism that make men selfish, and we can free ourselves from the prejudicial corners of our consciousness of false and inhuman morality. This is the struggle.[15]

Drawing on the principles of nineteenth-century liberalism and feminist theory, Sabas Alomá offered her own version of women's liberation:

> Feminism is the supreme and high effort that women give to emancipate themselves morally, legally, and socially from men. Feminism redeems women from their role as slaves, and it elevates them to a category of a conscious person. Feminism is, then, essentially, liberation. Until now women have only been the judged members of civilization.[16]

Yet in contributing to a new Cuban morality, Sabas Alomá did not imply that women should become men's equals in any sphere, and certainly not in politics.

> Women do not wish to be men's enemies, equals, or inferiors. . . . women want to be men's companions. This is all. Women wish to be free from the lessons established by a passé and bankrupt civilization. Women are the

creators of a new morality, a morality that is without the abominable monstrosities called property rights, the privilege of legitimate birth, and woman as nothing but reproductive uterus. We are for warmth, light, tenderness, joy, the fountain that quenches men's thirst in moments of intimacy, but only during intimacy. Women must be totally female. By being women we can make men more masculine.[17]

By preserving masculine and feminine functions in Cuban society, Sabas Alomá did not offend the sense of place and order but expanded old notions about women's influence over men. She hardly attacked the patriarchy. Women and men should be connected, and women should assume responsibility for designated tasks such as determining a sense of national morality *and* influencing men's public and private behavior.

Condemnation of the patriarchy for the repression of women was not a central part of Sabas Alomá's feminist argument, although it surfaced as a secondary theme. She believed that Cuban feminism had to be defined beyond the narrow battle between the sexes. Women had to resolve the problems of the poor, political corruption, economic disadvantages facing women, illegitimacy, work discrimination, education, and health. She therefore believed that feminism was:

> Against men when men are the masters. With men when they, like us, are slaves trying to gain their independence. Against men if they, just because they are men, adhere to the standards of bedroom *hembrismo* [sexual and submissive femininity], or purely sexual perceptions of women, which are morbid, humiliating, and sterile. With men, if they, riddled with the painful reality of exploitation at work, rise up against their exploiters, making a clean opening toward a "future without boundaries" that Lenin proclaimed.[18]

The links between feminism and revolutionary change were of utmost importance to Sabas Alomá. Anything short of new family relations, values, and beliefs would end in a society unable to free itself from hierarchical arrangements. But for Sabas Alomá revolutionary change was not modeled entirely after Marxist-Leninism. Women, she insisted, could not be subsumed in a genderless proletariat.

> The feminist movement is fundamentally revolutionary. We women, upon rebelling against the established order, form within the Left a social process of incalculable importance. . . . We modify the Marxist theory of historical materialism, without deforming it. We women fight in schools, shops, factories, and in our own homes with our underappreciated gift of spiritual delicateness. Delicateness does not exclude bravery, nor does it condone humiliation. Each woman is an *hembra* [female] in essence and a mother in potentiality, although the actual conditions of life strangle and deform the

feelings of motherhood. Upon incorporating ourselves slowly but surely into political life, we bring pure ideals, kind hopes, noble expectations, and enthusiasm in the best interests of the community. We also bring a quality that becomes increasingly rare in men—perhaps because they have exercised it for so long without getting results—and that quality is OUTRAGE.[19]

For her assault on traditional family and gender relations, Sabas Alomá's critics accused her of being a communist or a homosexual, antifamily, and heretical. But she insisted that her version of feminism was "maternal humanism" that assumed the central importance of the family. Families depended upon mothers, and mothers, by Sabas Alomá's definition, could not be lesbian or antifamily. She simply refused to be labeled.

Since Sabas Alomá considered the Catholic Church hypocritical and a morally coercive force that crippled women's capacity to excel, she took pride in being called a heretic. She raged at a clergy that manipulated women into subservience by setting for them the "unattainable, yet divine goals of chastity, sublime virtue, and vague notions of Christian morality" and condemning worldly love as "profane, carnal, and crude." Sabas Alomá advocated human and natural love that ennobled mother-hood. She accused the Church of blaspheming against motherhood, since it laid down the rules for when motherhood was acceptable and when it was not. She defied civil and ecclesiastical canons that con-demned children born out of wedlock. She also blamed the Church for condoning adultery committed by men while castigating unfaithful wives and ignoring the complaints of loyal wives. Men, the Church, and the law maintained *fueros* (special privileges), said Sabas Alomá, and women served. She exhorted women: "reconquistemos los fueros de la dignidad" (let us reconquer the privilege of dignity).[20]

More than any one issue, the rights of illegitimate children distin-guished leftist from moderate feminists. The birthright of the newborn affected every woman and child at the most intense moment of their union: the moment of birth. Conservatives believed distinguishing between legitimate and illegitimate children was appropriate because it preserved the symbols of marriage and the properly registered family. Sabas Alomá and the radicals believed that all mothers and children were entitled to legitimate civil status because motherhood in and of itself was sacred. The issue of illegitimacy incited reaction from every feminist and early became the dividing line between radicals and conservatives.

A controversy over continued funding for La Inclusa, a foundling hospital, provided Sabas Alomá with an opportunity to write eloquently about the rights of illegitimate children. Many feminists wanted to garner public support for La Inclusa as an act of charity for poor and

Mariblanca Sabas Alomá and Ofelia Rodríguez Acosta are honored for their writing. Both authors had stirred heated debate about free love and rights for illegitimate children. *From left to right:* Mariblanca Sabas Alomá, María Dolores Machin, Grace Thompson-Seton, and Ofelia Rodríguez Acosta.

illegitimate orphans. Sabas Alomá opposed the hospital and charity because she felt it continued the demarcation of status and demeaned certain mothers and their children. Sabas Alomá was passionate in her appeal for women to honor motherhood and denounce man-made rules of legitimate birth. She drew upon religion, not Marx, to defend her view.

> Woman, your child is yours. With your child in your arms, you dominate your own life, you are the conqueror of your own destiny, you are Holy Mary forever and always. It does not matter that a heartless man made you a mother, and then abandoned you to your own luck. It does not matter. Your child is yours, above all the laws, above all the codes of honor, above all the good and evil in life and death.

> The Holy Mother Mary lives in the hearts of all women, not as a virgin, but as a mother. With your child in your arms, defy all: the evil of men, the scorn of society.

> Do anything except abandon your child. Abandoning him will be your only crime.[21]

Sabas Alomá called for a change in the structure and morality of the family. Marriage, in her view, was not sacrosanct, and the contract was not binding. She was more interested in the essence and meaning of marriage than in the formal seal, and thus she allowed for divorce when love and respect ceased to unify a couple. To her, remaining unhappily married usually ended in adultery, which was considered natural for husbands but scandalous for wives. Sabas Alomá found the resignation expected of wives unacceptable; she argued for divorce and against the unfair sanctions against women in cases of adultery.

Her adherence to free love relationships aside, Sabas Alomá had to admit that Cuban society was not ready for mutual authority within marriage, and Cuban men in particular would not countenance independent-minded women. She, therefore, advised women to remain single.

> Enlightened solitude is preferable to relationships that are darkened by lies. . . . The brave and deep pain of living alone is preferable to the senseless pain of vegetating [which is what she believed women had to do if they were to maintain a marriage]. Our [women's] mental, spiritual, and physical faculties have never reached their potential. We have always been gagged, intimidated, shut off, tortured and always in the name of divine love.[22]

Sabas Alomá blamed women for their resignation and willing subjugation to men. Cuban women adhered blindly to the social convention called *hembrismo* that tied men and women together in a vicious cycle of sexual dependency. *Hembra* is the term used to indicate the biological female gender, but hembrismo implied that women should submit to men simply because of their sex, and that sexual desire and intercourse characterized men's domination of women. Sabas Alomá condemned the dehumanization of women that hembrismo engendered, though oddly she maintained that sexual intercourse should be the only aspect of gender relations in which the woman should surrender.

> *Hembrismo* is women's biologically determined subservience to men. Women must be sweet, demure, pure, and dependent. The *hembra* manipulates men with sex, yet the *hembra* must never be confrontational. Sex, therefore, becomes the only bond between women and men. *Hembrismo* is not the essence of femininity, and *machismo* is not the essence of masculinity. Women can be feminine and submissive in the bedroom, but no where else. It is humiliating to be dominated and to view sex as the only motive for men and women to form relationships.[23]

But even in her strident condemnations of cowardly, mean-minded, class-oriented women and her attacks on the Church, traditional family orientations, social conventions, and the patriarchy, Sabas Alomá took the original principles of maternal humanism as the foundations of feminism. She reified the mystique of motherhood and gave it purpose in modern Cuba. She made feminism the moral basis of a progressive movement, and she inspired her readers to sharpen their views on women's rights and national objectives, regardless of their political leanings. She also referred to sainted motherhood as the origin of social justice. She venerated the Mother Mary, not the Virgin, for her unwavering nurturance of all people: the poor, the illegitimate, the scorned and humiliated, who, in the radicals' view, were too often women. The image of the Mother Mary allowed some to adopt simultaneously Marxist and feminist principles by allowing a terminology of morality, not ideology, to stimulate recognition for radical change.

Sabas Alomá was passionate but not sentimental, compassionate but not weak. She expected Cuban women to adopt her views because of their merits, but she was also guilty of augmenting her own importance and amassing loyal followers. Her views were sometimes contradictory and confusing. She was, nevertheless, brilliantly perceptive about Cuban conventions of domination that kept women from rising to their greatest potentials. Colonial practices that gave the Church and the upper class special privileges had to end, and a cult of motherhood had to begin.

OFELIA BRODRÍGUEZ ACOSTA

Ofelia Rodríguez Acosta, a journalist and novelist, was as influential as Mariblanca Sabas Alomá in attracting attention to the feminist cause. Though she was not a member of the Grupo Minorista, she was widely recognized as a serious author. While Rodríguez echoed many of Sabas Alomá's views (such as the coalition of the woman's movement with socialist values and the fundamental importance of the economic liberation of women and the rights of illegitimate children), she reflected upon philosophical and psychological roots of exploitation and more clearly articulated the need for a revision of women's self-perceptions than Sabas Alomá did. Sadly, Rodríguez was a pessimist about social reform and believed that change had to be an individual matter and not a sweeping renovation dictated by law.

Ofelia Rodríguez Acosta was born in Pinar del Río on September 2, 1902. She received her undergraduate training at the Institute of Havana in 1925, and in 1927 she was awarded a grant from the Ministry of Education to study in Europe and Mexico. Between 1929 and 1932 she wrote for *Bohemia,* and her work also appeared intermittently in *Diario de la Marina, El Mundo,* and *Social.* Rodríguez also wrote novels that

Ofelia Rodríguez Acosta,
socialist-feminist writer
whose column in *Bohemia*
developed radical psycho-
logical challenges to the
prescribed behavior of
Cuban women. Taken
from *La mujer,* May 31,
1930. The Stoner Collec-
tion, Roll 7.

contained social commentary.[24] She gave public lectures, the most noted
of which was "La tragedia social de la mujer," given at the Lyceum Lawn
and Tennis Club in 1932. She also founded and directed the journal
Espartana in 1927. From 1923 to 1928 she was a member of the Club
Femenino de Cuba and later briefly belonged to the Unión Laborista de
Mujeres. In 1933 she traveled through Spain and France and finally settled
in Mexico in 1940 where she lived until her death in 1975.

Rodríguez was a child prodigy, and her talent was inspired by her
father Dr. José Rodríguez Acosta, himself a writer, artist, politician, and
intellectual. When she was twelve, Rodríguez wrote her first book,
Evocaciones, in which she demonstrated perception and curiosity that was
advanced for her age. She wondered about the lives of poor Blacks,
death, hypocrisy within the Church, and morality.

When she was thirty, Rodríguez took on a Russian philosopher,
Anton Vitalievich Nemilov, who had written a treatise entitled *The
Biological Tragedy of Women* (1929). Nemilov argued that women were
forever dependent upon men because they were confined to childbearing

and reproduction in their young adulthood. For that reason, and because menopause and old age rendered women unattractive and therefore less lovable in their later years, women's lives were tragic, and tragedy was determined by women's biology.

In a speech delivered at the Lyceum Lawn and Tennis Club on December 13, 1932, Rodríguez countered with the claim that tragedy was not created by nature alone but by the interpretation humankind imposed on nature. Therefore, menstruation, the loss of virginity, motherhood, menopause, and old age were not in themselves tragic, but the stigma men placed upon these functions was. Rodríguez sought to remove artificial constraints placed upon women's biological function by demonstrating that the force of nature, contained in the woman's body, was sacred.[25] Motherhood was a wondrous act of nature that existed beyond individual female personalities. Tragedy was social, not biological. The implication in Rodríguez's argument was that attitudes about biology and the resulting social norms could change and thus women's social status could improve.

In this speech and in her articles in *Bohemia,* Rodríguez argued that only free love would liberate women from limitations imposed by the Catholic Church and men's repressive instincts. She embraced Bertrand Russell's position that free love for women could lead even to eugenics, leaving women free to select the fathers of their children. Rodríguez believed that free love suited the nature of women and men. Men contracted relationships for the pleasure of the union, she insisted, and, when love's illusion diminished, they would find another woman. Women acquired relations to have children, and after that they too could have lovers at their pleasure, as men did. She justified her position by insisting that free love did not produce unwanted children or adultery as traditional Spanish and Catholic arrangements did.[26]

Rodríguez believed it imperative that women direct their loyalties to themselves and not succumb to the arbitrary authority of men.[27] Women's liberation began in the minds of women and not in attacks on the patriarchy. Changing gender relations first required women to believe in their own strength, integrity, effectiveness, intelligence, and the right to belong to the most powerful governing bodies. Like Sabas Alomá, Rodríguez challenged the notion of women's blind obedience to men; both insisted that responsible and able women could achieve independence while simultaneously being companions to men.[28]

Rodríguez's most controversial work, a novel entitled *La Vida Manda,* written in 1927, provoked such outrage that she devoted her column in *Bohemia* to the public's reaction. Some people thought the novel pornographic, or at least erotic. Others grasped her intended challenge to women to experience their own sexuality. The novel, potentially as important in criticizing Cuban culture as *Las impuras* and *Las honradas* by Miguel de Carrion or *Los inmorales* by Carlos Loveira, went beyond Cuban social veneer to identify the psychological motives for women's and men's behavior and to attack common mores. *La vida manda* achieved neither the attention nor the acclaim it deserved.

For all the turmoil over the alleged pornography, the novel contains no explicit descriptions of sexual encounters. Rather, it examines the feelings and thoughts, not acts, of Gertrudis, a young woman who belonged to a poor but respectable family. Gertrudis contemplated her own desires. From the beginning of the novel the reader is warned that Gertrudis is unique, given to depression, and alone. From a very early age Gertrudis knew that she would suffer because of men. She was, then, brash for her sexual independence and at the same time defeated by a system that prohibited women's freedom to know their own sexuality.

In her brashness she confessed to her uncle the real reason she agreed to have an unfulfilling relationship with a sweetheart, Antonio. She said that she allowed Antonio to visit her "for a horrible, scandalous reason . . . because I needed a boyfriend. I needed to be loved, kissed, caressed. I was twenty-three. When I could not find a good man to marry, I did what all women do: I gathered up my feelings, disfigured them, adulterated them and adorned them with flowers of spiritual necessity."[29] Her confession, of course, exposed women who had married for respectability and out of loneliness, but not for love. It challenged the assumption that women were passionately in love with their husbands and sexually fulfilled. This declaration made readers at least uncomfortable, if not angry, for women were supposed to be devoted to and satisfied by their husbands.

Gertrudis not only admitted her reason for flirtation, she also had an affair with what turned out to be a married man. Though the affair ended tragically for Gertrudis, for a brief moment her expectations of ideal love were met. She experienced sexual fulfillment and selfless loving, sentiments she had previously dismissed as impossible. The bitter end of the affair shattered Gertrudis's illusion, reconfirmed her cynicism, and threw her into a depression from which she never recovered. As a result, she became a stoic, yet she took no responsibility for her own life. She believed that all was predetermined by insensitive men and a society with no place for emancipated women. Her reaction was to invent her own morality that in no way honored virginity but that did acknowledge self-improvement, refinement, polish, and perfection, along with "the sterilization of feelings." She believed in goodness for the sake of goodness, life because one lives, but fantasy and passion no longer existed for her. She was indifferent toward people and issues. Her morality was "self-contained, unfragmented, intrinsic, and absolute." She was at peace, but also alone. She had no purpose.

The only stimulus to rouse her from her remoteness and depression was the thought of having a child. In fact, she managed a loveless affair with her old friend Antonio, and she bore a child who brought her maternal happiness for only four hours. The infant died. Suicide seemed to be the only release for Gertrudis from her unfulfilled life, but even suicide eluded her. A poorly aimed bullet severed her optic nerve, rendering her blind.

A reader who sought affirmation for sexual precociousness in *La vida manda* was doomed to disappointment. For daring to know her sexuality and test the limits of love, Gertrudis's life ended tragically. But if the book were understood as a cry for the flourishing of women's minds and bodies in Cuban society, then Rodríguez succeeded in uncovering a stifled but living force.

The novel provoked a sharp reaction immediately following its publication. Emilio Roig de Leuchsenring, a noted journalist and social analyst, praised the book, as did Sabas Alomá. The literary audience and the public at large were more skeptical; they reprimanded Rodríguez's introspection about women's sexuality. For the most part, Cuban literary critics ignored her work, and today it is all but forgotten.

In their journal articles, both Rodríguez and Sabas Alomá criticized the feminist movement for reflecting aristocratic values. Though Rodríguez admitted that the leaders of the movement made every effort to be moral, democratic, and forward looking, she held out little hope that the feminists could be revolutionary because they were wedded to traditional class and cultural values. As the movement stood in 1931, Rodríguez argued (perhaps incorrectly), it only undertook to emancipate women from men. But the challenge for Cuban women had to be much greater than that. Rodríguez's ideal for women's liberation was to teach women to take responsibility for their own lives and to place themselves at the center of all social, political, and moral issues.

An obstacle to women's independence and well-being was their economic reliance upon men. Rodríguez did not believe that electing a few women to Congress would affect the majority of humble women whose poverty and economic hopelessness would not be corrected through legal reform. Nor did she believe that privileged and powerful women could understand or solve problems of the poor. Thus, she disagreed with the bourgeois notion of liberation. But Rodríguez also doubted the efficacy of a socialist revolution that ignored women's concerns. Women's liberation had to emerge from a solitary struggle within each woman, an accomplishment that Rodríguez sadly believed was unattainable.[30] Rodríguez's concept of women's liberation was, by her own definition, stillborn, and she died hopelessly depressed, much like her character Gertrudis, in an insane asylum in Mexico.

MARÍA COLLADO

Feminist editorials in the popular press and women's publications recorded the close connections among feminists who debated the principles of Cuban feminism. Every partisan declaration elicited an opposing response, and every advocate had her detractor. The fiercest pretender for conservative feminist leadership was María Collado, who embodied the qualities of wealthy feminists so despised by Mariblanca Sabas Alomá and Ofelia Rodríguez Acosta.[31] Collado was undeterred by their abhorrence for things upper-class, as she took up the cause of the monied women activists, and she, like Sabas Alomá and Rodríguez, viewed herself as the savior of all women.

María Collado was born in 1899 into a wealthy Havana family. As a teenager she advocated women's rights in the *Revista Protectora de la Mujer,* edited by another society lady, Sra. Velacoracho de Lara. One of her first feminist acts was to immortalize Emilia de Córdoba, a mambisa who not only refused to accept U.S. military occupation but also was the first woman to demand political equality for women after independence. In 1920 María Collado, then a member of the Club Femenino, was appointed the Club's director of publicity, and she published her opinions on women's issues in *La Discusión,* a Havana newspaper. In 1924 the dailies *Cuba* and *La Noche* added her columns to their editorial pages.

In 1924 the president of the Partido Nacional Sufragista, Amalia Mallén, made Collado her vice president. In a difference over allegiance to President Gerardo Machado, Collado left the Partido Nacional Sufragista, formed her own Partido Demócrata Sufragista, and served as its first president. Collado defended Machado because he had agreed in 1925 to grant women the vote during his presidential term. She would remain loyal to him, even though he neglected to support congressional bills for suffrage.

In 1929 Collado founded and edited the journal *La Mujer,* which ran until 1942, making it the longest-running feminist journal in prerevolu-

Srta. María Collado, founder of the Partido Demócrata Sufragista and editor of *La Mujer*. Collado defended the position of upper-class feminists and asked all women to unify around gender issues and to forget about class distinctions. She sided with President Machado up to the moment of his overthrow. Taken from *Memoria del Primer Congreso*, p. 76. The Stoner Collection, Roll 2.

tionary Cuba. The stated purpose of *La Mujer* was both "to offer a forum to all just causes that affected women and to conduct a peaceful campaign for women's rights."[32] The editor pledged to pay special attention to working and university women's concerns. Putting those claims aside, *La Mujer* was the voice for conservative feminism, and María Collado wrote two to three articles in each issue, unless she were ill.

Collado basically believed that women should organize around gender issues and overlook class and caste division. She took every opportunity to scold the radical opposition, whom she identified by name in her editorials, for their defiance of class structure. By concentrating upon class and racial issues, leftist feminists divided the woman's movement, and Collado believed that such a division would weaken the movement's chances of success.

Compared to Mariblanca Sabas Alomá and Ofelia Rodríguez Acosta, or even many of the organized feminists, Collado was less philosophical and more political in her approach to women's issues. More than any other Cuban feminist, she focused on the vote as the vehicle for attaining progressive reforms. She was an apologist for wealthy feminists, who, she insisted, could work to benefit working and poor women as well as women of color. Collado repeatedly pointed to the quiet, philanthropic work that upper-class women did for the poor that went unnoticed and unappreciated.

Although María Collado was critical of the left, she rarely identified her opponents as communists or enemies of the state, an accusation commonly used by Machado's supporters against his opponents during those years. Instead, she wondered at what she called the radical feminists' misguided allegiances, invited them to come back to the fold, and expressed stunned insult when they attacked her values. She was arrogant and acted to humiliate all who disagreed with her. But just as she abhorred the use of violence by both revolutionaries and the state police, she limited her rage to her published invectives.

From the late 1920s through 1937 one main focus of Collado's consternation was Ofelia Domínguez Navarro. Collado's hostility toward Domínguez was unmerciful, and her attacks were relentless. Domínguez's socialist leanings had disrupted the movement and challenged authority of the privileged classes. In an article that reported on Domínguez's withdrawal from the Alianza Nacional Feminista, Collado concluded that such feminists were detrimental to the woman's movement.[33]

Not satisfied with simply writing against Domínguez, Collado tried to persuade women to oppose her. In 1928, as the Constitutional Assembly considered votes for women and as feminists kept vigil outside the capital, Collado went out to the demonstration to advise feminists against joining the newly formed Unión Laborista de Mujeres. Collado was rejected by many women in her own Partido who had joined the Unión because they disagreed with her defense of wealthy women. She was stung and angered by their decision. In her article, she sought to attract other feminists to her view. She also warned working-class women against cooperating with the Unión and becoming Domínguez's puppets and dupes of Marxism. Mostly she condemned Domínguez's egoism. Collado insisted that Domínguez had marginalized herself from the mainstream movement, which would solidify around respectable feminists like herself. True to her upper-class graciousness, however, Collado closed her article by professing complete disagreement with Domínguez, but also offering friendship.[34]

Collado also criticized other leftist women's organizations and leaders, such as the radical Unión Feminista Universitaria, Loló de la Torriente, and Ofelia Rodríguez Acosta, because they too gave preference to class and racial issues over the more simple gender concerns.

Nowadays feminism has become a movement that includes women of all classes who unify to advance the cause of women. Women who remain tied to their own particular social levels and who do not support universal women's issues detract from women's rights.

The Unión Feminista Universitaria is guilty of this factionalism because it takes on class issues before feminist issues. It does not declare in its charter that it is for the improvement of women's lives. Instead it declares in favor of the class struggle. It only states that it will study the problems of women within the class struggle.[35]

The inclusion of the Lyceum Lawn and Tennis Club among her enemies in 1931 revealed the extent of Collado's alienation from the mainstream feminist movement, for Lyceum women were nonpartisan intellectuals and members of the elite. In this case the Lyceum insulted Collado by excluding her and the Partido's membership from Lyceum meetings and cultural events. Collado guessed that this was because she and the Partido supported Machado. She demanded an explanation for her social rejection, and she wanted the Lyceum women to come to terms with the fact that they were entertaining leftists who were out in the streets in violent demonstrations. By contrast, Collado and the Partido were peacefully trying to attain votes for women. The implication was that the Partido was more virtuous than other feminist groups because they were polite about asking for women's suffrage. She pointed out that the Lyceum women had spoken to the president about passing suffrage, so they shared the Partido's views and association with the president.[36]

Apart from Collado's focus on the vote and her devotion to Machado, she supported some progressive causes such as abortion, divorce, and the rights of illegitimate children. But she did not make these issues central to her cause, nor did she use the motherhood myth to encourage people to support her position. For example, birth control to her was necessary because premarital sex was a reality and unwanted children resulted. It was not intended to enhance women's sexual freedom or to make motherhood a divine act.[37]

Collado, an indefatigable lobbyist, used *La Mujer* to identify politicians who supported women's suffrage and to mobilize advocates for the vote. She encouraged her readership not to lose heart because the Congress rejected the vote, and she invited them to take an interest in the political process that would eventually grant them the right to participate in national elections.[38]

María Collado was one of the few Cuban feminists who advocated gender equality over feminine self-awareness and empowerment. In her earliest profession of faith, she said, "I understand feminism to be more than a desire, it is a necessity. Women ought to be in every way, politically and socially, men's equal. And why shouldn't it be so?"[39] With this statement Collado separated herself from nearly every other feminist and feminist organization in Cuba. The literal equality between women and men found no resonance in values shared by most Cuban women, who enjoyed some status as mothers and wives.

Motherhood did not hold the mythical value for Collado that it did for Sabas Alomá and Domínguez. Collado did not make the Madonna her icon. Instead, the mambisa, who was the loyal wife and mother of Cuba's patriots and a warrior for freedom, became her symbol of political rights for women. Collado emphasized patriotism and individual rights and only secondarily concerned herself with family and community matters. She believed that suffrage and public charity would cleanse Cuba of corrupt political practices. For her, Christian and aristocratic giving and the mother/mambisa were central ideals.

Collado rejected Marxist strategies for social change. As an advocate for women's democratic participation and justice through legislation, she argued for leaving class structure in place. More specifically, she believed that the well-born should lead and that privileged ladies were the natural allies of poor women. Claims of class differentiation and conflict troubled her. She accused Mariblanca Sabas Alomá, Ofelia Rodríguez Acosta, and especially Ofelia Domínguez Navarro of heresy against the women's movement because they had broken away from a unified women's front. María Collado was the self-appointed guardian of class values and the inquisitor general against deviant forms of feminism.

Yet María Collado went to the streets as an investigator who visited stores, factories, and shops to oversee their adherence to labor laws. Her reporting seemed fair and free of political ideology, though the activity itself was self-serving insofar as it showed that upper-class feminists would look after working-class women. Clearly, Collado's cooperation with an undemocratic government, even as she fought for the vote, and confrontation with leftist feminists exposed her patrician rules for reform.[40]

Cuban feminism, represented by these three writers and organized feminists, had no ideological center. Sabas Alomá and Rodríguez Acosta exalted women's biological function and wanted to dignify femininity, even as they supported the destruction of class divisions and other socioeconomic prejudices in Cuban society. These two radicals found their ideological roots in values associated with the woman/mother. Morality for the socialists followed a Marxist analysis but also Catholic charity by broadening Hispanic regard for family to contain the national community. For progressive and moderate feminists predominant in feminist organizations, positivist values and individual rights exemplified by the mambisa held sway. Conservative feminists pursued equal rights for women but under the tutelage of wealthy women. All three groups presumed that women would continue in their capacity as guardians and models of morality, although they disagreed on what that morality should be. And all feminists wanted to convince the public that the subjugation of women was wrong.

Motherhood, so eloquently idealized by the feminists, symbolized social welfare, family unity, and national morality. As a feminist and nationalist icon, it stimulated sentiments about virtuous behavior, and it acquired diverse meaning. Motherhood was revered as life's force, and it projected onto an unstable and violent society the promise of wholesomeness, protection, purity, and new life. The nation needed these symbols, and feminists needed national prominence. That motherhood became a myth—because it was used to explain the essence of women's social function—and a metaphor for progress gave the feminist movement a positive forcefulness that transcended home life and offered some version of national morality to the Cuban political conscience.

6

Women's Suffrage and
the Question of Democracy

Diversity and dissent within the woman's movement did not ruin its chances for success. The strength of Cuban feminists lay neither in their numbers nor in their unity, for they were a small and factionalized group. Feminist success came from the broad appeal of messages, effectiveness in getting feminist views across, and women's adhesion to the diverse political affiliations so prevalent in Cuba between 1927 and 1940. Put another way, the disputatious woman's movement matched a divided and contentious society, and this allowed women with differing ideas about feminism to appeal to a corresponding sector of the Cuban polity.

A revolutionary setting was the catalyst for feminist reforms because it gave feminists some power over vulnerable politicians and political dissident groups. In the upheaval, feminists became power brokers who bartered their support in exchange for defense of feminist causes. No other political group was as amorphous and diverse as the feminists, and these qualities served to enhance their capacity to challenge restrictive legal tenets.

Suffrage was the most widely supported issue on the feminist agenda. Not until 1930 did any feminist group disapprove of suffrage. As historical circumstance would have it, the suffragist campaign reached its apogee at the same time as Cubans were ousting President Gerardo Machado. Votes for women and the end of the Machadato were inextricably linked in the minds of feminists and the Cuban people, making women's suffrage a metaphor for constitutional democracy.

The Feminists and the Machadato

By 1930 political tensions between the Machado government and the opposition had become strained past the point of tolerance. The cause of the tension was Machado's decision in 1927 to appoint his own constitutional assembly and rewrite the 1901 constitution in order to extend the presidential term from four to six years. He subsequently banned all political parties other than the Conservative, National, and Liberal parties.

Suddenly Cubans were faced with a crisis in democracy. Was Machado a dictator? Was democratic participation possible in Cuba? How could political opposition find expression, and who made up the opposition? These were central questions, and they were important to feminists, who were attempting to broaden democratic principles to include their own participation. Many would come to understand that a threat to democracy was also a threat to their chances to determine policies. Most feminists, therefore, sooner or later joined the insurgency against Machado, all, that is, but the Partido Demócrata Sufragista whose membership believed Machado's claim that he would step down in 1934 and proceed with a plebescite in which women could vote.

As early as March 1927 elements of the opposition protested Machado's irregular constitutional revisions. When the government announced its proposed constitutional reform, students at the University of Havana organized a demonstration at the home of Enrique José Varona, a noted intellectual and veteran of the independence wars. The police broke up the demonstration and took control of Varona's house. The following day a group of intellectuals signed a manifesto known as "Nuestra Protesta."[1] It objected to the proposed amendments, and it condemned Machado's appointment of the delegates to the constitutional assembly. The manifesto promised agitation until democracy was restored. Five of the twenty-four signatories were feminists and included Loló de la Torriente, Emma López Seña, Rosario Guillaume, Rita Shelton, and Beneranda Martínez.

The constitutional crisis dissolved the cohesion between moderate and progressive activists and startled many Cubans out of their complacency about the expanded control of executive office, social injustice, and U.S. domination. Under Machado, violation of the constitution was unmistakable and inexcusable. Cuban citizens understood that they had no real power and that democracy was an illusion. At the same time the Cuban economy collapsed as a result of Cuban links to the U.S. economy and the Great Depression. Students, workers, and campesinos organized strikes and demonstrations, and the government hit back with a reign of terror. From 1927 to 1933 violence begat violence: even unpoliticized citizens could not escape from an undeclared but pervasive civil war.

Machado justified his persecution of dissidents in terms of halting the "proceso comunista."[2] In his view, a threat to his government was communist-inspired and warranted brutal recriminations. More, he knew that the United States would tolerate repression of supposed communists and could be relied upon for help, at least in the short run. Machado's method was to terrorize anyone opposed to his administration for alleged revolutionary activities. He set up emergency courts to punish students and demonstrators who sympathized with the Directorio Estudiantil Universitario (DEU), a radical student organization. On July 9, 1927, Machado's police arrested fifty-six people under Causa 967, a law improvised to eliminate dissidents. Machado claimed that seditious people were infiltrating political organizations, writing pamphlets, and fomenting unrest through public demonstrations and speeches. These accusations were proof enough of insurgency. Machado believed that the most susceptible recruits of the proceso comunista were factory workers and campesinos, railroad workers, the military, and the students. Suddenly, working with the poor or writing and speaking against the government carried the risk of a prison sentence or worse: exile, disappearance, incarceration, or assassination.

By 1931 political tensions had driven members of the opposition, many of whom were feminists, to the streets in opposition to the government. It became increasingly difficult for Cubans to dissent peacefully, however, when the democratic system was in question. If they valued their lives, Cubans had to choose either tacit complicity with the government or radical opposition; there was no safe middle ground.

An array of dissident groups ranging from simple opponents of Machado to communist revolutionaries made up the opposition. Just as more people chose sides, so too the woman's movement polarized into moderate and extreme factions. María Collado and the Partido Demócrata Sufragista supported Machado because of his promise on women's suffrage and because Collado agreed with his anticommunist, reformist, but repressive policies. The Alianza Nacional Feminista actively opposed Machado for violating constitutional democracy and not granting universal suffrage in his first term of office. The Lyceum Lawn and Tennis Club, while launching no public campaign, heard speeches by Loló de la Torriente, Raul Roa, and Ofelia Domínguez Navarro, all avid Marxists and advocates of the revolutionary struggle against the government. Domínguez's Unión Laborista de Mujeres initially supported suffrage and opposed Machado but by late 1930 argued against suffrage and for radical change in governing principles. As strong personalities battled for control, the Cuban matronas became less cordial toward one another. No one group dominated. All groups advocated their own perceptions of social justice, and most of them demanded the removal of the regime, but no two groups agreed upon the order of post-Machado Cuba.

Cuban Suffrage and the Question of Democracy

Unlike North American and British suffragists who fought alone against established governments for the vote, Cuban suffragists joined a revolution and helped to bring down a repressive regime, using votes for women as evidence of Cuban adherence to democratic principles. Cuban feminists were moderates among radicals, not radicals among moderates, and they were thereby acceptable to most factions of the 1930s unrest. Feminists earned national respect through their calls for national order and their promises that "peace, honor, love, justice, and reform" would follow the ouster of Machado and acceptance of women's suffrage. The genius of the feminist leadership was in building associations between political stability, justice and morality, and votes for women at a time when a national consensus formed around order, reform, and democracy. Women presented themselves as the salvation of Cuban morality when men were discredited as public leaders. The historic moment and the insightfulness of the feminist leadership combined to make votes for women a real possibility.

President Gerardo Machado, like Alfredo Zayas before him, committed himself to passing women's suffrage, but Machado did it before the 1925 Second National Women's Congress. Yet by 1927 he had done little to effect the law, and the feminists were restless. Their presence in powerful circles meant that their dissatisfaction brought reaction, and their militance was not confused with leftist insurgency. Machado knew that the feminists were a political force to be used to his own advantage. In 1927, as disapproval of Machado's government increased with the appointment of the new constitutional assembly, the president decided to add votes for women to his proposed constitutional reforms to win feminist approval and assure the populace of his democratic intentions.

Machado's lack of commitment to suffrage discredited his sincerity about constitutional government. When introducing his constitutional reforms to the assembly, he never defended women's suffrage. The only public reference he made to the vote issue came in a speech in which he merely listed it among his constitutional resolutions.[3] After forwarding his proposal for women's suffrage to the assembly, Machado washed his hands of any further obligation. Responsibility lay with the assembly either to approve or reject his proposal according to the assemblymen's sense of politics and the political climate.

As the assembly met and debated the proposed constitution, citizens testified about the merits of change. Seizing the opportunity, feminists campaigned hard for suffrage despite their reservations about Machado's intentions. One of the more prominent witnesses before the assembly was Ofelia Domínguez Navarro. In May 1928 she argued that the franchise was a just cause, since it incorporated a previously marginal group into a democratic society.[4] Feminists held a vigil outside the capitol and packed capitol galleries to remind delegates of their commitment. Society women, suffragists, and feminists awaited the verdict. According to Domínguez, feminists knew they would not win the constitutional reform, but they wanted their presence felt through orderly demonstration.[5]

Despite the fact that the assembly essentially rubber-stamped the most grievous departures from democratic government in Machado's proposed amendments, the suffrage resolution failed. A few assemblymen used arguments such as women's biological inferiority and behavioral underdevelopment to justify their opposition to women's suffrage. The majority who rejected suffrage were afraid that women would become a voting bloc. Only one or two assemblymen defended women's right to vote, but without effect. The final legislation was an apparent compromise that, in fact, denied women the vote. Article 38 of the 1928 reformed constitution required a ratified constitutional amendment to grant women suffrage.[6] This action effectively killed any reform since amendments required a two-thirds majority in both houses, a majority that was virtually unattainable at the time.

When feminists and suffragists realized the implications of the 1928 constitutional amendments, some formed the Comité de Defensa de Sufragio Femenino to keep the issue alive.[7] The Comité held interviews with prominent members of the assembly to publicize their positions on suffrage in the press. The Comité also raised a petition to Antonio Sánchez de Bustamante, the president of the assembly, demanding that the delegates reconsider the suffrage issue.

In May 1928 members of the Comité gathered in the entryway of the national capitol, where the assembly was in session. Hortensia Lamar, Pilar Jorge de Tella, Rosario Guillaume, Rosa Arrendondo de Vega, and Ofelia Domínguez Navarro carried the petition to Sánchez de Bustamante and exhorted the assembly to reform the constitution to give equal rights to women and men. The Comité's efforts failed. The amended constitution extended the presidential term, allowed for Machado's reelection, suppressed political parties, and denied women the vote. As if the final document were not insult enough to democratic principles, Machado conferred upon himself the title of "Illustrious and Exemplary Citizen." His audacity forced many people into opposition who might otherwise have stood by him, and a period of political gangsterism began.

Since Machado had failed to deliver suffrage, opposition groups—including intellectuals, middle-class liberals, students, and Marxists—added the franchise to their programs. The Cuban Communist Party announced its support for universal suffrage as early as 1926. The Directorio Estudiantil and the Ala Izquierda Estudiantil both adopted suffrage as part of their programs. The clandestine, middle-class terrorist group, the ABC, included votes for women in its 1931 manifesto.[8]

In response to the failure of constitutional reform, the Alianza Nacional Feminista initiated a new, and less polite, effort to win the vote. In November 1929 the executive committee of the Alianza asked Machado to support a Senate bill to amend Article 38 of the constitution and give women the vote. The representatives met the president in the presidential palace and Machado listened to their presentation. Domínguez, speaking for the committee, asked him to recommend full suffrage just as he had promised in the Second National Women's Congress in 1925. In this speech Domínguez promised loyalty to President Machado in exchange for his support. (Within two years she would become one of the president's archenemies, and she would argue against the importance of suffrage.)[9] Machado assured the Aliancistas that he would send a message to Congress, but there is no evidence that he did. At the time, Machado believed that he was in control and did not need feminist support.

At this crucial juncture in Cuba's constitutional history, U.S. feminists could have joined their Cuban colleagues as they pressured the Cuban legislature to grant women the vote. International suffrage organizations, often initiated by North Americans, were forming to change electoral laws in all democratic nations so that women could vote. U.S. feminists could have appealed to their government to support suffrage and encourage a constitutional reform. But the North American feminists, acting out of their own cultural and political biases, demonstrated disdain for Latin women's inabilities to participate in politics. At the 1926 Interamerican Women's Congress in Panama, the North American delegation argued that Latin American women were not prepared to exercise their rights. They abstained from voting for a resolution to bring women's suffrage to all American nations, and they convinced a majority of Latin American delegates to reject the resolution. In 1929 Carrie Chapman Catt, the director of the Women's Struggle for World Peace and Friendship with South America, criticized Latin American women as "a threat to friendly and peaceful relations between the United States and South America."[10] She reasoned that Latin American women had not fought long enough to appreciate the responsibilities of an electoral public.

At the moment they needed support, the Aliancistas came to understand that their alliance with their North American counterparts was
troubled by Anglo and Latin cultural and political differences. What
surprised the majority of Aliancistas was the compliance of other Latin
American representatives, most notably the Argentines, with the U.S.
position.

By 1930 the North American position on suffrage seemed to soften,
perhaps because Doris Stevens, a feminist with broader views than Catts,
was president of the Interamerican Commission on Women and worked
for Pan-American women's suffrage. But for the Cubans, the moment
for peaceful constitutional reform had passed. In 1930 a revolution was
brewing, and votes for women had become a minor skirmish in a major
war.

While the Alianza publicly disapproved of Machado's assumption of
power in 1928 and his inattention to women's suffrage, the Partido
Demócrata Sufragista used another tactic to get the vote. The Partido
membership pledged steadfast loyalty to Machado because it calculated
that Machado would deliver on his promises. The Partido published
articles in *La Mujer* advocating votes for women and at the same time
extolled the virtues of the Machado family.[11] The intentions were clear:
women of the Partido would use feminine persuasion, flattery, and
loyalty to ingratiate themselves with the president and thus groom
themselves for political favors and the right to vote after the conflict was
resolved.

Paying homage to the president was not the Partido's only strategy.
María Collado and her contributors publicized the names of those
politicians who supported women's rights legislation and virulently
attacked those who opposed it.[12] Even though women had no formal
political authority, Collado was depending upon the subtle influence
women had when they made moral judgments about politicians and
political acts. She also assumed that women in powerful families would
take up the issue of suffrage with their husbands and fathers, thereby
gaining the necessary votes to amend the electoral law.

To the last, Collado believed that Machado's policy of "cooperation"
among the elite political groups held the greatest promise for women's
democratic participation, and she blamed the malcontents for jeopardiz-
ing women's rights by creating political unrest. She accused them of
collaborating with Marxists, who would only exploit the cause to amass
and never concede power or resources to women after a revolutionary
victory. In her determination to expel Marxist feminists from the movement, Collado appealed to Machado to grant suffrage and thereby

discredit leftist charges of dictatorship and violation of a democratic constitution.[13]

From Instability to Civil War

As the depression deepened in 1930, resentment over the way Machado had assumed power exploded into insurgency. Votes for women, a cause apparently betrayed by the Machado administration, became the symbol of Machado's infidelity to Cuban democracy and the metaphor for reform. Women from all social stations, advocating a return to democracy and an end to economic dependency and poverty, joined the opposition and thus linked the franchise, public dissidence, and revolution.

Between 1930 and 1933 Cuban political factions fought a civil war. Revolutionary groups and Machado's *porra* (secret police) engaged in public resistance and violent repression. The "Seccion de Expertos" (the department of the secret police responsible for assassinations and disappearances) participated in street fights, shoot-outs, bombings, and assassinations with the opposition. Heightened violence aggravated the argument about whether women had a place in politics. Senators and representatives, who had over time insisted that politics was no place for women, could now point to criminal political activities as proof that women should remain in the home, safe from danger. But the era of the mambisa had dispelled the taboo on women warriors, and hopes for democracy had given Cuban women the idea that they offered unique solutions for Cuba's political instability.

After 1931 feminist groups had to address the crisis in democracy, and they began allying themselves with political groups. The Alianza Nacional Feminista, for example, joined Carlos Saladrigas and Joaquin Martínez Saenz, founding members of the ABC, and influenced the ABC manifesto.[14] The Alianza insisted that the ABC agenda include women's suffrage, liberation of political prisoners, and protest against the kidnapping of dissidents.[15] Whether a formal alliance existed between the Alianza and the ABC is unclear, but contact and efforts to influence each other occurred. To credit the Alianza with approval of the ABC's tactics would be difficult, since they involved terrorism, but Hortensia Lamar, a prominent figure in the Alianza, wrote an article welcoming U.S. mediation of the conflict, which coincided with ABC strategy.[16]

Throughout the civil unrest, the Alianza never withdrew its commitment to the franchise. The official argument was that the woman's vote was necessary to rectify Machado's illegal claim to power.[17] The underlying assumption was that women's moral values would ameliorate men's tendencies to abuse power. But constancy in Alianza policies came at the cost of a purge of the more radical membership.

The Unión Laborista completely disagreed and in 1930 published a manifesto establishing its opposition to suffrage, bourgeois capitalism, and Machado. It challenged other feminists to set aside suffrage and take up the cause of a classless society. Since Machado was jailing communists and feminists alike, Domínguez urged all women to recognize their common cause with revolutionaries. In a word, she renounced the suffragist package because it encouraged women to support a corrupt system in exchange for a vote in it.[18]

Domínguez's secession from the Alianza provoked a belligerent response from María Collado's Partido Demócrata Sufragista. Being ever vigilant against socialist solutions to poverty and class ordering, Collado attacked Domínguez's position as one inspired by foreign dogma—communism. Collado published the Partido's official reply to Domínguez's Marxist faction, calling it the least suitable of all the women's organizations in the movement. Collado vilified Domínguez for having worked for suffrage with the Alianza only to renounce that work for other ideals. She urged women activists to see the Unión as "the last and the least" among feminists.[19]

By 1930 Cuban feminists, whether suffragists, progressive reformers, or socialists, had to balance the weight of the national crisis against the drive for suffrage. The majority chose to oppose Machado and turn that campaign into an effort to win the vote.

Feminism and the Overthrow of Machado

As violence escalated, respectable middle-class women took to the streets, some simply to express outrage over the carnage wrought by Machado, others to participate in opposition groups. Feminist opposition had remained fairly restrained until September 30, 1930, when Rafael Trejo, a student involved in a university protest, was shot six times in the back by a national policeman while trying to pull him off a fellow student. Until then, the moderate feminists condemned in writing political violence from any side. But the use of lethal force against students protesting University of Havana curriculum, faculty standards, and the Platt Amendment made many women militants who otherwise would have stayed at home.

Trejo's death prompted accusations of police misconduct. Students rushed to newspaper offices to publish their denunciations. Defying repression, Trejo's friends carried his body first to the emergency room of a nearby hospital and then to his parents' home where it lay for public viewing. Domínguez and the women of the Unión stood vigil by the body the night of the assassination.

Radicals began planning a protest demonstration at Trejo's funeral, and Machado responded by declaring a state of siege until after the body was buried. He ordered that only family members could accompany the body to the cemetery and threatened military force against anyone who defied his order. Word went out through the newspapers and radio stations that Trejo would not even get a proper burial because of Machado's "goons." As this was a great offense to Cuban Catholics, family and political mourners chose to defy the curfew. Women were recruited to join the funeral procession and lend legitimacy to the demonstration. On October 2, 1930, Ofelia Rodríguez Acosta, Ofelia Domínguez Navarro, Flora Diaz Parrado, and a former teacher of Trejo's led the funeral procession, and members of the Unión carried the casket on their shoulders from the chapel to the grave site. They were followed by over one hundred women, many of them moderate feminists, who defied the machine guns of government troops.[20] For once, being female had an advantage, for soldiers stationed along the route were loathe to fire on women who were doing what women are supposed to do after outbreaks of violence—mourn the dead. Ofelia Domínguez and Liliam Ojeda, another radical intellectual, delivered the eulogies directed at uniting all who objected to Machado's repressive tactics.[21]

In November 1930 a coalition of women opponents to Machado, including Loló de la Torriente, Sarah Méndez Capote, Candita Gómez de Bandujo, Flora Diaz Parrado, Ofelia Domínguez Navarro, María Teresa Casuso Brau, and Ofelia Rodríguez Acosta, sought to hold a memorial service for Trejo. They invited thousands of Cuban women to demonstrate their grief and their opposition to the government. A Cuban female worker, selected for her nonpolitical stance, was chosen to deliver the eulogy.[22] Havana city officials refused to designate a location, however. Realizing that another demonstration would certainly provoke violence, feminist leaders called off the service but made clear why they canceled. They encouraged women and students to avenge Trejo's death through future political action and alliance with the opposition.[23]

The forces for change were gaining respect from many sectors of Cuban society. Nearly everyone could find fault with repression, and, as the economy collapsed, most Cubans found no economic or political reason to support Machado. Only a small fraction of powerful people stood by the president, one of whom was María Collado. She responded to the Trejo assassination by discrediting the integrity of the student revolt. She accused the students of being out of hand when they demanded "free rights." Collado regretted Trejo's death, but she blamed the subversives, not Machado, for causing the unfortunate incident and called for an end to leftist resistance.[24] María Collado was critical of the proposed memorial service. She objected to having a working woman give the eulogy and claim to represent all Cuban women in their grief. She also attacked the planners of the service for their partisan views.

Machado was quick to realize that women had become a major force against him, and he began treating them as if they were genderless members of the opposition. For its part in Rafael Trejo's burial and for providing legal defense for jailed students and strikers, the Unión Laborista de Mujeres became a target of police investigations. Occasionally, policemen interrupted Unión meetings and disrupted the recruitment of new members. They also searched the Unión's offices at Lodge Washington on Jovellar 164 for evidence of seditious activities.[25]

As his administration came under increasing fire, Machado searched for a way to appease some of his opponents. An obvious ploy was to offer votes to women. As proof of his support for suffrage, he reminded the public of his 1927 constitutional resolution, blaming the Congress for rejecting the measure. Although few feminists believed Machado, his maneuver succeeded in maintaining a division between the Partido Demócrata Sufragista and the other feminist groups.

Machado's attempts at relieving tensions were unsuccessful, and through the year repression increased. The president outlawed public gatherings during the November 1930 by-elections and later that month suspended constitutional rights. Newspapers threatened with censorship closed. Police hunted down and killed students because they were members of the Directorio Estudiantil. They shot and killed protestors and suspected conspirators, several of whom were women, with their infamous "shots into the air." Stories of clashes, disturbances, protest demonstrations, threats, tortures, arrests, and deaths filled the press.

Women, many of them feminists, resisted government violence. In November 1930 the House of Representatives held hearings to review the university-ordered police action that resulted in Trejo's death. Women packed the House galleries to hear Carlos Manuel de la Cruz present a Unión Laborista de Mujeres motion to dismiss the secretary of Public Education and the university rector for their handling of the incident. Opposing representatives vehemently denied that anyone had been mistreated in the disturbance, a claim that almost no one could believe. In the midst of the defense's presentation, an outraged Unionista, Teté Casuso, shouted from the galleries, "Here are the blows I received, and they are still fresh, señores representantes."[26] The representatives looked up to see that she had bared her shoulders and part of her back, showing them bands of huge bruises and contusions that the police had inflicted several weeks before. Little came of her brash display. The House merely issued a caution to educational officials.

From her lofty perch among the privileged, María Collado condemned women for forming an opposition and protesting violence and the suspension of the constitution. By resisting the Machado administration, she believed, women would "forever bury their hopes for attaining women's rights." She supported Machado's suspension of the constitution, arguing that a state of emergency "would give the country time to put things right and to proceed peacefully after the radicals were rounded up and after the distorted press was restored to fair reporting."[27]

Government repression encouraged opposition groups to form coalitions. Hortensia Lamar of the Club Femenino and Pilar Jorge de Tella of the Alianza were the prime movers for the feminists to join forces with the Mujeres en Oposición. They received support from all but María Collado's Partido. Their first planned demonstration took place before the presidential palace where a united front of women, carrying banners and placards, demanded Machado's resignation. In January 1931 representatives of the Lyceum, the Club Femenino, the Alianza, and the Unión marched. Some came with single-minded political zeal and others with feelings of ambivalence about their action and the possibility of arrest. One Lyceum member, Piedad de la Maza, fearing a disheveled appearance as a result of detention, had her hair done before venturing into the demonstration.[28]

The united front gathered outside the presidential palace and called Machado to appear on the balcony and acknowledge their presence. Believing that he was greeting friends, the president waved to the crowd. At that moment the women unfurled banners and signs reading, "Down with tyranny!" and "Resign executive power. The people demand it!"[29]

The action of the Oposicionistas unleashed a wave of aggression against women that defied earlier sensibilities about not brutalizing women to the same degree as men. On February 16, 1931, for example, two young women were victims of Machado's renovated *porra*. The porra had devised a special division for action against women. Sarah Benítez and Hortensia de la Cuevas, two women in the opposition, were attacked as they left Benítez's home in Vedado about midmorning. The attackers, two women and four men, surrounded Benítez and de la Cuevas. While the women porristas used metal fingernails to hit and scratch the suspected revolutionaries and to strip them nude in the street, the men surrounded the ambush to ward off intervention. The purpose was to terrorize and humiliate the Oposicionistas.[30]

The Unión Laborista de Mujeres offered legal assistance to the two women, but Benítez's father who was chief justice of the Havana Audiencia refused to carry the incident to trial, saying that he feared a scandal.[31] His daughter's sexual humiliation was an affront to his own honor, so he retreated into silence and compelled his daughter to do the same.

While Dr. Benítez bowed to the threat of scandal, the revolutionaries did not. Members of the Directorio Estudiantil took matters into their own hands, and the incident had a tragicomic ending. Several male students disguised themselves as women and went to an area where the special porra operated. The decoys began making antigovernment statements within earshot of the porra, and they were attacked. This time, however, the students exchanged punches for scratches, and they fended off the guards. The brawl apparently discouraged the activities of the special porra.[32]

The Congress was undecided about how to handle the suffrage issue. Feminism and the feminists were forces with which to contend, but they posed a dilemma for members of the Liberal Party who had cooperated with Machado, trading their autonomy for loyalty to him. Liberals wanted to secure women's votes, but women were going out into the streets against Machado. If women got the vote, Liberal Party members feared that they would elect progressive leaders other than themselves. They hedged their bets by introducing suffrage limited to municipal elections or the political appointments of favored women. Their alliance with the feminists was unreliable, and feminists continued to take a hard stance for the ouster of Machado and his officials.

In March 1931, for example, Senator Gustavo Parodi proposed a bill seeking an executive appointment for a woman nominated by designated feminist organizations. This proposal was roundly rejected by all feminist organizations, even the Partido Demócrata Sufragista, as an attempt to get women to settle for a gesture and dispel their determination to win the vote.

Following a year of warfare between the government and the allied opposition, the bankruptcy of the legal and executive branches was obvious. In March 1932 the chief justice of the Supreme Court resigned because he could not carry out the law. In an atmosphere of lawlessness, most feminists declared themselves in favor of the restored 1901 constitution with a suffrage amendment. Unfortunately, Congress never considered reverting to the original constitution, but it continually heard bills proposing universal suffrage.

The Alianza took advantage of one such hearing to publicize which congressmen favored or opposed universal suffrage. On June 12, 1932, *Bohemia* published the Alianza list of congressional supporters and opponents of votes for women.[33]

On June 8, 1932, the proposal for the franchise went before Congress. As before, congressmen debated the merits of women participating in politics and rejected the bill. The usual arguments concerning women's biological inferiority and their unsuitable political constitution were resurrected, but they had a flat ring given the extent of women's involvement in the civil war. Since women had become more active in contemporary politics, opponents had to concede that women were capable leaders and couch their objections in more indirect terms. Several congressmen objected to women assuming high political posts because it transferred "those fine feminine minds away from the positions they hold on local education boards." Holding to the notion that giving women the vote should proceed slowly, another congressman suggested that limited suffrage be granted whereby women could vote in municipal elections.[34] Liberal congressmen feared that women would vote as a radical block, and conservatives were concerned that women would favor costly welfare reforms. Although a majority of congressmen supported the franchise, there was not the two-thirds majority required to pass the bill. The final vote was fifty-two in favor and forty-two opposed.

Eulalia de Miranda, a member of the Partido Nacional Sufragista, made one last stand for a compromise: limited suffrage. She tried to gain support for a law permitting Havana women to vote in the municipal election. Nearly all the feminist organizations in the country denounced de Miranda's proposal. The Alianza called her strategy "a mutilated concession" that was "oppressive of and discriminatory toward all other Cuban women, who were the majority, living outside Havana's metropolitan limits."[35]

After the bill's second defeat, infuriated progressive feminists followed the Unión into open rebellion. The Alianza, while maintaining its commitment to the franchise, issued a manifesto calling for an alliance of all opposition groups. The Alianza preferred a peaceful change of power, but its shift to the nonnegotiable demand for Machado's removal and its willingness to organize popular action against him were unmistakable.[36]

From July 1932 to September 1933, Cuba fell into political chaos and

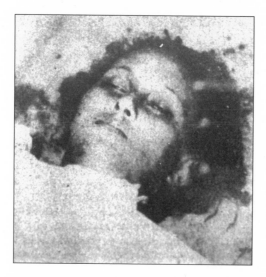

América Labadi, a member of the Cuban Young Communist League who was shot to death August 1, 1933, by President Machado's *porra*. Taken from *La mujer cubana*, p. 49. The Stoner Collection, Roll 1.

martial rule. Sugar workers initiated a general strike, and people disappeared daily or were killed and their bodies left on the streets. Suffrage stayed alive as an issue only because parties sought approval for their violent opposition to the Machado regime, and feminists used their alliances with opposition groups and recognized political parties to ensure that suffrage was not forgotten. The Liberal Party, for example, invited Gustavo Gutiérrez, secretary of justice, to speak on the suffrage issue. The secretary defended suffrage and condemned congressional cowardice with the argument that Cuban women were ready to assume the responsibility of voting.[37]

The year 1932 was a time of hunger in Cuba. With the economy completely disrupted, many people had nothing to eat. In Havana people sat in their doorways begging for food. The standard fare for those people was bread without butter, humorously referred to as "cram and swallow" (*aprieta y traga*). The large trees surrounding the national capital that were originally intended for shade also provided shelter for the homeless. Public employees received salaries every fifty to sixty days rather than by the month, and what they received was sometimes reduced to 70 percent of their contracted monthly earnings. Responding to the desperate conditions, members of the Directorio Estudiantil went on a hunger strike that won sympathy from the public but that had essentially no effect on political policy. As more young people were martyred, more funerals became political spectacles and occasions for political eulogies. Cuban women were prominent speakers at these funerals. The bier became the podium for feminist and political activists.

By late 1932 it appeared that, despite general dissatisfaction, Machado would withstand the popular revolt. Thousands of people had been arrested or had disappeared. Emergency courts were authorized to hold perfunctory trials within twenty-four hours after the arrest of dissidents to hinder the accused from preparing an effective defense. Though violence and disruption continued, progress toward removing the president had stalled. Life had become intolerable for the average citizen, which left the moderate with little other choice than to appeal for U.S. intervention under the provisions of the Platt Amendment.

In July 1933 various subgroups of the opposition met with Sumner Welles, the U.S. ambassador dispatched to Cuba to end the rebellion, to solicit his support. On July 14, 1933, the Full Opposition Committee, presided over by Hortensia Lamar of the Club Femenino, the Alianza, and Women in Opposition, met with the ambassador and discussed the illegitimacy of the Machado government and attempted to convince the ambassador that Machado's ouster was imperative to the survival of Cuban democracy.[38] The absence of women's suffrage counted as evidence that Machado's regime was undemocratic and his claim to the presidency dishonest.[39]

Welles offered concessions to Machado and to the opposition. The beleaguered but recalcitrant president needed economic relief to alleviate the effects of the depression. Welles promised a revision of economic trade treaties with the United States and an opening of the U.S. domestic market to Cuban goods in exchange for Machado's guarantee of an election in 1934. To the moderate opposition groups, Welles promised that Machado would not succeed himself and that open elections would be held at the end of his term in exchange for an end to insurgency. Radical leftists, who were not invited to the meetings and who demonstrated their opposition to mediation with a ceremonial boycott, had no bargaining power, and thus they were excluded from the negotiation.

The left had no alternative but to call strikes, thereby damaging the relationship between Sumner Welles and the president. In response to the general strike, Machado began negotiations with the Cuban Communist Party and the National Committee of Campesinos and Workers. He agreed to release political prisoners and legalize the radical organizations. He also consented to allowing leftist organizations to participate in future elections. Machado's command of domestic policy and his resolutions were unacceptable to Welles, who neither understood nor accepted the Cuban left. In response to Machado's concessions, Welles committed himself to the overthrow of Machado with the support of the moderate opposition. Welles and the moderates believed that, if the president did not resign, the country would be faced with a communist revolution. To secure a resignation, Sumner Welles threatened to withdraw U.S. recognition of Machado's presidency and throw Cuba into unending economic chaos. The mere threat of U.S. action sent the last supporters of Machado into a panic.

Welles's strategy produced the desired effects. Members of the political elite resigned their positions, which created a political vacuum to be filled by the moderate opposition. The military, also tired of holding the line for the unpopular president through force, mutinied as they observed the very people against whom they had fought assuming office. The army also feared U.S. military intervention, since the army would have to fight or surrender, neither of which was an attractive alternative.

On August 12, 1933, an army coup ousted Machado. The interim president, Carlos Manuel de Céspedes, reinstated the Constitution of 1901. The old organic law required elections as soon as they could be scheduled. Cubans celebrated the end of the Machadato and pondered better guarantees of regular democratic elections. Harking back to the days of Martí for inspiration, they made much of justice, social reform, and the cancellation of the Platt Amendment. In this atmosphere the Alianza appealed to President Céspedes in the name of Ana Betancourt, who had raised suffrage with President Céspedes's father (who had presided over the revolutionary government in 1869), to grant women the vote. The Alianza also asked the Congress to reinstate all social reform laws that had passed since 1902.[40]

President Céspedes provided ineffective leadership, and, in the confusion, a five-man junta replaced him. On September 9, 1933, the Student Directorate appointed Ramón Grau San Martín, one of the junta, provisional president. Grau, professor and a reformist, had the support of the students and, for a short time, the military. Aided by Antonio Guiteras, a radical but noncommunist reformer, he began issuing executive decrees aimed at social restructuring and redistribution of wealth. Grau represented the reformist attitudes of progressives: he was a nationalist, a socialist but not a Marxist, and an anti-imperialist. Within the context of democracy, Grau passed decree-laws intended to rectify social injustice and placate Cuba's most outspoken activists: anti-imperialists, laborers, students, and women. Among his most dramatic reforms were abrogating the Platt Amendment, establishing the eight-hour workday, redistributing land, nationalizing the labor force, and granting women the vote.[41]

Grau's reforms were not extensive enough to please the radical left, and they threatened the right's and U.S. business interests. By with-holding diplomatic recognition of the Grau government, the United States hoped to erode support for the new regime. The radical left carried out strikes and conspired to involve the army in a coup. Because the end to Cuba's economic depression depended on U.S. cooperation, mode-rates and progressives began withdrawing their support for Grau. The interim president's popularity among peasants and workers increased despite leftist activities, but his influence among students fell when the Student Directorate dissolved itself. Initially, Batista hesitated to inter-fere, but with prodding and flattery from Washington he came to oppose Grau. On Sunday, January 15, 1934, after being convinced that the army would overthrow him, Grau resigned and took up exile in the Domini-can Republic.

U.S. cooperation with the ouster of presidents Machado and Grau assured that government would once again be imposed by Washington and not determined by a majority of Cubans. Between 1933 and 1939 the rapid and irregular succession of Cuban presidents supported by the U.S. left open the question of the legitimacy of each regime. For six years feminists battled to keep their concerns before the provisional adminis-trations, and politicians, in their frantic search for support, promised to comply with feminists' demands.

On January 18, 1934, Carlos Mendieta became the next provisional president. The irregular transfer of power threw into question the validity of Grau's presidential decree giving women the vote. The legal question was: could a short-term and internationally unrecognized administration promulgate a long-standing law? Did the succeeding administration have to accept the laws passed by a temporary and ousted regime? Would Mendieta honor women's suffrage rights?

As the Mendieta administration worked to establish order, women's groups held a vigil outside the presidential palace hoping to influence the president to sustain the suffrage law.[42] A coalition of political groups called the Commission of Oppositionist Sectors passed a provisional constitution on February 3, 1934, which formally extended the vote to women.[43] Article 38 of the constitution read: "All Cubans of either sex have the right to active or passive suffrage under the conditions and exceptions that determine the law."[44] The formalized Constitution of 1940 restated that women could vote and be elected to public office.

Women's voting rights were obtained via presidential decrees during a revolutionary period and not through normal democratic procedures. Presidents Machado, Grau, and Carlos Mendieta, interested in legitimiz-ing their administrations, used suffrage to bolster support and moral approval for their policies. Cuban feminists took advantage of political unrest to press their cause with incumbent regimes and dissidents alike. Most men, faced with the inevitability of women's suffrage, did not dare to say that women were incompetent or unable to assume political responsibility, but, citing political reasons, they did avoid endorsing the bills. It took one insincere resolution from Machado, a decree law from Grau, and an interim constitution from Carlos Mendieta to affirm that women could vote and hold public office.

Not all feminists were pleased with the outcome. In 1934, from her position on the sidelines, Ofelia Domínguez Navarro railed at the middle- and upper-class suffragists who were satisfied with their achievement. In an article in *Bohemia,* Domínguez recanted her initial support for the franchise and accused suffragists of being responsible for social injustice. She disregarded the breadth of some of the feminists' social programs and asserted that women had been given the vote and had not earned it. She charged that suffragists and middle-class feminists had the mistaken impression that new laws would reform society. She rightfully pointed out that suffrage had little appeal to working-class women. Domínguez was also one of the first to show how the franchise had been used by male politicians to justify their own policies, although she refused to admit that women had used Cuba's unstable conditions to advance suffrage.[45]

Like the divorce and property laws, suffrage served as a statement of governing principles. Suffrage symbolized democracy at a time when presidents were violating democratic principles. But, unlike divorce and property laws, suffrage was passed because feminists made it a cause and a national symbol. As a result, Cuban feminists had to struggle for only ten years after women's groups declared their intention to win the vote. They also continued to adhere to broad programs of social reform for women and children. Before Cuban women even began voting, they had already moved on to organize for health, education, and welfare guarantees.

Feminism and Social
Motherhood

⌇

The period between the ouster of Gerardo Machado and the writing
of the 1940 constitution was a time of national introspection.
Relieved of a dictator and spared the trauma of radical reform, moderate
Cubans debated among themselves the terms of social justice appropriate
for Cuba. Once again José Martí's nationalist directives stirred Cubans to
reflect upon their political and social circumstances and to demand
democracy and social equity. Between 1938 and 1940, as Cubans antici-
pated writing a new constitution, newspapers and journals reported the
controversy over the meaning of Martí's message, direction of government, and imperatives for social change. Controversies indicated that
Cubans understood that within the next few years they would be setting
legal standards for their society and that many disagreed over the terms of
social justice.

Having just won the vote and having been instrumental in overthrow-
ing Machado, most Cuban feminists assumed new responsibilities and
exhibited a new political identity. They wanted to reconstruct social
values to give women a place in policymaking, support women's professions as well as domestic responsibilities, and protect women and
children who no longer found refuge in traditional social institutions
such as the Church and family. Feminists, therefore, participated in
forming welfare policies and creating the enabling government agencies. In the areas of education and welfare, they developed political authority.

National circumstances propelled women into political administrative
positions previously beyond their reach. A decade-long economic depression, changing modes of production, the increase in population and
decrease in wealth, and changing roles of the Church and charity
organizations left many Cubans poor and increasingly unable to find
assistance. Colonel Fulgencio Batista, chief of the military and the power
behind four puppet presidents (Carlos Mendieta, 1934–35; José A.
Barnet, 1935–36; Miguel Mariano Gómez, 1936; and Federico Laredo
Brú, 1936–40), sought to restore peace and stability through social

welfare programs. Batista was a demagogue who at once brutally repressed his opposition while providing liberal reforms to aid those most devastated by economic setbacks. He shrewdly invited women to run some of the education and social welfare programs, thus appearing committed to social justice and co-opting the feminists.

Batista's dual policies of repression and reform succeeded in suppressing the radical elements until 1953. With opposition leaders either in jail or exile, members of ideologically antagonistic groups such as the ABC, trade unions, radical student groups, and the Communist Party began cooperating with Batista. More, the campesinos and common laborers identified with the former military sergeant, who referred to them as "los humildes" and himself came from a lower-class and ethnically mixed background. (Batista was of black, white, and Chinese lineage.) Feminists too joined ranks with what they hoped would be a progressive government headed by a popular reformer. The Pax Batistiana gave the feminist activists the opening they needed to implement their programs.

The period of reconciliation made possible the healing of divisions between feminist organizations. Not that feminist groups unified under a single rubric, but tensions that separated Collado from the progressives subsided, and Domínguez was either in jail or exiled in Mexico until 1937. That year she returned to Cuba and affiliated again with the Unión Radical de Mujeres, renamed from the Unión Laborista de Mujeres. But her experience in Mexico with labor radicals who found ways to cooperate with President Lázaro Cárdenas's government ameliorated her revolutionary zeal. Her softening corresponded with international adjustments within Marxism-Leninism. Between 1937 and 1940 Domínguez helped organize nongovernmental labor unions, and in 1940 she returned briefly to Mexico to help prepare the legal defense for Leon Trotsky's murderer, but she also ran for a seat in the Cuban House of Representatives in 1938. Hence, while feminist groups did not renounce their political preferences, they did cooperate under a troubled and imposed governing order.

Literacy, social welfare, school lunch programs, medical provisions, and the cultural advancement of women concerned progressive feminists most. These issues complemented their natural interests in the family, and they extended women's philanthropic programs into reformist policies. Feminist social reform programs evolved in two steps. Between 1901 and 1934 the feminists filled in where charity was inadequate and where the state had not yet assumed responsibility by funding their own education and welfare programs. From 1934 to 1940 they obtained legal agreements that the federal government would fund women's education,

Mothers and children who benefited from the milk program supported by the Club Femenino de Cuba. Taken from *La mujer moderna*, January 1926, p. 43. The Stoner Collection, Roll 10.

provide welfare and maternity services, and correct the horrors of women's prisons.

The question for these progressives was whether they would demand entirely new ruling structures with values that reflected women's moral views or whether they would only repair or modify the traditional system that constantly challenged the validity of their values and undermined their political power. Could organized feminists alter governing priorities so that the well-being of citizens would take precedence over war activities and commerce?

In most cases feminists supported traditional political values. They involved themselves in resource allocation and projects within the departments of education, health, and welfare, and many supported Batista's limited reform programs. Progressive feminists, then, settled for inserting welfare and education reforms into a crowded political agenda. Their solution to poverty and exploitation was to create a place for themselves within the existing political framework as the overseers of welfare matters and to apply mild ameliorative measures to the harsh realities of poverty and male domination. These women proved themselves to be classical democrats who believed that popular will would govern, even in a weak nation dominated by a foreign power. They were, in the end, using their energies to build a modern Cuba without challenging men's political morality and authority. For their efforts, they, and not the women they represented, gained power and influence. These Cuban feminists thus preserved Cuba's patriarchy, class structure, and foreign domination while they reformed certain aspects of a national welfare program.

Feminism and Social Reform

After gaining the vote, feminists referred to the 1923 and 1925 women's congresses to guide their new campaigns. Depending upon the preferences of individual organizations, feminists took up a variety of causes, and the various groups functioned both in cooperation with and independently of each other. While debate between the various groups over political ideology was often acrimonious, feminists agreed on the fundamental importance of improving chances for poor and working-class women to live safely and in health.

The women's congresses' directions in social reforms emphasized: (1) secular public education with special programs for teaching scientific child care and home economics; (2) reform of civil and penal codes; (3) protective legislation for children and the formation of a juvenile court system; (4) civic volunteering by women; (5) an end to drug trafficking, gambling, alcohol, and prostitution; and (6) a revision of the adultery law. In all areas except the social vices, the feminists made observable differences. Their failure to correct drug, gambling, and prostitution problems might be explained by their inept and unambitious campaigns against vice. As ladies, they did not speak strongly or in depth on topics about which they were purposefully ignorant. They condemned the existence and results of these crimes, to be sure, but they did not administer public health clinics for prostitutes, close casinos and bordellos, nor expose police and politicians for their complicity with underworld business. Perhaps their close connections with politicians precluded effective action to stop Cuba's infamous nightlife.

The Club Femenino de Cuba, the Lyceum, and the Alianza Nacional Feminista developed formidable campaigns for improved education and social work. The Unión Laborista de Mujeres worked with organizations of women workers and the rights of illegitimate children. Feminist authors attacked the adultery law and the limited rights of illegitimate children. National social reform campaigns increased between 1925 and 1940 when the legal means of governance was in question and no one knew the extent of government involvement in social assistance. The main body of the feminist movement joined a popular national movement that was progressive and dealt with the crushing effects of the depression. By 1940 feminists had influenced massive legal reforms and established schools and health services in such numbers as to qualify Cuban ideals, if not Cuban reality, as one of the most progressive in the Western Hemisphere.

EDUCATION

Ideals of national sovereignty, democracy, an educated citizenry, and feminism converged in the twentieth century as Cuban patriots took education as the cornerstone of independence and democratic rule and tapped women as the educators of future generations. Political leaders had to provide a place for women's contributions to the new society both because they recognized the influence women had and because they feared women's allegiance to the Catholic Church. Patriots held parochial education, administered by Spanish clerics, to be a means of suppressing democratic principles. If contemporary examples in Latin America carried any message, it was that democratic government required the separation of Church and state and secularized schools. Because women seemed to have the strongest affiliation with the Catholic Church and because they influenced the morality of youth, patriots believed they had to offer women new authority as secular educators of young nationals.

Remembering María Luisa Dolz's directives that women would be liberated through the study of science and physical education, feminists worked to modernize school curricula and make it accessible to women. Feminists themselves were educated, aware of discrimination, and bent on empowering women through modern education. In an era when positivism challenged Hispanic Catholic thought, feminists placed great importance on teaching women to shed colonial, patriarchal values that isolated them in the home, made them dependent upon men, and kept them fatalistic and attached to Hispanic Catholic mysticism or folk superstitions.

Before organized feminists initiated educational programs for girls and women, Cuban public education had raised Cuba's literacy rate to relatively high standards for both girls and boys. By 1919 Cuban women had attained the same level of literacy as men. Table 6 reflects advances the public education system made in increasing Cuba's literacy rate for women and men from the first year of independence to 1943. General literacy rose from 36 percent in 1899 to 75.4 percent in 1943. From 1899 to 1919, slightly more men were literate than women, but between 1919 and 1931, the years when the feminists were actively building schools and libraries for women, women surpassed men by nearly 1.8 percent in the rate of literacy.

Table 7 demonstrates that in rural areas women tended to be more literate than men. No doubt feminists' efforts to educate women produced some improvement in women's literacy, since feminists did build

Table 6   Expansion of Literacy for Persons Five Years and Older, by Gender, 1899–1943

Year	Total	Female	Male
1899	36	—	—
1907	56.6	54.6	58.3
1919	61.6	61	62.1
1931	69.3	70.1	68.3
1943	75.4	76	74.2

Sources: United States Bureau of the Census, *Cuba: Population, History, and Resource, 1907* (Washington, D.C.: U.S. Government Publication Office, 1909), 206. República de Cuba, Dirección General del Censo, *Census of the Republic of Cuba, 1919* (Havana: Masa, Arrango, Caso), 743. República de Cuba. *Informe general del censo de 1943* (Havana: P. Fernández, 1945), 926 and 930–31.

Table 7   Literate Population Five Years and Older, by Province and Gender, 1931 and 1943

Province	1943			1931		
	Total	Females	Males	Total	Females	Males
Pinar del Río	66.5	63.4	68.4	60.3	59.2	61.2
Havana	87.8	87.8	87.8	85.8	85.9	85.7
Matanzas	79.4	81.2	78.6	72.3	74.0	70.7
Las Villas	74.7	75.9	74.3	62.6	70.0	62.2
Camagüey	75.5	77.8	71.4	67.6	73.9	63.5
Oriente	68.5	70.2	65.7	64.4	68.1	61.4

Source: República de Cuba, *Informe general del censo de 1943* (Havana: P. Fernández, 1945), 930.

schools for women in provincial capitals. But other forces also obtained. The higher literacy rate for women in the rural areas reflected rural work conditions whereby adolescent boys worked seasonally in the cane or tobacco fields and then migrated to cities during the dead season in search of work in factories or docks. Girls remained at home longer and took advantage of the rudimentary education available in the countryside.[1]

Federal emphasis on public education notwithstanding, schooling beyond primary education was virtually unavailable in the countryside for girls and boys. According to a U.S. research team's report in 1933, six of Cuba's seven provincial capitals had public secondary schools, and these graduated only 15,000 students in a year. Private schools conducted by religious bodies, mutual benefit societies, patriotic philanthropic groups, and individuals compensated for the lack of public high schools. Private schools educated those who could pay tuition, and over 25,000 students were enrolled in these schools. Feminist contributions to higher education were significant and certainly welcome, since only one of twenty Cuban youths went beyond the fifth grade.[2]

In the 1920s a significant portion of the students graduating from the University of Havana were women. In 1927, 23 percent of the graduating class were women, and, between 1929 and 1933, 19 percent were women. This figure compares to 27 percent women in all North American universities.[3] Thus, Cuba had an unusually large percentage of women in the graduating classes of the university, but that group represented only a small percentage of the general population (see Table 8).

Feminist leaders had graduated from universities aware of their changing roles and believing in the importance of education as the key to personal liberation and social progress, and they were committed to extending educational opportunities to working-class women. Following the example of the wealthy benefactresses of the nineteenth and early twentieth centuries, feminist organizations established night schools and free classes for working-class women. The Lyceum, the Club Femenino, and the Alianza Nacional Feminista, in particular, contributed enormously to women's education without legislative or financial support from the government.[4]

Individual organizations founded their own schools and educational programs. In most of the provincial cities the Lyceum established excellent night schools for working women, stressing literacy, elementary mathematics, and home skills. Other courses taught preschool teachers hygiene and child care, preparation of food, washing and ironing and mending children's clothes, and instructive children's games.

Table 8   Enrollment at University of Havana, by Race and Gender, 1929–30

	White		Colored		Total		Grand Total
	Men	Women	Men	Women	Men	Women	
1. Civil Law	653	30	40	4	693	34	727
2. Public Law	91	8	4	0	95	8	103
3. Notary	101	11	4	0	105	11	116
4. Lawyer	231	9	7	0	238	9	247
5. Political, Social, Economic Sciences	190	4	6	0	196	4	200
6. Medicine	1,356	18	150	9	1,506	27	1,533
7. Pharmacy	202	111	18	23	220	134	354
8. Dental Surgery	638	36	99	21	737	57	794
9. Veterinary	252	3	15	0	267	3	270
10. Philosophy and Letters	169	188	10	22	179	210	389
11. Pedagogy	268	573	32	61	300	634	934
12. Physics and Math	86	20	4	0	90	20	110
13. Chemistry	102	29	2	0	104	29	133
14. Natural Sciences	135	64	3	2	138	66	204
15. Civil Engineering	271	11	9	1	280	12	292
16. Electrical Engineering	124	2	1	1	125	3	128
17. Architecture	152	7	8	0	160	7	167
18. Agricultural Sugar Engineering	119	5	6	0	125	5	130
19. Chemical Expert	44	3	2	0	46	3	49
20. Agricultural Expert	37	1	3	0	40	1	41
Total	5,221	1,133	423	144	5,644	1,277	6,921

Source: Commission on Cuban Affairs, 155.

Courses were taught by specialists, some of whom were graduates of the Escuela del Hogar. The plan was to educate poor women so that they might find better employment and an improved station in life. The Lyceum also built one of the best lending libraries in Havana and subsequently established libraries in all provincial cities.[5]

The Alianza also was active in women's public education. By 1933 it had founded seventy-two schools for women. In 1938 its schools offered courses in primary education, civics, clothing design, English, typing, shorthand, embroidery, and weaving. The Aliancistas stressed women's voting rights in the civics course. In 1945 the Alianza organized a course for teachers and superintendents on teaching methods, which had an attendance of 1,500 students. A year later it sponsored a national course on nutrition, and in 1947 it expanded courses on social assistance. Like the Lyceum, the Alianza established a lending library and it was called the Ana Betancourt de Mora Library.[6]

As early as 1929 feminist intellectuals turned to the government with demands for equal educational opportunities and state funding for women's education. Under the Machadato the Central Executive Committee of the Alianza Nacional Feminista publicly protested the resolution of the secretary of education, General Alemán, that excluded women from classes at the Industrial School in Oriente province. They protested on legal grounds, for Decree 837 of May 1928 stated that women could not be denied entrance into industrial school. Pilar Jorge de Tella not only protested the resolution, she petitioned for government funds to begin the Arts and Business School for Women. Her efforts required intense lobbying from the Alianza. In 1929 Machado granted the land, and Rosalia Abreu, niece of the great patriot and philanthropist Marta Abreu, donated 150,000 pesos for building construction. The school was run and subsidized largely by the Alianza with occasional support from the government.[7]

Feminists did not educate poor, working-class women for highly professional jobs, nor did they indoctrinate them with ideas about women and men being equal. Their approach was more pragmatic. To ameliorate men's domination of women, feminists educated women to become men's companions. They believed that women's natural instinct to nurture would temper men's urge to combat and destroy, women's protection of the weak would restrain men's egoism and penchant to exploit, and women's revulsion for violence would chasten men's brutal forcefulness. Thus, feminists believed that women of all classes had public usefulness, if they were trained to exert it.

The Escuela del Hogar was a project supported by the Club Femenino de Mujeres. After consulting with club members in 1927, Representatives Alberto Berreras, Ricardo Dolz, Carmelo Urquiaga, and Manuel Tomé presented a congressional bill establishing the escuelas in all the provincial cities and Havana. The escuelas' objective was "the advancement of women, whose scientific, artistic, and practical knowledge [would] give them general cultural information to prepare them for life in the home as caretakers and mothers and outside the home as responsible people in industry appropriate to their gender." The bill outlined five major areas of preparation: practical home skills, domestic arts and sciences, commercial preparation, artistic-industrial lessons, and occupations and responsibilities appropriate for women.[8] The escuelas were free and open to girls over the age of seventeen and of good health and moral background. With practically no objections, Congress approved the Escuela del Hogar and appropriated funds for the physical plant.

The bipartisan support for the Escuelas reflected general approval for women becoming scientific mothers and motherly professionals. Most agreed that women's functions as wife, mother, and creator of future generations deserved respect in modernizing Cuba. The curriculum encouraged practical education intended to strengthen the home and the family. The positivist approach to education created the field of home economics that challenged folkways with courses on nutrition, cleanliness, first aid, orderliness, and wise consumption. A degree from the Escuela del Hogar also prepared women for professions in interior design and service management outside the home. Women, then, received permission from legislators and feminist activists to expand their traditional roles into professional ones, but, as yet, they had no public approval for challenging feminine activity by redefining male and female interests.

In addition to educational opportunities for women, a long-term project for the Club Feminino was the school breakfast program, commonly called the Gota de Leche program. In 1913 Congress passed a law (Decree-Law 312) allocating subsidies for it.[9] The breakfast program did not materialize, however, because funding never reached school districts. Members of the Club continued to petition after 1917 and made public demands for the promised support, but Congress did not react until 1934, after the revolutionary upheaval and during the progressive one hundred days of the Grau San Martín government.

The decree—the Desayuno Escolar—was passed by Executive Decree-Law 115 on January 8, 1934. It established morning meals in all public schools and appropriated sufficient funds for the service.[10] Decree-Law 17, passed on February 16, 1934, issued the program's regulations and enforcement legislation. Subsequent interim administrations chose to uphold Grau's commitment to free and balanced breakfasts for schoolchildren.

Feminist organizations sponsored education projects for the poor, but they also promoted courses for their membership in literature, the arts, and crafts. The Lyceum created a forum for women artists and intellectuals to display their work. It sponsored women's recitals, literary readings, and art exhibits, and it created scholarships to educate Cuba's more accomplished performers. Believing that art expressed the conjunc-

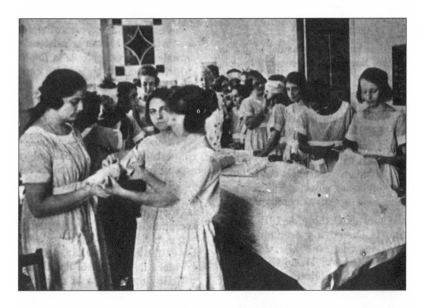

The Escuela del Hogar was established by the Club Femenino. Women who graduated were able to be scientific mothers or professionals in welfare services, nutrition, cooking, and hygiene. Taken from *La mujer moderna,* April 1926, pp. 14, 17, and 18. Stoner Collection, Roll 10.

tion of culture, morality, and self-expression, the women of the Lyceum offered a forum and an appreciative audience to young artists. Because the Lyceum was apolitical and not religious, it supported art from all political and religious views.

The Alianza did not emphasize membership courses or exhibitions to the extent the Lyceum did. In 1932 it held an arts and crafts exhibition entitled Exposición de Defensa Feminina, yet its social and cultural projects focused more on establishing services for a diverse community. The Cultural Commission helped create a Psychological Institute, rural schools, schools for the mentally handicapped, and schools for advanced children. It also broadcast educational programs and pro-feminist information over radio channels.[11]

Feminist efforts to reform education were in keeping with the general progressive, positivist attitudes that prevailed throughout the 1920s and 1930s in Cuba, which endorsed the connection between feminism and Cuban culture. Feminists were able to implement their programs because they integrated reform projects with national public education programs. They also emerged as directors and teachers because of the precedent for women to serve at various levels of authority within the education field, and they had less competition from men. They emphasized education for women because they were feminists.

Feminists supported the idea of liberated, educated women who were also mothers and sources of morality and social justice. In fact, feminist organizations founded the very schools that emphasized domestic skills and homemaking professions, thereby protecting traditional woman's roles. Liberation signified the aggrandizement of and respect for feminine endeavors, which meant that, through education, women should get jobs and receive fair salaries for their work, that women complemented men at home and in the work force, and that the public respected women's feminine qualities.

SOCIAL WELFARE PROGRAMS

Feminists predicted constructive social reform after women got the vote. As society's nurturers, women were expected to mold their mothering instincts into political theories and programs to serve the needy—that is, feminists expected that they would tidy up the disorder caused by limited national sovereignty, political corruption, and economic collapse. Work with social welfare programs was an appropriate mission for active feminists because it fulfilled their promises to add care for the disadvantaged to state political responsibilities, a welcomed activity during a period of deep economic and political distress. More importantly, it provided an outlet in social work for educated women without forcing them to renounce class allegiance.

Cuban feminist writers, ranging from conservative to radical, agreed that women should aid the poor because poverty destroyed families. María Teresa Bernal, an upper-class poet, argued that granting women their rights would formalize and enhance women's social contributions.[12] In a 1930 address to the Alianza, Graziella Barrinaga y Ponce de León, vice-president of the Alianza and a doctor of philosophy from the University of Havana, repudiated the possibility that because of feminist beliefs women would renounce roles as mothers and caretakers of the young to compete with men. On the contrary, she claimed that they would invent national programs insuring the welfare of people and opposing destruction through war, degradation, and poverty.[13] In "La maternidad transcendente," Ofelia Rodríguez Acosta interpreted the objectives of women's movements as a transfer of

their [women's] morality from the individualism of yesterday to a frankly socialist point of view. Theirs is a choice of being either a mother to their own flesh and blood and teaching their children how to exploit others or a mother to all children. If they choose the latter, they must raise their children with a social conscience. They must believe in complete equality. Women are the force of change, and they must take their task seriously.[14]

María Collado remained faithful to the idea that class and race divisions among women could be resolved as long as women honored biological ties and ignored class and ethnic origins. She believed that a unified woman's movement gave rich women the chance to understand the plight of the poor in ways they had never known before, and through that knowledge they could become advocates for the poor.[15] Many writers claimed that humaneness, charity, and love would exert a positive influence on national policy. But theorists such as Mariblanca Sabas Alomá and Ofelia Domínguez Navarro warned against leaving social rectification to charity and ignoring the causes of poverty, ignorance, crime, and class and racial hatred.[16]

Feminist involvement in social reforms grew out of upper-class philanthropy of the colonial period when social welfare functioned through philanthropic groups, patronage, self-help societies, and the Church. The Asilo San Vicente de Paul, an orphanage for illegitimate girls, exemplified charitable provisions for abandoned girls. Founded in 1872 by a group of distinguished Habaneras, the orphanage cared for seventy girls who were taught embroidery and sewing, skills used to bring in funds for the home.[17] The founders raised money for the orphanage by going door to door in good neighborhoods until they had collected the $14,000 to buy a ranch and build the school. According to descriptions of the school, its comforts rivaled those accorded to daughters of the privileged. The Sisters of Charity oversaw the daily responsibilities for the girls' educations, and the Junta de Señoras administered the school's financial accounting. The girls were taught to read and write and do figures. They also learned a trade to support themselves and help pay for the school. For that purpose, a cardboard box factory employed some of the girls as well as poor women living in the vicinity. By 1922 the orphanage had failed because of insufficient funds.

Following independence, women's work in social welfare activities and legislation can be divided into two historical periods: 1901–23 and 1923–58. The first stage was characterized by private acts of charity and very little organized effort to force governmental provision of social service programs. The second stage was marked by feminist organization and legislative and institutional reforms providing welfare guarantees.

Between 1901 and 1923 women's philanthropic groups fulfilled their public duties by singling out favorite charitable causes and donating money, time, and handicraft.[18] Their responses to poverty were often symbolic, religious, and personal, as they took upon themselves the task of evaluating need, developing and implementing programs, serving as project facilitators, and directing aid to the indigent. Philanthropic works were often limited projects with no long-lasting effects. Girls' orphanages were managed by lay and Catholic sisterhoods or philanthropic associations. President Mendieta's wife and her friends, for example, opened a community for undernourished girls near Varadero. One hundred girls received a primary education, room and board, and medical treatment. The advantage of these schools was in the personal interest sponsors took in their work and the imaginative programs they developed. The disadvantage was the irregular and uneven service to the poor.

Charitable works served also to draw public attention to the social status of club members. Lowry Nelson described the Christmas gifts for the poor as follows:

> During the Christmas season the First Lady of the Land distributes gifts to the "poor people" in front of the Presidential Palace. Thus the poor congregate ostentatiously before the palace in great numbers to receive their gifts. The point is not that the gifts are given to the poor—an act that is done in most countries—but solely in the manner of public giving, which amounts to

official recognition of a class called "the poor." While this may be dealing with reality, it makes a public spectacle of it.[19]

Early philanthropists had special interests in women's and children's concerns. In September 1913 the Damas Isabelinas sought permission to establish a lying-in emergency room on the first floor of a widow's house. The room would be open to indigent women in need of a sanitary place to give birth. The Damas wanted to have a physician on duty to prescribe treatment and the length of convalescence for mothers and children.[20] In May 1928 the Comisión Nacional de Protección de la Maternidad e Infancia, founded by Angela Elvira Machado de Obregon, established an ill-woman's clinic in the Hospital Calixto García.

Feminists in the early republic viewed themselves as Good Samaritans, elevating community work to one of the raisons d'être for their political organization. After 1923 and the formalization of the movement, feminists differed from their antecedents in their demands that the state, rather than the Church and wealthy individuals, underwrite programs for the poor. For these public-spirited feminists, women's emancipation from feudal tradition was closely linked with social improvements. They promoted as best they could the idea of better medical and welfare services. Their work identified social and economic injustices borne by the poor, and they insisted on humane solutions to basic needs and problems. They sensitized themselves to the problems of the poor and publicized their belief in public responsibility. Thus, while they were not socialists, they raised the question of social responsibility, and their solutions often expanded state involvement.

Women's entrance into social welfare programs elicited little negative response from men or conservatives, since care for the needy subverted no Cuban notions of femininity and signaled no revolution. In fact, this aspect of the woman's movement was so acceptable that feminists used their commitment to social works projects to refute charges that they were becoming like men or communists. The social welfare movement softened the feminists' strident image during the initial phases of the movement when ventures into public issues were potentially threatening to male political leaders.

The first Cuban Women's Congress in 1923 marked the second phase of the feminist welfare efforts. Feminists pledged to make social welfare their major concern after they won the vote. By 1928 women's organizations formed the vanguard of public welfare campaigns. The Club Femenino de Cuba, the Alianza Nacional Feminista, and the Lyceum combined the initiative for suffrage with public stances on social welfare, which made the link between women's causes and political participation obvious.

Relief work, both public and private, needed direction and funding, but no sooner had the associations undertaken welfare programs than economic collapse began in 1929. The depth of the depression was unforeseen as real wages in 1931 and 1932 fell to 60 percent of wages at the beginning of the republic in 1903 and 56 percent of wages after the economic disaster of 1921.[21] Evidence of destitution was visible everywhere. In Havana, city parks became makeshift homes for vagrants. Shantytowns, called *llega-y-pon* (come-and-flop), grew up around Havana, causing problems of sanitation and overpopulation. Public health and sanitation services, begun during the U.S. occupation, could not adequately respond to the economic depression of the 1930s, and what relief they had offered was hampered by budget cuts. Welfare and social services, even at the national level, were often left to charity. The National Committee for the Welfare and Defense of the Needy, founded in 1931, depended upon some government but mainly private funds. By 1934 beggars roamed the streets and stole to survive. Policemen, not social workers, handled problems caused by unemployment, vagrancy, and poverty.

Cuba's first federal elections in which women could vote and be elected were held in 1936. Several of the six women elected to the House of Representatives were advocates of social welfare. In the House of Representatives, Alicia Hernández de la Barca and María Gómez Carbonell, both of the Alianza, were faithful proponents of social reform. Hernández de la Barca presented bills for the integral reform of education and social service and on vocational education in public schools. Gómez Carbonell, a representative from Havana province, introduced legislation for the juvenile delinquent rehabilitation centers, the establishment of children's libraries, and the foundation of the Institution of Education Psychology.[22] Thus, there was a sense of formality and permanence to feminist reform issues.

With the beginnings of feminist organization came an altered stance on the handling of public services. As community-minded groups made more demands on the government, the terminology for social services and social works changed. *Asistencia social* replaced terms such as *caridad* and *beneficios*. However, the real progress on government-supported welfare programs began in 1934 when the leaders of the Lyceum Lawn and Tennis Club responded to an article by Miss Helen Hall on women's civil responsibilities.[23] The Lyceum immediately organized a subcommittee, the Social Assistance Division, and investigated international social assistance programs.

At first the division supplied financial help to the poor in the Mercedes Hospital and offered courses on basic first aid and self-help through the hospitals, particularly during World War II.[24] Concomitant with these initial projects, Elena Mederos de González directed a campaign to formalize public responsibility for social welfare through the establishment and accreditation of the School of Social Welfare at the University of Havana. Mederos, herself a doctor of pharmacology, founding member of the Alianza Nacional Feminista, and officer of the Lyceum, devoted her efforts to developing sophisticated training programs for welfare and social workers, educators, and administrators to staff government and private programs for public assistance. Mederos spent several years examining social welfare curricula in the United States and Latin America, attending courses, and conferring with Cuban health specialists and educators. Finally, a team of experts agreed upon an academic program that would prepare social workers and educators and selected a skeleton faculty. In July 1943 after Mederos presented her well-planned program, the University of Havana regents, with little debate, passed a resolution establishing a School of Social Welfare at the university, and the federal legislature appropriated funds for staff and material requirements.

The effects of the school were significant. Graduates qualified for employment in public service agencies, such as Public Sanitation and Hygiene and the National Office of Labor for Women and Youth. But success for the program did not stop there. Government agencies doing studies on the status of public welfare hired School of Social Welfare graduates as researchers and analysts. Women shared in establishing welfare programs and in carrying out the projects. They were also the recipients of welfare aid.

Mederos, whose skepticism about the efficacy of the law and devotion to public action made her an outstanding figure in welfare reform, wrestled honestly and forthrightly with the complexities of privileged feminists' involvement in problems of poverty, racism, and class divisions. Her solution was to give poor women opportunities to define their own programs, which meant educating them and providing respectable work and a democratic government through which they could express their opinions. Mederos did not think it appropriate for upper-class women to represent all women, as María Collado did. She understood that wealthy women should serve the poor by offering tools for empowerment. She knew that her work would not produce immediate results, but she hoped that in time it would effect lasting change.[25]

WOMEN'S PRISONS

One group of women was far beyond the reach of welfare, education, and democratic reforms: prostitutes and prisoners. The period of political repression had educated the well-to-do about prison conditions because some otherwise law-abiding women went to jail and reported on the horrors there.[26] The Alianza and the Lyceum developed active programs intended to make the women's prison more like a reformatory than a penitentiary. The Alianza pressed for a separate women's prison, and in 1934 it succeeded in creating Guanabacoa Prison for Women, a separate building with a woman warden and women as trained guards. Both the Alianza and the Lyceum sent teachers into the prisons to offer practical courses in sewing and basic literacy. Radios, supplied by the Lyceum, broadcast selected programs intended to teach new values to the inmates. Texts chosen for the reading courses were often value-laden so that the prisoners might be instructed in moral tenets to lead them away from their criminal pasts. The Aliancistas and the Lyceumistas, concerned about the reassimilation of prisoners into society, maintained files recording the health, education, and deportment of each inmate's performance in jail so that the prisoner might convince employers to give her a job.[27]

To make Guanabacoa a healthier place, feminists provided specialists who advised prison officials about exercise yards and sanitary washrooms and kitchens. They placed their own representatives on the Penal Advisory Council to advise on women's legal and rehabilitation matters.[28] They also paid for a physical exercise instructor who led the prisoners in calisthenics. On holidays many feminists volunteered to go into the prisons with presents for the inmates and their children. Christmas parties often consisted of music, party games, prizes, gift exchanges, and inspirational readings.

Most often women were incarcerated on charges of prostitution and drug use. Unlike their Argentine or North American cohorts, Cuban feminists had very little to say about a society that made prostitution lucrative; they merely decried its existence. They did not denounce it because it corrupted society and exploited women, nor did they respond to prostitutes by offering them medical information or politicizing the medical threats prostitution posed to the Cuban public health. Feminists voiced their disapproval of police corruption and exploitation of prostitutes but failed to develop a campaign with specific objectives to eliminate prostitution. Their relative indifference is all the more remarkable since Cuba had a reputation as a "whorehouse with a view of the sea" where prostitution and gambling were prevalent and accessible. The only attempts feminists made to address the issue of prostitution was to talk with women prisoners about health and the spread of venereal disease and offer them other means of making a living.

Feminists made the women's prison a healthier and cleaner place, but they failed to obtain women's courts or to establish permanent rehabilitation programs. They placed the onus on prostitutes to change their way of life, but they did little to alter circumstances that made prostitution necessary. The writers criticized social values that stigmatized women as sex objects and exploitable, but their sharp words could not correct the double standard. Men continued to escape moral condemnation, while prostitutes stood accused of immoral behavior. Only a few feminists blamed Cuba's international alignment with the United States for making Cuba a sexual resort for vacationing businessmen or a perennial dock for foreign sailors.

Once again women's roles as mothers translated into social and political authority for feminists. Responding to economic depression, feminists advocated and won legislative reforms that aided poor women and children. Their activities were acceptable to powerful men because they were moderate, helpful during economic crisis, and appropriate for women. Social welfare programs aided the poor, but they also employed a professional class of women as administrators. In terms of promoting social change, however, welfare reforms were limited at best, and they often reinforced class and gender systems that stifled women's sense of independence. As national matriarchs, many feminists reproduced social values and class relations even as they provided for some poor people and opened bureaucratic positions for educated women.

8

Legislating Morality

~T~

Conventions of male domination were the most repressive and pervasive aspects of Cuban culture to affect women, and they were also the most difficult to overcome. Men's power over women began at the level of individual interaction, and it ended with laws that governed women's and men's public roles and family responsibilities. Individual lives were shaped by it, personal identities were founded in it, and social values emanated from it. At every level women had to assume a subservient role, and in extreme cases women could lose their lives for offending men's honor. Men could control women legally as well as emotionally, physically, and psychologically. But for all their authority, patriarchal codes required men to be responsible for their families, protecting and caring for women and children, and managing matters of state.

Men's domination of women should have been a central concern for feminists, for it established that men were powerful and women were not. Most feminists did not launch a direct attack against male dominance, however, not because they were unaware of its deleterious effects, but because they would have had to transform the most intimate conventions of their culture, some of which afforded women their livelihood and protection. Instead of dismantling the patriarchal system, most feminists appealed to the ideals of patriarchal protection and only secondarily to principles of gender equality as restraints on men's abuse of authority.

Male domination, harmful as it was for women, was an important component of male identity. Honor and shame were directly linked to a man's ability to control the sexual behavior of the women in his family, which meant that wives had to be loyal to their husbands regardless of their infidelities, and sisters and daughters had to remain virgins until marriage to worthy men, which had to be authorized by male family members. Men also impressed other men and acquired a powerful reputation for themselves by appearing as captivators and seducers of women.[1]

To limit men's sexual domination of women, which was a public and a private phenomenon, would have threatened male identity. Yet by 1940 political and economic conditions had convinced Cuban legislators, all of whom were men, to change the family laws that not only awarded them power but preserved the gender double standard so necessary to their identity. For example, legislators determined that adultery should not be practiced by men without the threat of divorce and that adulterous women should not be murdered by offended husbands. Negligence of family on the part of either spouse became grounds for divorce, and illegitimate children obtained the same rights to support as legitimate children had.

Family laws changed during the chaotic decade of the 1930s, a period when the federal government had little legitimate claim to power. Politicians reformed laws in pursuit of social justice and also as a means of garnering support for their positions and legitimizing the government. U.S. hegemony after independence limited the actions of the government in matters such as treaty making, financial borrowing, commerce, international relations, and even domestic control. The only area where the national government had uncontested power to formulate law was in matters of the family. Legitimating family associations became a measure of the federal government's social control and political authority.[2]

Between 1930 and 1940, in the midst of a deep depression, the state took on increasing responsibility for welfare issues. Unwed mothers and their children were among the poorest of the poor, and prostitutes made up the majority of prisoners in women's jails. Illegitimate children, 25 percent of the population in 1943 and only 10 percent in 1899, made up a growing number of street urchins with little hope of attending school or finding a profession beyond street peddling or crime. Civic public works such as maternity hospitals and health clinics were permanent fixtures of federal expenditures. In 1931 there were 7,372 prostitutes in Havana alone.[3] The costs of poverty and crime were depleting government funds at a time when it was least affordable. Congress had to deal with a welfare class that had emerged, and it sought to do so at its source: moral attitudes and family relations. As a result, laws emerged that curtailed men's sexual exploitation of women while still constraining women's sexual freedom. Feminists went along with these reforms even though new family laws also preserved principles of patriarchal authority by conferring power upon the state to establish family associations and by ignoring cultural attitudes and economic structures that guaranteed men the power of patria potestad.

Feminists played an indirect role in changing family laws. They identified social problems and argued passionately for reform. But they operated outside the context of a national movement, such as the ouster of Machado, through which to broker their cause. Without political leverage to force new laws, feminists had only the power of persuasion, which meant that men reformed family codes.

The Adultery Law

Men's authority over women was nowhere more absolute than in family law. Under the patria potestad, the male head of household had the authority to guide his children, determine their careers and marriage partners, avenge their honor, and punish their transgressions. Patria potestad extended to wives. Husbands could send wives to convents, manage their property, represent them or not in legal suits and business contracts, and insist upon obedience and fidelity. Within the family a man's unmitigated authority was accompanied by the expectation that he would support and preside justly over his family.

If a man's authority within the family were absolute, then under the adultery law it was lethal. In this one law resided the most deep-seated elements of male domination: sex, honor, and ownership. Article 437 of the Spanish Penal Code stated that a husband who encountered his wife in the act of committing adultery could kill her and the offending lover without being tried for homicide; the maximum penalty was exile. If he only wounded the wife or lover, he suffered no penalty. The law also entitled a father who encountered his minor daughter with a lover to murder her or the lover under the same rules of sanction.[4] The adultery law exemplified the close alignment of the notions of a man's honor with his need for complete authority over the behavior of the women in his family. It also determined that women could not expect to resolve their own sexual needs. The adultery law clearly framed the boundaries of sexuality for men and women.

The removal of the adultery law was among the first priorities established by feminists at the 1923 National Women's Congress. Two women lawyers spoke out against Article 437 of the Penal Code. The more eloquent and better known of the two, Dr. Rosa Anders, a lawyer from Camagüey, offered both moral and practical reasons for changing the adultery law.[5] Anders argued that even the mild sentence of exile was rarely handed down against a husband who had murdered his wife.[6] As a result, men could murder their wives for any reason, claiming adultery as the cause, which made women the victims of arbitrary aggression.

Dra. Rosa Anders, a femi-
nist lawyer who argued eloquently for an end to the
adultery law. Taken from
*Memoria del Primer Con-
greso,* p. 338. The Stoner
Collection, Roll 2.

Anders also argued that, since Cuba had a divorce law, adultery should be considered an offense against marriage and not against a man's honor. Adultery, therefore, should be grounds for divorce, and the guilty party could be either the husband or the wife.

Anders struck out against the excesses of patriarchal privilege when she criticized the Hispanic notion of honor that made men restrict the behavior of women in their families while having full freedom to commit adultery themselves. She pointed out that husbands could bring their illegitimate children into their wives' homes but that the reverse was inconceivable. Anders spoke for most feminists, regardless of their political persuasion, when she asked that adultery be made a cause for divorce and not an excuse for wife-killing.

Anders struck a chord with legislators when she compared Cuba's adultery law with modern legal codes in other countries, showing that, by retaining the barbaric custom, Cuba could not claim to have entered the modern league of nations.

In a country like ours, after a redeeming revolution destroyed the old and corroded edifice of the *ancien régime* and after accepting the three principles of liberty, equality, and fraternity of the French Revolution and the influence of all modern constitutions, we cannot accept in our legal codes an article that is based exclusively on illegitimate male egoism. This, in effect, is a public and legal recognition of an ancient feudal right, which [is inappropriate] in a period like ours, a period of liberty and progress.

Our constitution establishes, as a beautiful egalitarian principle, that the Republic does not recognize institutional or personal privileges.But do not men have special privileges simply because they are born men? How can the constitution and the Penal Code Article 437 exist simultaneously?[7]

Anders was one of the few speakers at the 1923 congress who suggested that women and men should be equal before the law and as human beings. She claimed that the existential experience of suffering was the same for women and men. Men, therefore, should not think that after they were married they could take mistresses and not consider the emotional consequences for their wives. Anders wanted Article 437 of the Penal Code erased and adultery to be considered a legal justification for divorce for both women and men. Her resolution passed unanimously.

Beyond their call to throw out articles in the Penal Code, feminists did not make a public issue of the adultery law, perhaps because women of their status did not speak openly about sexual relationships. The feminists spoke about the hideousness of *femicidio* (feminicide), as they called it, but they did not mount a campaign as they had with suffrage, social legislation, and labor laws. Only occasionally did feminists take patriarchal privilege to task. One such exception was Leonor Martínez de Cervera of the Partido Demócrata Sufragista, who publicly accused men of heinous behavior.

Martínez de Cervera was outraged by the adultery law and roundly condemned men for their cowardice in dealing with marital problems. In a letter printed in *La Mujer* she wrote that jealous husbands were cowards because they could not face the causes of their wives' dissatisfaction with their marriages. She berated husbands who only had the nerve to kill defenseless wives and not their lovers, which she claimed was often the case. Martínez argued that the law placed different values on women's and men's lives since men could kill women for adultery but women could not kill men for the same offense. If women had the same rights as men, according to her predictions, the number of widows in Cuba would be "uncountable." Resorting to the rhetoric of a morally offended woman, Martínez condemned men's behavior: "Women must always forgive and forget. Men are not required to do this because of their concept of honor and pride. Because of this character flaw, men are not worthy of divine or human law."[8]

Mariblanca Sabas Alomá wrote consistently about women's sexual freedom and men's domination of women. While she decried the effects of men's control of women, she tended to blame women, men, the Catholic Church, and patterns of love and courtship for the problem. Her response to adultery was to avoid attacking Hispanic interpretations of honor and shame. Instead, she believed that adultery should become a divorceable offense, and wife killing would become first-degree murder. Sabas Alomá accused the Catholic Church, and not men, of making adultery unavoidable. By prohibiting divorce, the Church forced unhappy couples either to live celibate lives or to commit adultery.[9]

Progressive men joined feminists in their condemnation of the adultery law, and, like feminists, they often differed among themselves about why the law should change. As early as 1902, law student Manuel Secades defended before the law faculty at the University of Havana his thesis that family laws should change. A doctoral thesis normally would not be a document of much importance, but in this instance it was read by legislators and law professors who entered their remarks in the introduction. Many of them built their positions upon Secades's conclusions.[10]

Manuel Secades combined nineteenth-century romanticism and utilitarianism to suggest legal reform to end men's abuse of women while preserving women's purity and gentle character. Secades blamed men for being insensitive to their wives' sexual needs and for not financially maintaining their families. These abuses and men's proclivity to be unfaithful were, according to Secades, an unfortunate part of the male ego that required men to exploit women as a means of demonstrating their authority. Their behavior drove women to commit adultery. Secades sympathized with wives who sought the love of men other than their husbands, men who would respond to their desires and who would not abuse them.[11]

Secades advanced the romantic notion that women, in general, were pure and men were not. He believed men were only interested in sexual conquest and thus "needed a gallery of lovers." For their exploits they received the approval of other men, simultaneously corrupting women and themselves.[12] Secades accused patriarchal custom of malevolence and excess, but he nonetheless turned to patriarchal ideals for an antidote to the problem.

Sexual promiscuity left many women abandoned and dishonored. As unprotected heads of households, they lived in poverty and sometimes turned to prostitution. Secades's solution was to guarantee mothers a subsistence living, regardless of their marital status. With shelter and nourishment, Secades believed, most women would turn away from vice and behave as "beacons of morality."

Secades believed that, in all circumstances, it was men's mission to save both themselves and women from lasciviousness and prostitution. Men should love, respect, and support their wives. Like feminists, Secades advocated adultery as grounds for divorce, but unlike them, he argued that unless marriages were based upon religious morality they were worthless. Secades defended divorce but only because an infusion of secular society had rejected religious morality. The new, modern values, he believed, had made marriage an economic and social, but not a moral, contract.[13] Thus, Secades did not support egalitarian society in a strict sense, and he berated the effects of modernization. He constructed a hierarchy in which men were dominant economically and politically and berated them for not being morally superior as well. He also insisted that jurists and the public stop viewing women as property and begin defining them as people. Only then would women be "emancipated from slavery, no longer the property of men, and free of the life and death authority of the law."[14] But viewing women as people did not imply gender equality.

Emilio Roig de Leuchsenring, one of Cuba's leading journalists and intellectuals, detested the adultery law and argued for its removal, but his was a progressive, more egalitarian view than that of Secades.[15] Roig was no less outraged by men's abuses of women than Leonor Martínez or Manuel Secades, but his argument emphasized the anachronistic characteristics of the law. He portrayed the adultery law as a throwback to Spanish society under Moorish rule, when religious tradition kept women hidden in seclusion and under the domination of the men in their family. A woman who defied her master could be killed. The subsequent seven hundred years of Christian Reconquest had changed the Moorish justification of men's domination of women, but not its reality. During the Reconquest, Spanish nobility upheld strict codes of honor to indicate social position. Wives and daughters fell in the category of property and therefore had to submit to men. A woman's unfaithfulness besmirched a man's honor, and that honor could only be avenged by shedding the woman's blood.

Under Spanish law, men could bring their wives before the courts if women ignored men's instructions, rejected them, or committed adultery. Women's powerlessness in this regard was based on an assumption that it was women's plight to suffer and be forever tied in the bonds of marriage. A saying from that period that was repeated in twentieth-century Cuba encapsulated this belief: "matrimonio y mortaja, del cielo baja" (marriage and death are predetermined by God, and from them there is no release). This aphorism conveyed a fatalistic view of life and marriage by warning that marital felicity was capricious and beyond human control, but marriage itself was inescapable.

Roig also pointed out that since the Middle Ages men had ignored their responsibility for the well-being of the family. This omission had turned a medieval custom that balanced authority with accountability into a convention of immoral exploitation. Wife-killing was an anti-quated custom, according to Roig, and it was repugnant to those who wanted to see Cuba advance into the twentieth century as a modern nation. The Spanish were no longer the conquerors. They had been defeated, and a modern Cuban society with new models for social justice was emerging.

By the time Roig entered the debate, an important element had been added to opposition to wife-killing. Citizens and politicians were recognizing that state-given rights superceded patriarchal authority. This more than any attack leveled by opponents of Article 437 convinced legislators that wife-killing should end and that the state had the authority to stop it. Women, of course, benefited from the view, and ending men's punitive power as well as having legal rights liberated them from colonial bonds of oppression.

Roig opposed the adultery law because he viewed women as people, not property. He was put off by the longevity of medieval habit that made women symbols of men's honor and spared men the burden of establishing independent integrity. Like Secades, Roig hoped that men would assume greater moral responsibility within the family and the community, but, unlike Secades, he did not view women as the fragile wards of men.

Both Manuel Secades and Emilio Roig claimed that adultery was an evil patriarchal habit and that wife-killing had to stop. But Secades was interested in nineteenth-century concepts of public morality and Roig in modern, socialist views of society and laws. Both looked to the state to govern impartially, insisting that the ruling come from a divorce court and not a criminal court. The issue was finding cause for divorce and not pleading mitigating circumstances for homicide. Both men opposed the conservative religious position that divorce was not permissible. Secades found a place for religious sentiment, if not religious ruling, on divorce. Roig held the Church and religious teaching in contempt, and only acknowledged the Church to the extent he could blame it for promoting adultery. As regarded women, the two men disagreed. Secades argued against the equal status of women, and Roig was in favor of it. Both agreed that women should be viewed as human beings, but in Secades's case this did not imply equality.

Communication between intellectuals and politicians was fairly routine, and there is a high likelihood that men such as Secades and Roig influenced the debate surrounding Article 437. As a law student, Secades attracted the attention of Cuba's leading jurists. Lawyers and politicians entered their remarks in his thesis. After graduating, Secades served the government as an executive appointee to the Secretary of Agriculture, Commerce, and Labor. His work in political service placed him in contact with many of Cuba's lawmakers, both in the academy and the Congress.

Roig belonged to progressive clubs, and his articles were featured in *Social* and *Carteles,* two major journals. He was a well-known advocate for legal and social change who fraternized with progressive politicians, when he was not criticizing their policies. Senators and congressmen were no doubt aware of Roig's position, as lawmakers were also aware of Secades's treatise. While the extent of their influence cannot be measured, their opinions were public and important enough to have come to legislators' attention. In the final analysis, legislators used both arguments to abrogate Article 437 of the Spanish Penal Code.

In 1928, Dr. Ramón Zaydín and Manuel Márquez Sterling introduced a resolution in the Senate subcommittee to abolish the adultery law, arguing that the law no longer applied to Cuban society. They blamed custom for allowing men in twentieth-century Cuba to use the law to avenge their honor and force women into submission. Zaydín and Márquez Sterling accused men of abuse of power, hypocrisy, and cynicism. They also suggested that Cuban society would be better off if women's motives for committing adultery were understood. Wife-killing was also an embarrassing indictment of primitive values they hoped to erase along with the colonial past. Their final argument was that in an era of no-fault divorce, the lethal adultery law had no place. Since marriage was a civil contract and since women as well as men were heads of household, the old notions that men were heads of family and women were property no longer obtained.

Resistance in Congress formed around the concern that, by making adultery a reason for divorce, women would commit adultery as freely as men did. Conservatives argued that the law discouraged adultery, since women could pay for their transgressions with their lives. No one excused the double standard, but no one moved to give women the right to avenge their honor by legitimately murdering their husbands.

The bill was introduced to the Congress in February 1930 and revoked Article 437 that had sanctioned wife-killing. The bill passed on February 16, 1930, but President Gerardo Machado did not sign it, not wishing to be associated with the loosening of sexual standards. He did not veto the bill, however, and it passed without presidential signature.

Nullifying Article 437 ended the legal basis for wife-killing, and it mandated equal treatment of women and men before the divorce law in the event of adultery. Such action was possible because three new assumptions about life and liberty were current: (1) jurists and congressmen believed that women were more than symbols of men's honor; (2) marriage was not necessarily sanctioned by God, and therefore, undissolvable; and (3) legislators had the responsibility of intervening in domestic affairs and protecting the weak, who were women and children, from the excessive abuse inflicted by common men.

In 1930 men's abilities to avenge their honor by murdering adulterous wives was no longer acceptable before the courts. Crimes of passion, while understood, were not excusable, yet the resulting modifications did not abrogate all vestiges of paternalism. None of the politicians contended that adultery committed by men was wrong. Only Secades wrote about the destruction of trust between wives and husbands, and he supported strengthening male authority. Ending infidelity by men, or sanctioning it for everyone, was a radical feminist view rejected by most men, except for a few leftists such as Roig. Most men in public office felt obliged to protect women, and so they abrogated the adultery law to correct an acknowledged abuse of privilege, but not to endorse women's expression of independence or autonomy. Legislators were more concerned with Cuba's international image. There was in all of this a patrician and paternalistic abstraction of equality. To politicians, equality was not a measure of parity between women and men, or the rich and the poor, or the powerful and the weak. It was, instead, a show of respect for separate spheres, for privileged responsibility, and it acknowledged women's importance, not independence, in Cuban society.

Revisions of the 1918 Divorce Law

The 1918 divorce law, intended to defy Church authority, opened a dispute about the responsibilities family members had after marriages ended. The principle reason for adopting the divorce law had been to separate Church and government and to declare independence from a colonial past. Adherents of this policy paid insufficient attention to provisions for women and children after divorce. Some feminists and progressive men defended divorce on moral grounds. They argued that divorce would preclude separations and adultery and that the law would hold parents accountable for their children. The first divorce law left children largely under the tutelage of their fathers, while the economic future of wives was left uncertain, and this concerned feminists.

The 1918 law satisfied neither the Church nor the liberal community. The Catholic Church opposed the law because it defied religious canon and reduced the Church's role as arbitrator of marital conflicts. More, divorce broke the moral and religious covenant between men and women, a contract that symbolized patriarchal ordering. Priests continued to speak out against the evils of divorce from the pulpit, in church meetings, in pamphlets and newspaper articles, and through petitioning of legislators and even presidents.

Liberals were not happy with the law either. They complained that divorce was difficult because it was a costly procedure and because judges were instructed to reconcile the spouses by imposing a six-year waiting period. Women complained that judges sympathized more with men by expecting women to endure adulterous husbands and by siding with men whose wives had committed adultery.

Despite the clergy's predictions that Cuba would become another Hollywood and that people would leave marriages with no remorse, Cubans did not make great use of the divorce law. Table 6 charts the total number of divorces in Cuba during the first seven years of the law. The middle years—1919, 1920, 1921, and 1922—showed the highest incidence of divorce, while 1925 registered only slightly more divorces than the pre-1918 period. Thus, the availability of a liberal law did not have an immediate or sustained effect upon the number of couples who legally terminated their marriages.[16]

In 1930 legislators reviewed the divorce law with an eye toward making it protective of the family. Feminists, who had long sought child support, custody, and alimony, joined progressive men in the debate about how and why the divorce law should change. They outlined the rights of mothers and acquired the icons of rectitude for their side. Liberal men echoed the righteousness of the women's cause and promoted mothers' rights in the family to prove their commitment to the public good. They also hoped to acquire the feminists as constituents. Under these circumstances, equity for women under family law became a symbol of social justice.

It is instructive that feminists rarely wrote about divorce. Instead, they wrote about marriage, family values, and love. Mariblanca Sabas Alomá was the most direct, and probably the most radical, feminist in expressing her views about modern marriage. She hoped that women and men would come together in voluntary love and call that relationship a marriage. She wrote about "the freedom of a true home" in which women were not economically dependent upon men, in which women had their own "social energy and individual will," and in which women could take on responsibilities outside the home.[17]

But Sabas Alomá also understood that many marriages were not happy. A recurring theme in her essays was the chicanery of "divine love that prohibited women from becoming men's companions and taught them to be subservient." Sabas Alomá preferred divorce to living in unhappy and often adulterous marriages and viewed it as the only hope of forming better unions later. She also admitted that many women would not take advantage of divorce because of the social stigma attached to it and because they could not afford to support their children alone.[18]

Sabas Alomá wanted guarantees from the state that women and their children could survive after divorce. In cases where a divorcing couple owned an estate, enforced alimony, fair distribution of the estate, and shared parental responsibilities were in order. Impoverished couples should be entitled to state assistance for child support. Her position was clear: protecting mothers and children should be the central principle in family law.

Ofelia Rodríguez Acosta also supported divorce, but her pessimism about the sincerity and permanence of love relations precluded her choosing divorce as a means of finding a happy marriage. She was cynical about constructive love between women and men. Love, respect, trust, and pleasure were illusions, and women and men were doomed to destroy one another. Divorce was little more than a diversion in the unavoidable march toward human destruction as a result of gender associations.

As with the adultery question, feminists lacked leverage with politicians to reform the divorce law, thus leaving the reforms to men. Legislators differed on the divorce issue. Conservatives wanted to roll back the divorce law altogether, returning marital problems to the clergy. Liberals supported divorce as a means of protecting the sincerity of marriage and sparing society the problems of separation, adultery, and illegitimate children. They also wanted to see the divorce laws guard more carefully the principles of marriage and provision for single mothers and children. Radicals preferred the honesty of free unions, which, because people could leave them easily, promised genuine affection and commitment. None of the protagonists favored indefinite separations, which were commonplace. All claimed to have the moral high ground in the debate.

In 1930 Heliodoro Gil, a Conservative Party congressman, introduced legislation to reinstate the 1901 marriage law giving the Church sole authority over marital relations. Naturally, Church canon forbade divorce. Gil challenged the separation of the Church and government on this specific matter when he held that the clergy and not judges provided better marital instruction.

Gil's outspoken opponent, Roig de Leuchsenring, advocated voluntary relations. He was not adverse to marriage but objected to maintaining a marriage after love subsided. The Church was the target of Roig's attack, since he, like Sabas Alomá and Rodríguez, believed the Church forced people to remain in marriages well after their emotional commitments had ended. He referred to marriage vows as "religious blackmail" practiced by priests, and he was therefore resolute in his opposition to Gil's petition.[19]

Between Gil and Roig other arguments about the divorce law emerged. For many progressive men modernization meant a move toward social justice, and the degree to which women were emancipated in a given society measured the level of a society's modernization. Secades blamed moral decay and perceived looser commitments practiced by North Americans and Europeans for destabilizing the family, not divorce.[20] To deter the collapse of the family, Secades recommended giving women more authority, which meant expanding the role of *mater familias,* or mother's moral leadership within the family, to *mater potestad,* or the empowerment of mothers before the law. He openly supported giving women the same family rights and responsibilities as men, which meant that the divorce law should consider women's custody and financial rights.

Despite his concentration on religious morality, Secades disagreed with the Church about divorce. He argued on philosophical and theological levels that marriage was not eternal but temporal and subject to the caprice of human passion.[21] At the same time he supported religious commitment to marriage until it proved unworkable. Ultimately, Secades challenged the state to govern wisely and not deny religious doctrine directly but to recognize that some marriages always fail and thus divorce was necessary. He argued that, by allowing divorce, the state could uphold religious principles by eliminating the need for prostitution, adultery, and illegitimate children.

In 1930 and again in 1934 Congress revised the divorce law. As a result, husbands and wives had to share responsibility for the stability of the family. Although the 1918 law acknowledged voluntary abandonment and the husband's lack of support of the family as justification for divorce, the 1930 law expanded the causes to include separation of spouses for a period of five years or more. Derelict spouses of either sex became the object of the 1934 divorce reform, as it included the corruption of one marriage partner by the other, the use of drugs, bigamy, and abandonment of only six months as grounds for divorce. Further, the 1934 law made it clear that both partners were responsible for family subsistence.

Property settlement regulations also changed. Alimony, established in 1918, awarded a subsistence pension to innocent wives. The 1930 law contained no changes in alimony legislation, but the 1934 law allowed for the liquidation of the husband's estate or the assumption of the estate by the wife in the event that the husband could not meet the alimony payments. The guarantee of a property settlement was a step forward for women; it assured financial solvency with access to real estate wealth.

Of all the reforms, those affecting child custody regulations were the most dramatic. The 1918 law made both parents responsible for the children after divorce. Children under the age of five stayed with the mother unless she was proved unfit on the basis of moral character or mental stability. Children between the ages of five and twenty-three could choose to live with either parent. In the event that both parents were unfit, the court assumed responsibility for the children to assign them either to next of kin or to boarding schools.

In 1930 the law established that parents not only had to support their children, but that children maintained their rights as members of the family. The law preferred that mothers retain custody of daughters, although children could choose with whom they would live, and unfit mothers were still denied custody. The parent who lost custody retained the right to communicate with the children.

The 1934 law emphasized the economic well-being of the children. Financial solvency weighed more in custody decisions than did the gender of the parents or children. The guardian obtained the usufruct and administration of a child's property. In the event that both parents were denied custody, both contributed to each child's pension, with child care payments not exceeding one-third of the parents' income. Thus, the more refined divorce law insured both parents' responsibility for the survival of the marriage, and, failing that, insured that both would contribute to the financial support of the children. Women, of course, were the least financially solvent, so they stood to lose custody more readily than men under the solvency provision.

By 1934 the liberal divorce law of 1918 had been tempered by amendments emphasizing domestic responsibility of both parents, which corresponded to demands consistently voiced by Cuban feminists. In the course of reforming the law, feminists directed attention to family stability. They agreed that people should marry in good faith, but, in the case of a dysfunctional marriage, they could divorce, and women could expect financial support and authority over children and property. Progressive men promoted revisions in the divorce law because they wanted to preserve the ideals of the Hispanic family and shelter women and children from poverty and destitution.

The Rights of Illegitimate Children

Between 1925, when Domínguez Navarro and the more radical feminists walked out of the Second National Women's Congress over the issue of the rights for illegitimate children, and 1940, when illegitimate children received expanded rights, a number of moderate feminist groups decided to openly adopt the issue. The Lyceum Lawn and Tennis Club and the Alianza Nacional Feminista undertook an educational effort to convince the nation of the case's merits. The Lyceum held a number of lectures on the topic, and the Alianza broadcast radio programs on the plight of illegitimate children.[22]

Feminists' work on illegitimate children's rights had a high political price. The emotional and moral responses to the issue ran deep enough to create schisms between progressive and moderate feminists as well as between feminists and women of the general public. The major dividing points were the social and religious interpretations of marriage, the respectability of wives, the rights of all women to be mothers, and the moral implications of the association of rights of illegitimate children with free love.

Ofelia Domínguez's departure from the Second National Women's Congress in 1925 did not silence her support of equal rights for illegitimate children. She moved her campaign from feminist groups to university campuses and to international women's congresses. In 1925, as the student movement organized around issues of inadequate education, political corruption, and political ideologies such as socialism, Domínguez inserted rights for illegitimate children into the agenda. In 1926 Julio Antonio Mella, the organizer of the Cuban Communist Party, invited Domínguez to speak several times at the Universidad Popular, where she argued for the rights of illegitimate children before a radical student gathering.

Mariblanca Sabas Alomá continued urging women to take motherhood as their most sacred mission. Women, she said, should not allow marital status to undermine their pride in being mothers nor poverty to obstruct the nurturing of their children. Men and the state should respect the fundamental right of women to have children, and they should provide a livelihood for women and children.

Marío Collado did not demonstrate an active interest in the rights of illegitimate children, although she did support charity for orphans and work schools for orphaned girls.[23] Collado was more interested in suffragist issues and political gains for women of her class than in deep moral or intellectual questions, particularly when these questions offended the conservative faction within the woman's movement.

Legislators did not respond to the calls for the rights of illegitimate children until 1928 when House Representative Guas Inclán presented a bill to Congress. It proposed the equalization of the status of illegitimate and legitimate children, and it was approved by the House of Representatives. It was rejected by the Senate as impractical, however, the major obstacle being the proof of paternity.[24] The issue was too controversial to reintroduce until the constitutional assembly met in 1940 to write Cuba's new constitution.

The atmosphere of the 1940 Constitutional Convention was charged with political purpose. After the instability and turmoil of the first thirty-eight years of the republic, Cubans wanted to address the issues of social justice and Cuban sovereignty that had eluded them. Living with uncertainty about the constitutionality of their government since 1928 led activists to reflect deeply about social rights and principles their new constitution would guarantee.

Cubans had been promised a new constitution since 1934. Newspapers, journals, and radios communicated Cuban hopes for laws that met expectations for reform. The election of leftist candidates to the constitutional assembly was the first indication that the constitution would be a progressive one.

Feminists intended to keep their issues before the public and held their Third National Women's Congress in February 1939. In the sixteen years since the first congress, feminists maintained themselves as a force for increasingly radical reform, and their strategy had hardened into a set of issues for which they received popular support: the protection of women and children and women's rights as citizens and mothers. Between 1923 and 1939 the women's movement had matured, and its programs had expanded from a narrow set of women's issues to an analysis of women's subordination which led to leftist political solutions. In 1939, previously moderate organizations such as the Lyceum and the Alianza espoused deep social and economic change.

The 1939 congress called for bold reforms in social welfare, education, labor, criminal, and family legislation. Under social welfare reforms feminists wanted free medical care and food and shelter guarantees for poor women and their children. They argued for extension centers to educate women in home care, human biology, and reproduction. Women workers needed equal pay for equal work, equal right to work, special protection of women in the workplace, a study of the needs of the *campesina*, and maternity benefits. Family laws should change so that women could have access to birth control, illegitimate and legitimate children would have equal rights, and wives would have the same legal authority in the family as husbands. They turned their attention to prostitution and female delinquency, and initiated studies of the social and economic context of women criminals. Establishing juvenile courts found similarly energetic support at the congress. Delegates spoke on the impact of racial prejudice on women. One of the least controversial issues before the congress was the rights of illegitimate children. What had been a disruptive issue in 1923 had become acceptable to the majority of moderates in 1939, but this did not mean that the constitutional assembly would give illegitimate children equal rights in 1940.[25]

By the time the constitutional assembly met in May 1940, the rights of illegitimate children had been a public issue for seventeen years. Various parties and coalitions introduced proposals for the fifty-fourth article intended to guarantee rights to all children regardless of the marital status of their parents. On May 18, 1940, at least six proposals appeared on the agenda, all supporting the elimination of illegitimate status, but all varied slightly because they were presented by opposing parties.

Santiago Rey introduced an article establishing "absolute equality among all children, in surname, in social considerations and in inheritance, thereby, erasing inequalities of any kind."[26] The Unión Revolucionaria Comunista formally endorsed his proposal, and Juan Marinello led the debate. Ramón Zaydín, a moderate reformist, supported equal inheritance rights with his own proposal, arguing that lineage is natural and common to all members of society and all children should have the same rights and responsibilities.[27]

José Manuel Cortina of the Coalición Socialista led the opposition to all proposals, purely for political gains. He claimed that communism, rights for all children, and destruction of the family would destroy Cuban culture. He also maintained that the preamble declared that all Cubans were equal, which was sufficient. He said that the constitution should regulate the contract of love through civil marriage and that recognizing the rights of illegitimate children would ignore the status of marriage and thereby negate the Civil Code and family life.[28]

After much impassioned debate, the Assembly voted on the amendment. With 47 members voting, the Rey amendment failed, 30 against to 17 in favor. Ballots did not fall along party or ideological lines, however. The opposition was composed of conservatives, liberals, and leftists, who, as later testimony revealed, were waiting for a chance to propose their own bills or simply to oppose any reform favoring rights of illegitimate children due to their own family circumstances. The issue had become a matter of political posturing on the one hand and moral accountability on the other, which made it difficult to predict how the delegates would vote.

Despite Cortina's linking support for the article with communist ideology, both women delegates, neither of them communists, voted for it. Alicia Hernández de la Barca, a member of the Alianza Nacional Feminista, explained her vote in feminist and religious terms:

> I voted in favor of the amendment, Mr. President and fellow delegates, as a consequence of the ideas that have been introduced repeatedly in this Assembly . . . and I thought that my vote was in accordance with these concepts, that is to say, with the concept of equality of all Cubans before the law and God who had been invoked to guide us in the writing of the Preamble. This God, Mr. President and fellow delegates, does not recognize distinctions between any of his children.
>
> I believe that the Preamble gives an irritating privilege to men, because men are the only people consistently covered by the law. The law gives men the choice of recognizing or rejecting their children. In contrast to my own selfish prejudices, I have extended my sense of responsibility and I have voted in favor of the amendment in order to defend all children, that they might have the same rights before nature and before God. I also defend women, because adultery has not been eliminated and because children are not equal. Adultery will be eliminated when there are more pure intentions, when men honestly wish to protect their young, and when the amendment presented by Mr. Rey is approved. Then all children will be protected, including natural children, when adultery does not exist, or when it is rare.[29]

For her speech Hernández received an ovation from the communist benches, a group she would oppose on other articles.

Other factions presented proposals, but the defeat of the Rey proposal demonstrated that the liberals and leftists were too divided to secure this constitutional right. A compromise did result, however. The Assembly admitted Article 54, which disallowed *social* distinction between legitimate and illegitimate children and permitted an illegitimate child capable of proving paternity to inherit 50 percent of the legitimate children's estate. This amendment meant that no child could be registered as illegitimate on birth or baptism certificates and that the illegitimate child's financial guarantees would be the same as those of a natural child, and half of those of the legitimate offspring.

Eusebio Mujal, the secretary of the Coalition of Cuban Workers and a member of the Family and Culture Committee of the Constitutional Assembly, offered comments about why the article was so difficult. Mujal favored absolute equality for all children, and he used his considerable influence to persuade other delegates to support the Rey amendment. When he met with members of the opposition to solicit their votes, he found that partisan objections took second place to personal preferences. A number of the male delegates (who ideologically should have supported the article) had illegitimate children whom they did not want to recognize publicly.[30]

Many Cuban women opposed the passage of the Rey article. Mujal reported receiving more than 14,000 letters from women expressing their objections. Mostly they felt that giving rights to illegitimate children was an assault on religious marriage and the stability of the primary family.[31]

Hernández did not accept the compromise passively. On May 21, 1940, she introduced Article 56, which established rights for children in general. The article laid out a set of strict rules for parental responsibilities and child protection that obligated parents to feed, help, educate, instruct, clothe, shelter, and respect their children. In the event that parents could not afford to care adequately for the children, the state would provide federal support. Her resolution came directly from the Declaration of Geneva on the Rights of Children, and it was supported by international groups and the Cuban teacher associations. Following a short debate, Hernández's article was passed by a voice majority.[32]

In the last analysis, the Cuban Constitution of 1940 prohibited classifying a child by the legitimacy of birth. Moreover, it insisted that, as citizens of Cuba, all children had rights to health, freedom, and the pursuit of happiness. Nevertheless, it continued to distinguish between the inheritance status of legitimate and illegitimate children.

From the standpoint of the improved status of the illegitimate child, the constitution was a start. Though there was no enabling legislation and the old Spanish Civil Code still had jurisdiction in some areas, the constitution was a statement of moral intent. Clearly, the lives of illegitimate children were affected slightly by removing the designation of "illegitimate" on birth certificates. Gender relations also were changed because unwed mothers could demand that fathers of their children take responsibility for the support of their offspring. But the problem of unsanctioned unions and illegitimate children persisted.

Conclusion

Women and men had different but complementary justifications for rewriting family laws, and both supported some aspect of patriarchal authority. Feminists encouraged stable, self-sufficient families with guarantees of safety and support for mothers and children. They wanted men to provide, and they wanted recognition for women's contributions to the community. From their congresses, feminists issued resolutions to give women authority when they headed families, and they unanimously opposed the adultery law. At first, feminists disagreed about the status of illegitimate children, but by 1939 most supported equal rights for all children. They unanimously supported mothers' authority over children and family finances. In the name of family stability, they suggested imposing new regulations that would give as cause for divorce either parent's neglect of family. Feminists were protecting mothers, regardless of marital status, and empowering women within the home.

Progressive men shared feminist concern over family protection, but they had other reasons for limiting men's domination of women. Following independence, ruling men were attempting to give order to chaos by writing new laws. Particularly troublesome were prostitution and the numbers of abandoned women and children. By controlling social behavior through legislation, congressmen hoped to change popular ideals from the sense of privilege and submission characteristic of colonial society to a more bourgeois notion of civic responsibility and family cohesion.

With the subordination of the Church to state rule, laws and courts became the sources of moral order. Legislators imposed laws as moral directives. Their referent, however, was neither the Scriptures nor social equality but, rather, Hispanic patriarchal values, which stressed men's obligation to care for women, children, and the state. Their target was the vulgarization of the patriarchy, which had become the *irresponsible* exploitation of women without the attending responsibility for their protection.

Modern legal and social concepts also impelled jurists and legislators to restrain men's domination of women. Independence brought with it the sense that Cuba had joined a modern community of nations in which its citizens partook of a worldview that emphasized education, participatory democracy, capitalist work ethics, market mechanisms, social welfare, and a rational and enforceable corpus of laws. Many legislators viewed progress in terms of a nation-state that valued intelligence over reckless emotion, science over myth, and orderly transferral of power over arbitrary or violent force. These goals were not always achieved, but they were pursued by some, as congressional records, public debates, and social unrest attest. Family law was an area of jurisprudence in which legislators could demonstrate their ideas of equitable relations. By 1930 colonial conventions that had governed the family no longer obtained, both because Cubans rejected the colonial past and because modern demands on women and men required that women have more responsibilities and privileges.

Between 1930 and 1940 a Cuban version of social justice emerged that incorporated two conflicting legal principles, patriarchal privilege (patria potestad) and equal rights for all citizens. As a result of the tension between the two principles, which was especially visible in family law, women and children won some rights. Men could not legally murder their adulterous wives, parents had to take responsibility for their families, women could sue for divorce on the same grounds as men, and illegitimate children attained more guarantees of protection. The reforms, awarded by a male legislature and a Constitutional Congress dominated by men, significantly limited men's authority over women, but nevertheless they rested on the assumption that a reformed patriarchy was the system of rule.

As a result, paternal authority within individual families evolved into the patriarchal authority of the state. Excessive abuse came under legal scrutiny. But fundamental assumptions, such as men's uncontested accessibility to women's bodies as well as women's acceptance of men's duplicity, went unchecked. Women still lived under social circumstances that prohibited sexual freedom and personal independence. The suppression of women's sexuality occurred despite the contradiction it created with the right of free expression and pursuit of happiness because women's sexuality was considered a private matter and therefore legally irrelevant and unmanageable. Men continued committing adultery, while women were punished psychologically, socially, financially, and legally if they committed such acts. Divorce was not practiced enough to curb husbands' abuse of wives, and illegitimate children continued to be born at a startling rate.

9

Fields, Factories, and Feminists

In June 1938 Dr. Antonio Bravo Correoso, a renowned jurist and the only surviving member of the independence constitutional assembly of 1901, observed the changes in Cuban society since the first days of the republic and recommended areas for legislative reform for the projected constitutional assembly of 1940:

> I believe that the most ideal social commitment of the constitution is socialist conservatism. . . . Today we have nothing, but we deserve and we desire a Magna Carta equal to that of 1901, which recognizes the principles of order and liberty, where new national necessities that continually emerge find solutions and remedies. In particular, two factions have appeared since the 1901 Constitution: workers and women. Not long ago these two groups had few benefits. Liberalism and conservatism have melted away and been replaced by two other movements: capitalism and the labor movement (obrerismo). Constitutional delegates must find room for these two movements in the new constitution.[1]

Bravo Correoso's statement summarized several characteristics of the feminist and labor reform movements: first, women and labor were new and important social and political forces; second, their demands required legal guarantees; and third, politicians should attempt to accommodate these groups with constitutional reforms and capitalist enterprise.

Cuba's labor and feminist movements evolved out of the conflict between democratic, egalitarian principles and social and economic destabilization. Both groups expected to attain new authority and improved living standards, but the failure of democracy and volatile economic conditions frustrated their aspirations. As economic and political crises deepened between 1928 and 1936, feminists found common cause with working women and formed conditional alliances based upon feminists lobbying for worker rights, founding professional centers for women, and leading a woman's movement that incorporated worker rights into its agenda.

Yet feminists and wage-earning women were not natural allies. Working women formed a socioeconomic group that shared relative poverty, low levels of education, and little hope of attaining power or wealth. Their oppressors were Cuban and foreign planters, industrialists, and politicians who suppressed wages and gave little relief to the unemployed. In contrast, feminists belonged to the privileged and educated classes that used cheap labor and aspired to power and influence over poor and inarticulate women. Feminist concern for working women was, nonetheless, a part of their ideology and a strategy for securing a following. The bonds of motherhood helped unite erstwhile antagonists. Sympathetic feminists advocated a progressive maternity code, protective legislation in the workplace, equal pay for equal work, and equal access to work.

Feminists, Working Women, and the Law, 1902–1927

The Wars of Independence marked the beginning of a cycle during which women of many classes took up work outside the home and established themselves increasingly in professional positions. During the War of 1895, they worked in munitions factories, hospitals, and schools, and they fought in the army. After independence, while the country was attempting to rationalize an industrial base and sculpt a national image, women joined the expanding labor force as business staff, teachers, nurses, and minor bureaucrats. Factories sprang up. Textile and tobacco enterprises, in particular, hired women in unskilled positions. In 1899 women made up 10.66 percent of the total work force, a figure that held constant until the early 1950s.[2]

In the first twenty-five years of the Republic, colonial patronage/peonage associations evolved into modern management/labor relations in ways that affected women. Immediately following independence, wives, mothers, and sisters of fallen heroes petitioned Congress for pensions. Congressmen, assuming that these women were dependent upon men, praised the heroes and doled out pensions. Within twenty years, however, government and business establishments had to respond to women's demands for better wages, work conditions, and employment benefits as women joined the labor force in search of an economic livelihood. Women increasingly joined the ranks of professionals, which made them an articulate and powerful faction to petition for legal change. Between 1898 and 1952 the percentage of professionally employed women grew from 3.6 percent to 45.3 percent of the total female work force (see table 9).

Medardo Vitier, a journalist writing for *Cuba Contemporánea* in 1917, commented on the changes in middle-class women:

Table 9   Distribution Increase of Women in the Female Labor Force
as Percentages, 1899–1943

Work Classification	1899	1907	1919	1943
White-Collar Jobs	3.6	9.0	13.2	45.3
Blue-Collar Jobs	61.6	58.0	40.2	32.2
Domestic Service	34.6	32.8	46.6	22.4
Other	0.2	0.2	—	—
Total	99.8	100.0	100.0	—

Source: Taken from raw data gathered from Appendix and the 1899, 1907, 1919, and 1943 censuses.

The Cuban woman has emerged [from the Wars of Independence] with extraordinary facility due to her ability to adapt and not to be conquered by tremendous struggles. Today she leaves the simple home for the factory in the growing industrial development; today she works and successfully earns a modest salary; today she invades the classroom and discovers her own solvency and well-being in public education; today she fits into the diverse spheres of administration, from municipal to federal levels, and she spends time working at the typewriter.[3]

Tension between working women and the government arose as early as 1909 when the Railroad Washing and Ironing Guild went on strike demanding uniform wages. Justa Martínez, the leader of the guild, formed a commission of strikers who demanded an audience with President José Miguel Gómez to inform him of their brutal exploitation. When Gómez refused to receive the commission, Martínez advised the women to continue their strike, and, as a result, she was arrested on charges of exhorting her associates to violence. The strikers responded by going into public parks in Havana to explain their position, and there the justice police attacked them, wounding ten women. The police later blamed the women for provoking violence.

Three U.S. invasions between 1907 and 1919 protected foreign business interests and undercut Cuban political authority, making significant dialogue between political dissenters and North American-supported administrations seem remote at best. Firmer resistance became necessary, and, under these circumstances, feminists and labor organizations formed. Initially, both of these groups were reformist, not radical. While feminists held congresses and passed resolutions, labor mounted isolated protests without clear agendas and held congresses requesting higher

Si orgullosos fueramos, es
seguro que en estos momentos
lo estariamos.
El Diario "El Mundo"; al
cual es inaccesible llegar, Aspiraciones, la modesta Escuela
de Tipógrafas ha llegado.
El retrato que publicamos es
el que publicó el "Mundo" con
la interview celebrada con la
Sra. Carmen Velacoracho de
Lara Directora de la Escuela.
Creemos que el mejor aprecio
que podemos hacer, es publicar
dicha fotografía en nuestra Revista, para que vean el agrade-
cimiento que sentimos.
Aunque pigmeos y ellos colo-
sos, pueden contar todos los
que integran el distinguido y
culto personal de "El Mundo"
que Aspiraciones está dispues-
ta siempre a librar campaña por
ellos, o cuando menos a sentir
admiración.

Poor women employed as typesetters. The Typesetting School was established
through the philanthropic efforts of the Partido Feminista de Aspiraciones,
and its magazine *Aspiraciones* was typeset by women in the school. Taken from
Aspiraciones (Año 6, No. 6): n.p. The Stoner Collection, Roll 6.

salaries, minimum wage, and an eight-hour workday. As yet, the majority of workers had not identified the origins of oppression, nor had they developed a class identity. Feminists, likewise, were confused about gender discrimination, although they recognized a common bond among mothers.

Feminists initially viewed poor and working women as victims who needed help, not power. In 1920, for example, the Club Femenino membership, concerned about sales clerks having to stand all day, went to the commercial district of Old Havana along Obispo, San Rafael, and Neptuno streets carrying chairs into stores. When sales clerks were not waiting on customers, Club ladies urged them to sit and rest until their services were needed. Using their privileged position to confront store owners and police, when the police were called, Club members demanded improved conditions for working women.

By 1921 the Club Femenino expanded its program to include labor reforms. That year Pilar Jorge de Tella, the chief of the Office of Work, testified about work conditions for women in a study conducted by Congressman Vicente Pardo Suarez. Besides establishing a Chair Law, she demanded an eight-hour workday, a maternity code, minimum wage legislation, female employment in 50 percent of jobs in industry and business, and the installation of nurseries in factories.

Feminist reformers assumed that factory conditions were dirty, unsafe, undesirable, inhuman, and antifeminine. They also portrayed women working in these conditions as abandoned mothers or poor wives who had to work so that their children could survive. At the Second National Women's Congress, Dulce María Borrero de Luján outlined the need for a maternity code for working mothers. She insisted that women be guaranteed health services and shelter. She believed that women's biological function—motherhood—was "above social law" and that it had to be protected by labor laws. But she asked for more than mere financial support for working mothers; she wanted moral support "to lift women from despair and to remind them that their greatest contribution to humanity is the replication of life." She recommended maternity care for working women and welfare houses for unemployed and destitute women.[4]

Congressional delegates agreed that working conditions were unhealthy and dangerous, that night work invited physical attack, and that protection during pregnancy was mandatory. In their speeches before the congress, Pilar Jorge de Tella and Ofelia Domínguez Navarro stressed the need for feminists to align themselves with female workers, who "suffered the greatest social injustice."[5] Feminists proposed to ameliorate working conditions through vocational education for domestics and factory workers and protective legislation. But even these well-intended benefactresses took on the same role as congressmen who awarded pensions to destitute women: they offered financial improvements, not economic or political autonomy. All this changed, however, after Machado failed to resolve Cuba's economic and political instability.

After 1925, when labor advanced from loosely organized, anarcho-syndicalist guilds to a trade union movement with some Marxist leadership, workers forced their demands on state and private enterprise, both foreign and national. Demands included everything from increased wages and improved work conditions to total surrender of commerce to a state-run economy. Methods for gaining reforms, if not power, were strikes, demonstrations, and, occasionally, sabotage. Government labor groups, such as the Confederation of Cuban Workers (CTC), formed to counteract the clearly Marxist orientation of the Confederación Nacional Obrera de Cuba and the Cuban Communist Party. Reform and revolutionary workers were divided in much the same way moderate and radical feminists were. Splits in the labor movement weakened its authority, but the pervasive presence of the movement in social and political events insured that reforms would pass.

Working women belonged to moderate and radical labor organizations, and thereby advocated reform policies as well as the revolutionary overthrow of capitalism. Whatever their political orientations, the increasing presence of women in the labor force and labor politics forced men to acknowledge women's work rights and include them in party manifestos.

In a limited fashion, working-class women began building their own representative organizations within the labor movement and independent of the feminist movement. The Sección Sindicato de Johnson, a syndicate of sales clerks in the Johnson Drug Store chain, and the syndicate of sales clerks in Woolworth's organized in the early 1920s to represent workers' demands. In 1926 the Federación de Obreros (the Workers' Federation) formed the Comité Proletario de Defensa de la Mujer (the Proletarian Committee for the Defense of Women) in Havana province. Its seven syndicates included 2,150 women, who represented nearly half of the female work force in that province.[6] The largest and most powerful independent union representing women was the Gremio de Despalilladoras (the Tobacco Stemmers' Guild). Within the CTC, women's largest representation was in the commercial guilds and the textile and weaving industries, although only 27 percent of women in the textile industry joined the union.[7]

Publicity generated by feminist congresses and the presence of working women in labor action encouraged politicians to pass reform legislation. On November 19, 1925, seven months after the close of the Second National Feminist Congress and two years after the formation of the CNOC and the Communist Party, President Machado enacted the Law Protecting the Woman Worker. It regulated health and sanitary conditions in the workplace, restated that women workers should have chairs for rest breaks, gave nursing mothers a morning and afternoon break to breast-feed children, and obligated employers to hire a fixed quota of women in particular jobs.[8] Many women were disappointed that it did not include an expansive maternity code. While the law regulated some aspects of health and safety for working women, it did not reflect labor and feminist concerns about authority between workers and owners, gender discrimination, or sexual harassment on the job.

The Feminists and Working-Class Women, 1927–1934

After 1927 loose alliances between feminists and working women firmed up to the extent that feminists attempted to recruit wage-earning women as members. Ofelia Domínguez Navarro, the vice-president of the Alianza Nacional Feminista in charge of labor issues, spoke at labor union meetings about women's issues, hoping to demonstrate to leaders and rank-and-file members that women formed a distinct and important group within the labor force. At Alianza meetings she reported on the plight of the tobacco stemmers, who, because they threatened capitalist control, withstood firings and physical threats from their bosses. Domínguez warned against complacency and dependence upon government inspectors to enforce labor legislation and against women's low salaries and inadequate work conditions.[9]

Taking on workers' rights did not immediately imply opposition to Machado or adherence to Marxist ideology. In 1927 Domínguez and even Inocencia Valdés, the respected secretary-general of the Tobacco Stemmers' Guild, hoped that Machado's constitutional amendments would include a maternity code, equal pay for equal work, child labor laws, guaranteed employment, and laws against sexual harassment and exploitation. They agreed with Machado's resolution for a unicameral congress on the grounds that too many politicians were paid for doing nothing. They both called for a united front of women, regardless of class and political affiliations, to influence the new constitution.[10]

María Collado of the moderate Partido Demócrata Sufragista openly sided with Machado, and she vowed to see that the 1925 legislation was enforced. To that end she took a job with the secretary of Agriculture, Commerce, and Work as an inspector who visited work establishments suspected of violating the law. She refused a salary for her work, and she publicized her findings in *La Mujer,* hoping that women would boycott offending establishments. Her message that upper-class women could serve the needs of the lower-class was intended to unite workers behind her leadership.

An increase in labor strikes brought feminists and working women into closer contact. In December 1929 sales clerks at Woolworth's went out on strike to demand a 33 percent increase in wages and to protest firings of union organizers and the use of strikebreakers in Camagüey and Oriente provinces. The Woolworth's representative in Cuba organized his own union with loyalties to the corporation. As strikebreakers crossed picket lines, conflict ensued. Strikers, nearly all women, defended themselves in bloody clashes with the police and paid thugs hired by the American firm and its newly formed union. The incident highlighted familiar labor complaints: foreign enterprise's disregard for Cuban labor laws, employment of foreign workers at the expense of the Cuban labor force, and the government's complicity with both of these violations.

Feminists did not remain on the sidelines, but they were divided in their response to the strike. Mariblanca Sabas Alomá writing in *Carteles* and Maria Collado in *La Mujer* squared off in a debate about the accuracy of worker complaints. Sabas Alomá got involved when she received a letter on September 19 written by Woolworth's employees asking her to publicize work conditions. They were protesting their $9.00-peso-per-week salaries, the 8-1/2 hour workday, the lack of chairs, no sick-leave provisions, and oppressive management.

Sabas Alomá published the letter and voiced her own indignation at the treatment of the women by a foreign firm. She pointed to the triple exploitation of the Woolworth's workers, since as laborers they were underpaid and overworked, as Cubans they were held hostage by their own government in behalf of foreign interests, and as women they were regarded as unimportant. She ran her own investigation of the charges and found that the 10 Cents store was even worse than had been reported. Management threatened the workers for having written to *Carteles,* and one boss humiliated a clerk by making her sweep up sawdust that he had thrown on the floor to punish her. Sabas Alomá called for a boycott and labeled anyone who ignored the boycott a traitor of Cuba and José Martí.[11] Important groups, such as the Alianza Nacional Feminista, the

Rotary Club, the Mason Lodge, and workers guilds, respected the boycott.

María Collado also responded to the Woolworth's strike, but she found in favor of management. Collado claimed that she was an expert at assessing work conditions because she was an inspector in the Office of the Secretary of Agriculture, Commerce, and Work. After interviewing Woolworth's clerks, she claimed that employers had not mistreated the staff, that work conditions were sanitary, and that the clerks had sufficient breaks for eating and resting. She also argued that salaries were in fact $25.00 pesos a week. Although some clerks did earn only $8.00 pesos, she argued that lower salaries could be augmented by working overtime plus a 10 percent bonus. When women got married, management gave them gifts. Collado also noted that Woolworth's workers got one sick day per year and fifteen days of paid vacation.[12]

Sabas Alomá, infuriated by Collado's loyalty to Machado and U.S. business interests, wrote a vitriolic essay in which she connected Cuban patriotism with an end to foreign exploitation and the rescue of the sales clerks at Woolworth's. She reminded Cubans that Cuba, because of its proximity to the United States, was obliged to be particularly vigilant about its nationalist ideology, implying that it should resist U.S. domination of politics and the economy.[13]

Moderate feminists not only joined boycotts, they also initiated self-help programs and, as always, sought new legislation. The Alianza, Lyceum, and the Partido set up vocational training centers to teach skills to domestics and unskilled laborers. Course curricula included reading and rudimentary math, nutrition, sewing, and home economics courses. The schools improved the lot of a few poor women who became seamstresses or sales clerks. But feminists could not offer educational opportunities to all poor working women, nor could they supply good jobs after graduation. Training centers prepared women for feminine employment that still paid low wages and did not encourage entry into unionized jobs or male-controlled professions.

The Unión Laborista de Mujeres opposed feminist labor reforms and espoused socialist revolution. Between 1930 and 1937, Unionistas spoke at strikes, unionized workers, and defended jailed students, workers, and campesinas. Ofelia Domínguez, Loló de la Torriente, and Bebé Darder, to name a few, went to jail for their work, and Domínguez and de la Torriente suffered exile. Until 1937, when Domínguez returned from exile in Mexico espousing a strategy of cooperation, Unionistas dedicated themselves to liberating working women through organized representation, not social welfare.

Protective Legislation:
Minimum Wage and the Maternity Law

A succession of presidents followed ousted president Ramón Grau San Martín, each falling because of his failure to control peasant and worker unrest. Finally, between 1936 and 1940, President Federico Laredo Brú, backed by Colonel Fulgencio Batista, resorted to a dual policy of repression and cooperation. Mainstream feminists, wittingly or not, aided the beleaguered president. Viewing themselves as peacemakers and progressives, they, not workers, promoted reform from the top down by promising new laws and obstructing revolution. Their work undercut radical efforts to empower laborers, and it placed power in the hands of the weak bourgeoisie.

Feminists were not the only leaders of women workers, but they were perhaps the most effective. So few women were unionized that labor did not give their demands high priority. In 1934, only 27 percent of women textile workers belonged to unions.[14] Interviews done by Ofelia Rodríguez Acosta in *Bohemia* revealed that working women in her small sample were not interested in a labor movement. Nearly all of them worked because they had to, and they looked forward to marrying, stopping work, and having children.[15] Thus, feminists led the faction of the women's labor movement that was satisfied with fiscal reform.

Feminists and working-class women agreed that mothers needed a maternity law guaranteeing them financial and medical support prior to, during, and following childbirth. Early evidence of feminist work for maternity care for poor mothers came in April 1917 when the Club Femenino sponsored a bill establishing a midwifery school in every province. Trained midwives would be available throughout the island to teach safe birthing techniques to other midwives and to deliver babies. Senators did not pass the law because they believed the demand for midwives did not justify the expense.[16]

Undaunted, feminists raised the issue of maternity facilities for workers and poor women in their congresses, and they supplied clinics at their own expense in poor Havana neighborhoods. At the first and second National Women's Congresses, participants agreed to promote maternity care for poor and working women. In 1923 Dulce María Borrero de Luján characterized the female worker as a victim of lecherous, irresponsible men. She proposed a complex, well-conceived resolution in which she wanted to: (1) Create special establishments, half clinic and half school, for poor and exhausted mothers who worked and whose salaries were always small. These women should receive adequate medical care for a reasonable period around birthing time to restore their physical health as well as improve their spirits, which are so important during a time when the morality and physical health of a new life unfolds. (2) Punish adults and minors alike who insult the sacred name of motherhood in public. (3) Influence the Cuban press to take interest in the social condition of mothers, who are also citizens of the country. (4) Expand women's education intended to develop their characters from an early age and put them in contact with their rights and responsibilities so that they can defend themselves.[17]

Borrero de Luján demanded state responsibility in caring for the health of pregnant working women. She insisted that maternity was an experience most women had, regardless of social class. Expectant mothers formed a class of their own that needed protection.[18] The more socialist-leaning feminists also asserted the proletarian woman's right to protection during pregnancy. Ofelia Rodríguez Acosta used arguments from Engels, who maintained that in early civilizations the role of motherhood was prized and valued, and only with modernization did women experience the reduction in status of their once-important position as mothers.[19]

The movement for maternity care first gained presidential recognition from Gerardo Machado. On February 3, 1929, as one of his public works projects, President Machado laid the cornerstone for the first municipal maternity hospital in Havana. The state-funded maternity hospitals, both municipal and provincial, provided medical care for mothers with normal and complicated deliveries. The Havana Maternity Hospital became one of the most highly respected maternity installations in the world. Built to the specifications of a medical team, the hospital operated with a staff of competent obstetricians and obstetric researchers. Furthermore, special funds subsidized the expense of needy women who required expert medical care such as surgery or toxemia treatment.[20]

On December 28, 1934, Carlos Mendieta signed Decree-Law 781 authorizing the first national maternity insurance for workers. It made up only part of a larger body of legislation on workers and working women, but the decree-law regulated the execution of an insurance policy covering the medical expenses of women in the labor force.[21] The law granted women six weeks' leave before and after giving birth. While new mothers were absent from work, maternity insurance paid a subsistence pension of no less than $1.25 pesos and no more than $4.00 pesos daily. The per diem corresponded to the woman's wages before her maternity absence. The law covered agricultural and pieceworkers, private employees, state employees, and factory and commercial workers. It excluded domestics, a group that composed 32 percent of the female work force in 1943. Finally, all public and private industrial factories employing more than fifty women had to maintain a nursery for children less than two years of age. The nurseries had to comply with stipulations of hygiene established by the secretary of labor, and they had to undergo periodic inspections by a medical doctor from the same office. Agricultural workers did not have access to the nurseries, however, and they formed 10 percent of the female labor force in 1943.

Decree-Law 781 lacked the subtleties required of such a far-reaching law. Cases came in questioning whether wives of workers could also have their medical expenses paid. Contributions of employers, employees, and state needed reworking. On December 15, 1937, on the recommendation of corporate lawyers, Congress rewrote the maternity law. The new Decree-Law 313 became the legal referent for maternity care through 1958. It added the provision that nursing mothers had one-half hour off in the morning and in the afternoon for breast-feeding until the children reached one year of age. The 1937 law also made it illegal for employers to fire female employees when they married because of potential maternity expenses.[22]

The government enforced much of the maternity law. In 1935 the Junta Central de Salud y Maternidad (the Central Health and Maternity Office) began with a small budget, but by 1940 it had distributed a total of $2.5 million pesos in the intervening five years. During that time 23,200 working women received payment for medical services, 7,320 claimed a simple pension for delivery, and 2,450 children had received treatment in dispensaries. Clearly, many women did not receive the services guaranteed them, but progress was underway. The 1940 budget apportioned new allocation of $1.3 million pesos for the following two years, or an increase of 25 percent over the expenses of the previous five years. National officials hoped that money would support 36,000 mothers between 1940 and 1942.[23]

Cuba's maternity code was one of the first and most progressive legal provisions for women in the Western Hemisphere. Mexico had passed a maternity code one year earlier, but it had only allowed women to take time off without pay, and it carried none of the benefits the Cuban law had. Argentina passed a maternity code the same year as Cuba. Its provisions were much like Cuba's except that the Argentine code was more generous in the provisions of prenatal care than the Cuban law. Fifteen other Western Hemisphere countries adopted a maternity code, but the first of these, Ecuador, passed its code in 1942. The United States has never provided for maternity care for working women.[24]

The maternity code was expensive, but the protection of motherhood was central not only to the feminists and working women but also to men who viewed women primarily as mothers. Cubans accepted the argument that motherhood was an act, a process, and an emotional and spiritual function that demanded legal protection.

Equal Work Laws

Setting sights on a maternity code did not deter feminists from arguing for equal rights for women in the work force. This effort involved direct contact with working women's groups. The Aliancistas, for example, worked with the Sociedad de Torcedores, the Sindicato de la Aguja, las Obreras y Empleadas de "El Encanto," "Fin de Siglo," "Casa Grande," "Isla de Cuba," "La Filosofía," the telephone company, and all agencies that hired women. Directed by Celia Sarra de Averhoff, the Labor Committee within the Alianza went into factories and talked with women, urging them to outline their needs and suggestions for action. In 1930, when hatmakers in Havana were fired for having gone on strike, Aliancistas protested to Antonio Ruiz, Havana's provincial governor. In 1933 the Alianza organized action against the bus company—Empresa de Omnibus Aliados—for not hiring women as ticket conductors. And in 1937 they organized and participated in a major conference between working women and feminists.[25]

These activities as well as President Mendieta's desire to heal the wounds of the overthrow of Machado influenced the promulgation of Decree-Law 589 in 1934, which included articles on hiring practices and equal wages. Congressmen writing the law intended to establish equal working conditions for women and men and equal opportunities for employment, including new legislation for the domestic servant.[26]

Article 2 of Decree-Law 589 assured, for the first time, that salary levels would correspond to the nature of work and not to the gender of workers, giving Cuban's legal precedent for equal-pay-for-equal-work regulation. Article 6 said that women should have equal access to work, with exceptions only in cases where protective legislation removed them from dangerous environments. Article 8 made it illegal to force women in industrial enterprises to do piecework at home. It also required domestic servants to register their employers' names and the salaries with the secretary of labor so that officials could detect underpayment and domestics would have access to national insurance. Finally, Article 17 made it illegal to fire a woman because she was married.[27]

Despite new regulations, women often experienced little change in salaries, benefits, or the ability to negotiate terms of employment. Between 1933 and 1937 women workers increasingly joined radical labor activists. After Grau San Martín's resignation, incensed workers went underground and formed La Joven Cuba. Two women, Xiomara O'Harrorans and Conchita Valdivieso, were with Antonio Güiteras on May 8, 1935, when he was assassinated. They were imprisoned. That same year Delia Echevarría and Charito Guillaume, two well-known labor activists and feminists, were arrested for supporting the revolutionary overthrow of the imposed government.

To quell unrest among workers, President Federico Laredo Brú signed Decree-Law 1024 on April 1, 1937. The decree restated law 589 by clarifying the equal-pay-for-equal-work provision and the protection of pieceworkers. However, law 1024 also limited jobs available to women by identifying new occupations that exposed workers to danger. Chapter 4 defined domestic work and established a means by which servants could register their employment, thereby regulating payment and insurance benefits.[28]

Political uncertainties between 1934 and 1940 cast doubt on the permanency or enforceability of laws passed during that period. Cubans called for a new constitution to clarify which laws would obtain. By 1938 constitutional reform was desired by even the most inveterate radicals, because revolution was no longer possible. Laredo Brú and Batista had jailed, killed, or exiled most insurgent leaders and co-opted their followers, and the Soviet Union was joining the Allied forces in Europe to defeat Hitler. Classical lines of division between capitalists and workers had become too blurred to continue the battle.

As a result, working-class presence in politics became institutionalized. Laredo Brú's government allowed for incremental gains in legal guarantees to workers, but he ultimately confined and regulated workers' power within capitalist conventions and under the control of business management. Because of effective repression of radical labor elements, labor leaders acquiesced and cooperated with government and capital. For its part, the government attempted to destroy labor's organizational base while conceding most of the social legislation approved during the insurrectionary period. The factions from which radical objection would ordinarily have come instead collaborated with the government. The Cuban Communist Party followed the lead of most communist parties during the Second World War, as they subordinated the struggle for socialism to a reform movement that included welfare legislation, democratic rights, modified colonial rule, and antifascism. Between 1936 and 1944 the Cuban Communist Party developed a close and cooperative relationship with the Batista regime, exchanging political support for legislation, organizational freedom, and access to cabinet ministers.

By 1939, therefore, labor, the communist and socialist parties, feminists, progressives, and conservatives agreed to come together and draw up a constitution. In anticipation of a constitutional convention, most political organizations published manifestos or platforms outlining their positions. Pamphlet after pamphlet and speech after speech confirmed nonpartisan interest in women's working rights. Most agreed that the promulgation of work laws in 1925, 1934, and 1937 only began a process that required widespread recognition and enforcement. The Cuban Communist Party put out numerous pamphlets arguing for expanded workers' rights, a free and democratic electoral process, and, to some extent, women's rights.[29] Other groups such as the Party of Republican Action, a more conservative group, did the same.[30]

The Constitutional Assembly of 1940 adopted a progressive stance in that it endorsed the rights of the worker and obligated the state to employ all citizens. The resulting constitution upheld earlier rulings regarding equal pay for equal work, minimum wage and maximum hours, as well as protective legislation. Specifically, Article 62 read: "Equal work under identical conditions will draw an equal salary regardless of sex, race, or nationality. Payment will be awarded on a daily or weekly basis." The article passed 36 to 27, with the two women delegates supporting the bill. Members of the opposition believed that the article gave too much power to the worker, who, they alleged, would forever sue business for improved salaries based upon what another worker might earn. They believed that owners would lose control, and production would suffer as a consequence. Those favoring the bill hoped to provide a more even and just distribution of income.[31]

Article 68 made it illegal to distinguish between married and single women in the workplace. Alicia Hernández de la Barca, a member of the Alianza and the most outspoken woman in the Assembly, proposed the article because she believed that the reason most often cited for firing women was their marital status. Hernández encountered no opposition to her proposal, which passed by a simple voice count.[32] Article 77 stirred the greatest opposition, since it dealt with setting maximum work hours. Conservatives and pro-business advocates believed that if a maximum workday were enforced, then industry would not grow. Although no one took offense at the protection of women, which included stipulations against night work and for the 8-and-$\frac{1}{2}$-hour day, the bill barely passed, even with guarantees that production would not fall.[33]

The 1940 Constitution was perhaps the most progressive charter in the Western Hemisphere. Born out of the chaos of the first thirty-eight years of statehood, it had to satisfy a majority of political groups, some of whom emerged in the twentieth century. Women and labor were two of these newly powerful groups. As a result of their pressure, the constitution guaranteed them rights. No other constitution in the Western Hemisphere undertook so much.

In Cuba constitutions and legal enforcement were never guaranteed. While the constitution might have outlined ideal governing principles, it also was a political tool. A liberal constitutional assembly and a progressive constitution appeased the left without threatening the right because congresses and the courts had to promulgate and try the laws. Old laws had to be challenged, regulatory agencies and legislation created, and individual cases tried before legal precedent became clear. The efficacy of the law fell into question, as working women continued to be poorly paid and overworked.

In 1941 Mariblanca Sabas Alomá wrote a series of articles in *El Avance Criollo,* a radical newspaper, in which she expressed continued dissatisfaction with the treatment of the woman worker. Despite the new constitution, she pointed out continued imbalances in the payment of labor. She insisted that Cuban women still worked an eleven- to twelve-hour day and earned only $2.75 pesos per week, while foreign women in foreign firms worked eight-hour days for $25.00 pesos per week.[34] Having criticized the middle-class feminist earlier for her limitations in understanding the plight of the working woman, she returned to feminism to form a base from which to demand enforcement of the legal rights of the female worker. She reminded middle-class women that feminism had three facets: economics, morality, and politics. With increased attention to women's economics, she believed that well-meaning people would not tolerate the exploitation of the Cuban female worker.[35]

Employment figures from the national censuses show that many working women remained outside the jurisdiction of the labor laws. Domestic servants continually made up about 33 percent of the work force, yet this sector lacked access to maternity provisions. Women continued to be paid significantly less than men because they clustered in "appropriate" jobs, which tended to earn less salary because equal-pay-for-work-of-equal-value laws did not pertain or they were not enforced. In 1956–57, 71.1 percent of women and 60.5 percent of men earned less than $75 pesos per month.[36] Cuba had the third largest national income per capita in Latin America in 1958, yet only 28.9 percent and 39.5 percent of female and male salaries, respectively, were above the $75.00 pesos per month average.

By 1940 labor and feminists had become assimilated into Batista's corporate state, as Batista attempted to fragment the social reform movement by separating feminists from working-class organizations. Cadres of feminist organizers turned their attention to holding public office and guiding policy rather than empowering working women. Middle- and upper-class women benefited increasingly from the Batista regime, as Cuba developed one of the most active corps of women diplomats and politicians in the Western Hemisphere. For these women there had been a revolution. Women in the lower classes, however, found themselves bound by economic constraints that made it impossible to go to court to protect their rights. For them the feminist movement was extraneous.

Cuban pride in the 1940 Constitution as well as cooperation with Batista effectively ameliorated civil dissent so prevalent in the 1920s and 1930s and anesthetized activist groups like the feminists for about a decade. By 1950 many feminists (even Ofelia Domínguez) and labor leaders formed part of the Batista government, and they became increasingly removed from the realities of working women and less familiar with socially marginal groups. Wage-earning women lost contact with their few advocates, and they had to make do with the few advances brought by legal change.

Conclusion

Cuba led the Western Hemisphere in the creation of progressive labor legislation for women. Only Argentina had a more generous maternity law, and by 1940 Cuba had compiled more protective and equal rights reforms than any Western country. Legislative success resulted from the need to accommodate workers in a rapidly modernizing society in which colonial conventions and attitudes no longer applied. With the advent of the new republic, workers replaced slaves, dignity became synonymous with sovereignty, submission connoted colonialism, and democracy and individual rights overrode monarchy and bestowed privileges. Workers and women had the most to gain under the new regime, and the increase in economic activity during the first two decades gave them reason to believe that new freedom was at hand.

Feminist and labor movements supplied platforms for working women's rights. The two movements, born within two years of one another, grew up through the Machadato as revolutionary fronts and later matured into reformist organizations in the post-1933 era. Their legacy bequeathed progressive law, but not social change. The leadership in both groups meant to influence gradual change, and, in the case of working women, liberate them from the grinding poverty so that they could choose the means by which they would live. Feminists wished health, education, protection from physical hardship, equal treatment at work, and maternity protection for working women. They also believed that, by working, women could find new dignity and self-sufficiency and less dependence upon men.

Critics of protective and equal working rights legislation for women speculated that improved work conditions would lure women away from their primary job in the home or that employers would refuse to hire women because of maternity costs. Each prediction no doubt occurred in individual cases. In the aggregate, however, relative constancy in women's employment statistics indicated that the percentage of women entering or leaving the work force changed substantially between 1931 and 1940. (The actual number did increase.) That predictions did not match reality suggests that legal provision did not significantly influence women's decision to work.

Enforcing the law was expensive and difficult. Of all the new laws, the maternity code was perhaps most observed by the government. It established a national maternity insurance policy, constructed hospitals, and reserved jobs for new mothers. Companies found ways to avoid providing nurseries or hiring married women. Enforcing equal pay for work of equal value and right-to-work laws required not only commmitment on the part of government and business but also by an informed and aggressive worker. Most wage-earning women were neither.

The value of labor legislation for women lay only in its statement of an ideal. Even the process of achieving progressive reforms lacked real contributions from women workers. Some of the laws, such as the Ley de Silla, reflected the interpretations of feminists and labor of what working women wanted and not a direct statement from the intended beneficiary. The maternity law, equal pay for equal work, and wage, hour, and hiring laws all directly pertained to women's abilities to provide for themselves and indicated that relief was at hand. Yet poverty and powerlessness abbreviated working women's opportunities to exercise their rights. As a result, Cuban working women experienced some improvement in work comforts but little social or economic change.

Blacks, Whites, and Women:
The Equal Rights Law

⚊

A statement of full legal equality for Cuban women did not exist until the passage of Article 23 of the 1940 Constitution. That article, which formally prohibited discrimination by sex, race, class, color, and creed or any transgression against human dignity, was more a conscious attempt to rectify racial inequalities and make a political statement after the 1933 revolution than to address issues of sex discrimination. The association between black slavery and racial and sex discrimination had deep historical and legal roots. Ana Betancourt's speech at the 1869 Revolutionary Congress was the first public statement that compared women's leagal status with that of black slaves, an association that is not trivial when the connection between slaves and married women is made.[1] After independence, social discrimination became part of the political agenda. Two factions, women and Blacks, sought redress of past injustices: feminists pressed for female emancipation, and Blacks demanded an end to racial discrimination. Although feminists rarely concerned themselves with purely racial issues and black women were not represented by the feminist movement, these two causes were again linked in the 1940 Equal Rights Article.

After independence, two contradictory tendencies surfaced: commitment to equal rights for all citizens and the fortification of special protection for women. Historically, the Cuban system of justice maintained separate legal codes for women and men because society and analysts believed that the abilities and functions of each gender were different. The advent of an equal rights law could have undermined protective laws, and it potentially challenged feminist arguments based on women's moral superiority and special status of motherhood. Yet feminists and legislators pursued an equal rights provision with little concern that it would abrogate special privileges for women.

Arguments against an equal rights law that were aired in the print media by women and men predicted the collapse of social order, corruption of women, breakdown of the family, and the disintegration of the Cuban community. Women becoming men's equals was at the core of the dispute. To appease these fears, feminists showed how women had worked in the public sphere alongside men and that it was good for society for them to have done so. In 1923 Mariblanca Sabás Alomá insisted that women expand the boundaries of their domain beyond the walls of their homes, which she viewed as prisons rather than palaces.[2] Ofelia Rodríguez Acosta insisted that women would take better care of the world's problems if they had power. She attacked the notion that political rights for women meant they had to fight in wars, which was a concern raised by opponents of the equal rights law. She said that women's struggle was to make injustice against particular social sectors difficult, and not to be like men and serve in the army.[3]

Cuba's dialectic of reform did not mean that women and men were equal. A literal interpretation of equality threatened the sex-specific biological, social, and economic roles accepted by most Cubans. Division of labor, not to mention the issues of maternity, required women to protect children and men to support the family. But a division of labor and social attitudes that devalued women's work encouraged feminists to redefine those duties and values. Enhanced employment in government, business, and the professions created a new feminine domain in which women attended to human needs in public agencies and work, and men operated banks, orchestrated international policy, and promoted technology.

Separate spheres were maintained and special provisions for maternity and safety were implemented. Equalization implied according *equal importance* to women's and men's social contributions and discouraging the deleterious effects of men's disregard for women's work. But the Cuban abstraction of equality preserved femininity within feminism and gender-specific roles in what Cubans called equal rights for women.

The Evolution of the Law

In 1917 the Cuban Judicial Congress met to discuss how to bring civil codes in line with the spirit of the 1901 Constitution, which discouraged social discrimination among citizens. Women's rights was part of the discussion. After considering a wide range of arguments, the jurists finally resolved that women had sufficient rights and left it to specific legislative changes to rectify injustices.[4] Reinaldo Sarabosa, a respected legal theorist at that time, dissented from the decision, maintaining that "hombre" used in the code should be translated as "man" in the generic sense and thereby extend legal authority to women. He rebuked those who believed that women should be denied rights on the basis of physical inferiority. He agreed that women tended to be smaller and weaker but asserted that they were no less intelligent than men.[5] Sarabosa criticized the other jurists by saying that the government's lawyers from the university law school had demonstrated their "conservative tendencies" by applying antiquated laws of the colonial past.[6]

At that time feminists had no organized response to the denial of equal rights. By 1923, however, Cuban women were working on a number of different levels for women's rights. Within the Western Hemisphere Cuban feminists led efforts to secure improved legal status for women, and nationally, they were outlining a platform with a number of equalizing objectives. In literary and theoretical debate, feminists questioned the intimate and psychological relationships between the sexes that subjugated women to men's wills.

At the Fifth International Conference of American States (Pan American Union) in 1923, representatives of participating countries adopted the first resolutions on women's rights at the plenary session of April 26. Representatives from Cuba took the floor and proposed a women's organization within the PAU. The resolution recommended that American countries seek ways to educate women, abolish constitutional and legal restrictions on them, and evaluate the status of women throughout the hemisphere.

In 1928 the Sixth Pan American Union meeting was held in Havana where a large contingent of Cuban women, led by Elena Mederos de González, chaired the plenary session to detail the civil and political status of American women and to request the establishment of an organization to study the situation further. On February 7, 1928, the final act of the Sixth Conference created the Interamerican Women's Commission (CIM). The Assembly resolved: "That an Interamerican Women's Commission be constituted to take charge of the preparation of juridical information and data of any other kind which may be deemed advisable to enable the Seventh International Conference of American States to take up the issue of the civil and political equality of women on the continent."[7] The commission undertook the preparation of an *Informe* on the legal position of women and, by the Seventh Conference, they were able to outline a study of the civil and political capacities of women throughout the hemisphere.

At the Seventh Interamerican Conference, the CIM commanded a great deal of attention and influenced the Assembly to pass two statutes to serve as guidelines to member states. The first allowed women the freedom to choose between their own nationality and that of an alien husband. The second stated simply that there should be no discrimination in the law based on sex. It was signed by the administrations of only four countries: Cuba, Ecuador, Paraguay, and Uruguay.

The PAU directly confronted equal rights for women at the 1936–37 Interamerican Conference for Maintenance of Peace held in Buenos Aires. There, the CIM encouraged the passage of Resolution 17, which stated that American governments should "adopt the most adequate legislation granting women full recognition of rights and duties of citizenship."[8] In 1938 the PAU passed the strongest resolution on women's rights to date. Known as the Lima Declaration in Favor of Women's Rights, Resolution 20 proposed:

1. To declare that women have the right to:
   A. Political treatment on the basis of equality with men.
   B. Equality of civil status.
   C. Full protection in and opportunity for work.
   D. Full protection as mothers.
2. To urge the governments of American Republics, which had not already done so, to adopt the necessary legislation to carry out fully the principles contained in this declaration, which shall be known as "The Lima Declaration in Favor of Women's Rights."[9]

Cuba's first attempt to pass an equal rights amendment came in November 1927 when Antonio Bravo Correoso, a senator and a member of the 1901 Constitutional Assembly, introduced an amendment to the 1901 Constitution giving women and men the same rights before the law. Bravo argued that women had accepted numerous responsibilities in society and, in fact, had been granted many rights since 1901. He referred at length to women's rights to conduct business, to sue and be sued, to own property, and to marry and divorce. He also pointed out the tremendous contributions of female activists in preparing all Cuban women for public and private responsibilities through educational and work programs. Bravo offered an amendment to regulate all laws that discriminated by sex, since rewriting individual laws would be a slow and incomplete way of approaching the problem of gender discrimination.[10]

Close examination of the proposed equal rights amendment shows several limitations. First, Article 1 pertained to single women only. It determined that single women would have the same rights as all men, regardless of the male's marital status. This amendment would have established once and for all that single women could represent themselves in court and take responsibility for their own financial matters, rights that they already had. It left married women largely under the legal jurisdiction of their husbands. Married women bore the same duties and responsibilities as their husbands, but husbands had final authority in matters of finance and jurisdiction over legitimate and illegitimate children. Married women had control over their own property and counsel over common property. The amendment allowed for the revision of prenuptial agreements when both parties consented. Additionally, married women could reclaim any private property they brought to the marriage. The proposed amendment, then, incorporated earlier property and parental authority legislation, cleared the way for reform of specific laws, but restricted married women's legal rights.

The amendment failed to pass because it repeated the Dictamen of the 1901 Constitution that all Cubans were equal before the law.[11] Senator Bravo's final argument, that the Dictamen and the Civil Code conflicted and an amendment was called for to establish constitutional authority, was ineffective. Congress shelved the equal rights amendment until 1940 when the Constituent Congress debated its passage.

In the interim feminists worked on the franchise, divorce law, labor laws, educational and welfare reform, and children's rights. An equal rights law was not their main concern. In the press, feminist writers tended to connect the struggle for equal rights with the U.S. movement and not their own. They looked at the individual components of women's legal reforms—labor laws, education reform, welfare, and the vote—more than at a comprehensive statement of general rights.

In anticipation of the 1940 constitutional assembly, feminists had called the Third National Women's Congress in February 1939. Fourteen years had passed since the disputatious 1925 congress, years fraught with violence and conflict. To avoid the dissension that had divided them previously, leaders insisted that the agenda "exclude any political, religious, or idiosyncratic inclination that would create divisions among feminine ranks."[12]

At that time Ofelia Domínguez Navarro, the main dissenter against reformist policies in the early 1930s, had returned from exile in Mexico imbued with the possibilities of a progressive corporate state like that orchestrated by President Lázaro Cárdenas. She agreed to cooperate with democratic regimes. Moderate feminists had softened their attack against Domínguez because the Left no longer seemed to be a threat. Under these circumstances, the Congress passed progressive resolutions peacefully, one of which was a constitutional guarantee for equal rights for women.

A few months later and amid high expectations, Cubans elected a Constituent Congress to write a new constitution that would bring the long-overdue social and political justice promised by the independence fighters. Dr. Gustavo Gutiérrez Sánchez, president of the House of Representatives, ex–secretary of justice, and past professor of the law faculty at the University of Havana, characterized the expectations of the new constitution as follows:

> the Cuban people must know how to take advantage of the opportunity that events offer them to adequately build its society, its national economy, its political organization in the upcoming Constituent Assembly. The determining factors of Cuban reality must be understood in the historical transcendency of the moment, and we are called to determine [law] for the Republic through freedom and self-conscious expression of popular will.[13]

The election of delegates to the Constituent Congress followed strict guidelines designed to provide for the broadest political representation. Fair elections took place on November 15, 1939, with a large voter turnout. Delegates with progressive leanings composed the majority of the congress, while radical activists made up the largest minority faction.[14] The professional composition of the delegates showed a majority of doctors, lawyers, and professionals, although members of the working class also participated.[15] Only two of the delegates were women: Alicia Hernández de la Barca, a teacher from Santa Clara, member of the Alianza, and later to become a national congressional representative from Santa Clara, and Esperanza Sánchez Mastrapa, a lawyer later to become a congressional representative from Oriente province. Both were moderate feminists interested in women's rights. They were joined by a number of men who supported women's rights and who introduced some of the most radical articles of the constitution.[16]

Preceding the deliberations of the constitutional assembly and during the campaigns to elect delegates, most political parties and coalitions declared in favor of equal rights for women. At the meetings themselves, however, equal rights for women was a nonissue, since debate focused on racial discrimination only. The Cuban Communist Party offered Article 23 to the constitution that specifically forbade social discrimination of any kind. Delegates, for the most part, supported constitutional statutes against discrimination, but the majority intitially felt that the 1901 Dictamen already ruled against such prejudice. It said:

> All Cubans are equal before the law. The Republic recognizes neither special privileges [fueros] nor selective legal advantages [privilegios]. It declares illegal and punishable by law all discrimination based on sex, race, color, class and any other prejudice against human dignity.[17]

Progressive and radical delegates wanted a stronger constitutional guarantee, since the Dictamen did not have the force of law that constitutional provisions had. Conservatives, however, maintained that proposed Article 23, guaranteeing *all* Cubans equal rights, was too broad. After quarreling over semantics, delegates called for a straw vote. Article 23 failed by a 23-to-20 count, with both women delegates voting with the minority for its passage. Explaining her vote, Alicia Hernández de la Barca made the only reference to nonracial discrimination. She said that the constitution had to be exacting and it had to correct the "many prejudices that existed."[18]

Conservatives held the majority until Delio Núñez Mesa explained his rejection of the article in terms no one could accept. He said he did not want a specific constitution. The constitution, he argued, should only indicate a direction, leaving to elected congresses and the judiciary the job of practical application. Besides, he added, "racism does not exist in Cuba. Blacks simply do not claim their constitutional rights. They do not know how to claim their rights. . . . neither a constitution nor any law of the land can make it so that these citizens will understand how to defend themselves like dignified men."[19]

Núñez Mesa's remark prompted heated debate and made it difficult for conservatives to hold ground. Progressives and radicals attacked, insisting that racism and social prejudice did in fact exist. They amended the article to remove the word *all* and to specify "gender, race, color, class or any prejudice against human dignity." (Race and color signified de jure and de facto discrimination, respectively.)

On the final day of debate, when it was clear that conservatives were losing ground, José Manuel Casanova informed delegates that the Communist Party had publicized the results of the straw vote with the purpose of provoking popular disapproval of the Assembly's work. He insisted that delegates forget that the article was a Communist Party proposal and vote for it on its merits. Euselio Mujal of the government-supported trade union confederation agreed. Juan Marinello, a communist, announced that the police were barring observers from entering the galleries and that many were keeping vigil in the rain. Under these circumstances, Article 23 of the constitution passed by a majority vote.[20] The center of debate had been racial injustice, but, when the article was passed, it covered every form of discrimination imaginable. The law read: "All Cubans are equal before the law. The State does not recognize special privileges or status. It declares illegal and punishable by law all discrimination based on sex, race, color, class and any other prejudice against human dignity."

An equal rights constitutional provision declared all Cuban citizens to be equal, but the conception of equality was Ana Betancourt's and José Martí's, not Susan B. Anthony's or Thomas Jefferson's. Cuban society still rested on the Hispanic corporate model in which social groups, not individuals, held power. Groups had rights, privileges, and responsibilities based upon their functions. The Church, the military, and political administrators had been the principal powers under Spanish rule because they oversaw spiritual and moral ordering. In modern Cuba the power of traditional groups declined, and new groups such as industrialists, workers, students, Blacks, and women demanded rights. But they struggled as members of groups and not as isolated individuals.

Women made up the group of women/mothers. As group members, they derived the same rights as members of any other social group—that is, equal status before the law—but, as mothers, they required special provisions. Thus, Cubans viewed women in two dimensions: they were at once equal with and distinct from men. The importance of motherhood and family to Cuban society and Cuban's propensity to embrace dual and seemingly contradictory principles allowed an equal rights law to pass with no controversy about whether it would abrogate the maternity code and protective labor laws.

The passage of Article 23 did not initiate a revision of legal discrimination against women, as might have been expected, since enabling legislation rarely followed. Rather than marking the beginning of massive legal reform, the 1940 Constitution ended the feminist movement for legal change. Believing that the major battle had been won, feminists turned their attention to welfare, education, and health projects. Their political activities prepared some to become part of the diplomatic corps, federal and provincial legislators, and political activists. Others were community activists concerned with resolving problems of poverty and disease among women and children. Others made social welfare part of women's domain by instituting a School of Social Welfare at the University of Havana that graduated mostly women and placed graduates in governmental and bureaucratic posts. After 1940 the feminist movement turned away from legal reform efforts and directed its attention toward community and social activities. The feminist movement for legal change was over.

Conclusion

᭶

Following the extended wars of Cuban independence and the intrusion of political chaos that followed, a Cuban woman's movement emerged, promising stability and justice. Given the small number of women who called themselves feminists and the deep roots of male domination in Cuban society, these women had every opportunity to fail. But they did not. Their own acuity in managing political alliances, their definitions of feminism, and cooperation with men won them progressive legal reforms.

At the 1923, 1925, and 1939 national women's congresses, participants outlined a feminist ideology that made motherhood the cornerstone of a women's revolution. The idea that motherhood could inspire revolution challenged Hispanic conventions that preferred women in homes raising children, responding to their husbands' needs, presenting a pious and chaste example for their children, and teaching their offspring simple but strict moral values. Yet only student and labor movements elicited the attention feminists did during a period of insurrection. Family laws, suffrage, equal rights guarantees, education and social welfare laws, rights for illegitimate children, and labor legislation changed to reflect women's new status in an emerging nation.

Clearly, a number of factors contributed to the success of the feminist movement. National sensitivity to José Martí's calls for social justice, a general agreement to rewrite colonial legislation, political instability, the overthrow of a dictator, and communist challenge to government control gave feminists opportunities to press their demands. They chose their opportunities judiciously, and they were successful because they presented themselves as moderates from the intelligentsia. They offered a definition of feminism that preserved family and Hispanic morality, helped women in a modernizing society, indirectly challenged male authority, and left intact a class-based society.

Operating out of the relative safety of the privileged classes, Cuban feminists forged a brand of feminism that was pro-women, pro-family, and pro-children. They also supported reforms for working women so that wage earners could earn a decent wage in healthy conditions.

Feminist advocates saw motherhood, respectable professions for women, political activity, and feminism fitting as one piece. They sensed no conflict between professionalism and motherhood, nor between motherhood and feminism, because, in their own lives and owing to their wealth and the existence of a servant class, they never had to exclude one option for another.

International women's organizations supported Cuban feminists in their efforts to get the vote. Some groups more than others were influenced by North American emphasis upon political participation and borrowed heavily from U.S. organizational tactics and political strategies. But Cuban feminists never put aside their age-old devotion to women's roles as wives, mothers, and guardians of morality. Indeed, they used these images and functions to justify their movement and argue for reform. Selling themselves as reformers for social justice, they convinced male politicians of their political importance and functioned as legitimizers of political movements. Therein lay their power.

Women did not win new legislation single-handedly. For different but complementary reasons, progressive men used women's support to secure public office and constitute a modern state. Under these circumstances, men changed family laws in ways that limited the grossest aspects of male domination. Men created a divorce law that promised alimony, child care, and an end to wife-killing for adultery. They even gave illegitimate children improved social and financial status.

As a result, feminists did not strive to eliminate the patriarchy. Rather they constructed a feminine domain in government and society that benefited them and, to a lesser extent, other women. Feminists aimed to strengthen the convention of *mater familias* (women's authority within the family) because it gave individual women power to manage family matters. More importantly, public acknowledgment of mater familias gave feminists the moral authority to place themselves in national leadership positions as social welfare and women's rights advocates.

Feminists remained dependent upon the patriarchy to achieve their goals. As a result, they had no philosophy to guide them away from a paternalistic society. The most they could do was claim morality and the sanctity of motherhood as both their cause and their domain. Thus, they and progressive men invented a new form of governance, state familialism, that imitated family ordering. At the state level, women had authority over welfare issues, and men directed financial and foreign policy matters. Women's and men's roles were not unified, but the notion of separate and occasionally equal spheres did apply.

It would be wrong to condemn Cuban feminists for their class orientation and their accommodation to patriarchal standards. During the early republic, living through a period of economic and political crises, middle- and upper-class feminists were the only ones able to form a woman's movement. They held social positions necessary to make their views known, and they could broker their demands during a period of constitutional revision and heightened national consciousness about social justice.

Their good work was not without contradictory consequences, however. The feminist ideal was to create equal opportunities for all women, but the process of change they advocated provided welfare and education out of the good sufferance of privileged feminists. As a result, class and ethnicity were maintained as a means of social discrimination. Feminists were rewarded most from social welfare programs because they were empowered as political and social matriarchs. Other women, even those who benefited from political, social, and labor reforms, were not significantly more powerful than before.

Not that feminist reforms were insignificant. They marked a beginning that produced positive results. Women could vote and hold office. Education and welfare work proved that women could manage national programs. Labor legislation, both protective and equal, reflected Cuban reverence for motherhood *and* recognition that women had joined the work force in new positions. Feminists provided a social consciousness that gave voice to community commitments and moral obligations. This was, perhaps, their greatest contribution, since they were substituting women's moral objectives for Catholic teachings.

The woman's movement found its place in the currents of change sweeping Cuba between 1920 and 1940. While men viewed these critical decades as a time for establishing bureaucratic control, feminists considered it a moment for expanding nurturing principles of the home into goverment and placing women in positions of responsibility.

Feminism in Cuba had at least one unique quality: its juxtaposition with North American feminism and feminists. The presence of U.S. influence in Cuba, marked by military invasions, a sizable foreign presence, and cultural domination, pervaded nearly every aspect of life. Cuban feminism could not be simply a matter of women's rights; it had to contain nationalist overtones that colored ideals of women's social roles. U.S. interventions made it difficult for some feminists to embrace aspects of U.S. feminism, such as individual rights, that they might have admired. Other feminists desired U.S. presence for reasons of stability and defended U.S. feminist principles, such as gender equality and attacks on the patriarchy, that could not transfer easily to Cuba's postcolonial society. It also made concern with race and class difficult, since North Americans viewed those issues as Bolshevik, not Cuban, concerns. Geography and the U.S. obsession with Cuba meant that U.S. feminism was a constant consideration for Cubans.

The importance of the emergence of the Cuban women's movement was not so much the fact that elite matriarchs fostered causes that protected family, children, and women. Rather, it was that feminists took restrictive social and religious principles and made them into imperatives for women's liberation. Only sixty years earlier, women holding public office would have implied the disruption of an ordered society. In the 1920s women activists symbolized political order, social stability, and moral justice. Bourgeois feminism did not alienate the majority of politically powerful men, who throughout the 1930s needed feminist support. Indeed, since the feminist movement was nearly universally accepted by political groups contending for power, feminists won significant legal rights for women and raised the consciousness of a generation of political activists. Moderation, a reverence for mother-hood, and the historical moment combined to produce a dynamic movement that affected legal change for privileged women and welfare for poor and working-class women while leaving aspects of male domi-nance, capital exploitation, and class structure in place.

Appendix

ॐ

Occupational Distribution of Employed Cuban Women by Class, 1899–1953

	1899	1907	1919	1943	1953
White-Collar Jobs (Total)	2,401	6,388	11,079	61,352	79,674
Actress	18	26	66	366	95
Artist	53	104	86	13	372
Bookkeeper-Accountant	4	—	—	183	1,880
Hotel and Restaurant	4	4	366	—	—
Literary and Scientific Figures	4	2	74	—	—
Merchants	414	—	779	—	—
Musicians and Music Teachers	46	51	71	1,057	745
Nurses	284	576	727	657	3,286
Photographers	7	4	—	111	123
Saleswomen	36	554	235	—	—
Stenographers, Typists	6	134	—	1,253	7,084
Teachers, College Professors	1,502	3,832	5,122	16,780	34,845
Telephone and Telegraph Employees	5	55	321	392	9,040
Lawyers and Judges	—	2	6	391	533
Agents (Travel and Real Estate)	—	1	16	—	1,023
Architects	—	1	—	66	77
Dentists	—	5	11	152	352
Engineers	—	1	10	23	6
Newspaper Reporters and Writers	—	5	4	23	148
Medical Doctors and Surgeons	—	3	35	105	403
Bank Officials, Brokers, Landlords	—	144	31	—	—
Clerks and Copyists	—	884	901	—	—
Office Employees	—	—	740	680	7,956
Government Officials and Employees	—	—	1,274	4,050	5,043
Pharmacists	—	—	200	378	1,275
Surveyors and Appraisers	—	—	4	—	—
Optometrists	—	—	—	16	—
Sugar Chemists	—	—	—	1	—
Veterinarians	—	—	—	13	—

Table—Continued

	1899	1907	1919	1943	1953
Other Professionals	—	—	—	958	55
Professional Athletes	—	—	—	154	31
Pilots	—	—	—	5	—
Librarians	—	—	—	24	114
Chemists and Laboratory Technicians	—	—	—	732	493
Editors	—	—	—	128	—
Radio Operators	—	—	—	41	—
Chiropractors	—	—	—	93	—
Other Semi-professionals	—	—	—	402	—
Owners of Large Ranches	—	—	—	10	—
Planters	18	—	—	—	—
Proprietors and Managers	—	—	—	5,575	4,040
Clerks and Public Employees	—	—	—	26,550	—
Social Workers	—	—	—	—	375
Blue-Collar Jobs (Total)	40,607	41,205	34,253	43,665	66,680
Boarding House Keepers	2	34	204	—	—
Charcoal Burners	11	5	—	—	—
Laborers	8,860	—	707	—	—
Laundresses	20,980	24,016	8,680	2,538	—
Operatives in Cigar Factories	1,580	—	4,905	—	—
Seamstresses	8,329	9,464	9,317	—	—
Shirtmakers	3	3	14	—	—
Strawworkers	322	—	—	—	—
Bakers	18	—	—	—	—
Dressmakers	419	—	—	—	—
Gardeners or Florists	7	3	11	—	—
Housekeepers	15	—	—	—	—
Printers and Lithographers	18	33	204	131	56
Shoemakers	40	19	—	1,740	—
Confectioners	3	10	94	251	1,845
Agricultural Workers	—	3,110	7,523	13,690	11,799
Railroad Workers	—	3	190	—	—
Sweepers	—	1	—	—	—
Woodcutters	—	2	—	—	—
Day Laborers	—	591	—	—	—

Table—Continued

	1899	1907	1919	1943	1953
Fisherwomen	—	4	—	—	—
Doorkeepers	—	262	—	—	—
Tobacco Workers	—	3,340	—	1,023	—
Weavers	—	95	202	—	—
Bricklayers	—	2	—	—	—
Apprentices	—	10	57	97	—
Beauticians	—	28	92	853	2,518
Carpenters	—	2	—	—	—
Painters	—	6	14	120	—
Watchmakers and Jewelers	—	2	1	81	76
Leatherworkers	—	22	2	—	—
Shepherds	—	2	7	—	—
Bookbinders	—	2	39	—	273
Plasterers	—	1	—	—	—
Tailors	—	17	154	301	272
Manufacturing	—	116	420	—	—
Boxmakers (wood)	—	—	9	250	250
Broom and Brush Makers	—	—	530	—	—
Dryers and Cleaners	—	—	7	—	—
Engravers	—	—	6	—	—
Messengers and Office Help	—	—	137	123	182
Gold and Silversmiths	—	—	12	—	—
Packers and Shippers	—	—	15	—	—
Porters	—	—	59	—	—
Ropemakers	—	—	134	—	—
Sail and Awning Makers	—	—	507	—	—
Skilled Workers	—	—	—	747	—
Quarry Workers	—	—	—	10	—
Decorators and Varnishers	—	—	—	1,713	—
Electricians	—	—	—	22	—
Tobacco Pickers	—	—	—	636	—
Butchers	—	—	—	33	—
Chauffeurs	—	—	—	65	609
Transportation Workers	—	—	—	60	500
Tobacco Stemmers	—	—	—	8,713	17,321
Unskilled Workers	—	—	—	10,282	12,468
Military Service and Police	—	—	—	35	274
Waitresses	—	—	—	151	—

Table—Continued

	1899	1907	1919	1943	1953
Construction	—	—	—	—	110
Food Services	—	—	—	—	1,247
Mechanics	—	—	—	—	320
Textile Workers	—	—	—	—	3,647
Day Laborers (factory)	—	—	—	—	3,740
Day Laborers (construction)	—	—	—	—	450
Day Laborers (transportation)	—	—	—	—	6,062
Domestic Servants (Total)	22,807	23,378	39,679	30,347	69,874
Others (Total) Hucksters and Peddlers	115	140	25	201	771

Sources: U.S. War Department, Director of the Census, *Report of the Census of Cuba, 1899* (Washington, D.C.: U.S. Government Printing Office, 1900), 462–63, 465; Oficino del Censo de los Estados Unidos, *Censo de la República de Cuba, 1907* (Washington, D.C.: U.S. Government Printing Office, 1908), 545–46; República de Cuba, Dirección general del censo, *Census of the Republic of Cuba,* 1919 (Havana: Maza, Arroyay Caso, 1919), 666–67; República de Cuba, Dirección general del censo, *Informe general del censo de 1943* (Havana: P. Fernández, 1953); Repúblic de Cuba, Oficina Nacional de los Censos Demográficos y Electoral, *Censos de Población, Viviendas y Electoral, 1953* (Havana: P. Fernández, 1953), 204–5.

Notes

Preface

1. Nancy F. Cott, *The Grounding of Modern Feminism* (New Haven: Yale University Press, 1987); and Paula Baker, "The Domestication of Politics: Women and American Political Society, 1780–1920," *American Historical Review* 89, no. 3 (June 1984): 620–47.

2. Karen Offen, "Defining Feminism: A Comparative Historical Approach," *Signs: Journal of Women in Culture and Society* 14, no. 11 (Spring 1988): 119–57.

3. Asunción Lavrin identifies femaleness and femininity as the bases for women's understanding of themselves in Latin American society. According to Lavrin, the feminism articulated by feminists between 1898 and 1950 for some meant equal civil rights with men. For others it implied education and economic parity with men. For most feminists, however, equality before the law did not imply "gender assimilation" or the adoption of male models of behavior. These women viewed themselves in a community with men in which gender roles were distinct but equally important. See Asunción Lavrin, *Female, Feminine, and Feminist: Key Concepts in Understanding Women's History in Twentieth-Century Latin America* (Bristol, England: University of Bristol, Occasional lecture series no. 4, 1988).

Chapter 1

1. The manigua and mambises are images as central to nineteenth-century Cuban patriotism as Antonio Maceo and José Martí. *Irse al manigua* or *estar en el manigua* meant to take up arms, usually the machete, against the Spanish army. The manigua referred to the untamed countryside, which consisted of dry, mountainous landscape in Oriente; flat fertile farmland in Camagüey; and mountainous jungles in Pinar del Río. To be in the manigua meant to live in the wild under the most crude conditions with only hammocks and provisions gotten from peasant communities for subsistence. To go to the *manigua* meant to suffer deprivation in order to be free. *Mambí* originally referred to Blacks from Santo Domingo, and the word connoted bad, repulsive, vile, dirty, cruel, evil men, who made their living by conniving and cheating. The Cubans used the term affectionately for themselves during the Wars of Independence. Their troops were dirty, malnourished, yet fierce independence fighters who contended with the superior Spanish forces with

cunning trickery. Cuban patriots proudly called themselves mambises. The women who fought were mambisas.

2. Prescribed behavior was intended for all women, but it could only apply to the upper class. It was an ideal. The importance of the Wars of Independence was that the ideal ceased to exist for most women, regardless of class, and the mambisa served as an admired example for Cuban women.

3. Sociedad Económica de La Habana, "La educación de las niñas," *Memorias* (Havana: Sociedad Económica de La Habana, 1843), 157.

4. *Patria potestad,* a Latin legal concept of the family, was established in Spain in 1252–64 in the *Siete Partidas.* Male authority became law in the New World in 1680 in the *Recopilación de Leyes de Indias,* and it was reestablished through the Napoleonic Code of 1809. In Cuba the Spanish government affirmed the patria potestad in the Spanish Civil Code of 1886.

5. Republic of Cuba, *Código Penal vigente en la República de Cuba* (Havana: Casa Editora, Librería e Imprenta "La Moderna Poesía," 1916), 191 and 195–96.

6. For informative sources that describe the lives of early nineteenth-century Cuban women, see Verena Martínez Alier's *Marriage, Class, and Colour in Nineteenth-Century Cuba* (Cambridge: Cambridge University Press, 1977). Cirilo Villaverde's *Cecilia Valdes,* vols. 1 and 2 (Havana: Editorial Letras Cubanas, 1984). For the English translation of *Cecilia Valdes,* see Villaverde, *Cecilia Valdes, or Angel's Hill* translated by Sydney G. Gest. (New York: Vantage Press, 1962).

7. For a detailed cataloging of nineteenth- and early twentieth-century women writers, see Antonio González Curquejo, *Florilegio de escritoras cubanas,* vol. 3 (Havana: Imprenta "Siglo XX," 1919). Antonio González Curquejo, *Florilegio de escritoras cubanas,* vol. 1 (Havana: "La Moderna Poesía," 1910). Antonio González Curquejo, *Florilegio de escritoras cubanas,* vol. 2 (Havana: Aurelio Miranda, 1913).

8. Evelyn Picon Garfield, "Periodical Literature for Women in Mid-Nineteenth Century Cuba: The Case of Gertrudis Gómez de Avellaneda's *Album Cubano de lo Bueno y lo Bello*" (paper delivered at the Latin American Studies Association conference, Miami, December 4–7, 1989).

9. Anita Arroyo, "Presencia de la mujer en la vida cubana," *Diario de la Marina. Siglo y cuarto* (Havana: Diario de la Marina, 1955), 192. See also Mirta Aguirre, *Influencia de la mujer en Iberoamérica. Ensayo* (Havana: P. Fernández, 1947), 68.

10. The Ten Years War, initiated by Carlos Manuel Céspedes's liberating his slaves and declaring Cuba free from Spanish rule in the "Grito de Yara" in 1868, was led by creoles. Many of the creoles belonged to the Reformist Party, later the Autonomist Party, which favored effective political representation in the Spanish court, free speech and association, the removal of unjust and burdensome taxes, the reduction of a heavy and costly Spanish bureaucracy, and the discrimination against Cubans seeking bureaucratic positions. Some creoles were revolutionaries who demanded complete independence from Spain, but they were not as powerful as the Autonomists in the Ten

Years War. Other creoles in the insurgent forces were Annexationists, who wanted to secure Cuba's economic and political future by placing Cuba under the domain of the United States. The differing objectives of the patriot army weakened its effectiveness.

11. James O'Kelly, *The Mambi-Land or Adventures of a Herald Correspondent in Cuba* (Philadelphia: J. B. Lippincott, 1974), 248.

12. Ibid., 237.

13. Ibid., 238.

14. Ana Moya de Perera, *La historia de la mujer cubana* (unpublished manuscript now in the possession of the author's daughter, Ana Perera. N.p., n.d.).

15. *Bohíos* were and are houses built by campesinos. They are rectangular and wooden, usually with a dirt floor. There are one or two bedrooms and a living room. Cooking and washing are done outside the house or in a lean-to. There is no bathroom, and the roof is made of thatched palm leaves.

16. James O'Kelly, *Mambi-Land*, 182 and 184–85.

17. Ibid., 186.

18. Nydia Sarabia, *Ana Betancourt* (Havana: Editorial de Ciencias Sociales, 1970), 55. For the actual copy of the speech, see Ana Betancourt de Mora in the Donativos y Recibos in the National Cuban Archives (Archivo Nacional de Cuba).

19. Paul Estrade's work, "Les Clubs Feminins dans le Parti Revolutionnaire Cubain (1892–1898)," *Femmes des Amériques* (Toulouse: Université de Toulouse—Le Mirail, 1986), 82, is an excellent and unique source for a study of the activities and composition of the women's revolutionary clubs up to and during the War of 1898.

20. Ibid., 88.

21. "Libro de Actas del Cuerpo De Consejo de Key West, Florida," 256–61, as cited in Estrade, "Clubs Feminins," 103.

22. Armando O. Caballero, *La mujer en el 95* (Havana: Editorial Gente Neuva, 1982), 17–23.

23. Ibid., 24. Numbers confirmed in conversations with A. O. Caballero, June 1988.

24. José Martí, "La recepción en Filadelfia," *Patria*, New York, August 20, 1892.

25. Caballero, *La mujer*, 32–46.

26. Caballero, *La mujer*, 123–24.

27. Ana Moya de Perrera, "La historia de la mujer cubana" (Unpublished manuscript). Caballero, *La mujer*, 123–24.

28. Maria Collado, "La revolución femenina en Cuba," *Bohemia* 19, no. 50 (December 11, 1927): 58.

Chapter 2

1. Comité Provincial del Partido Comunista de Cuba en la Habana, *La mujer cubana en los cien años de lucha, 1868–1968* (Havana: n.p., 1969), 44.

2. Carlos de Velasco, *Aspectos nacionales* (Havana: Librería "Studium," 1915), 107.

3. Fernándo Portuondo, *Estudios de historia de Cuba* (Havana: Editorial de Ciencias Sociales, Instituto Cubano del Libro, 1973), 9.

4. Speeches made by María Luisa Dolz, many of which are found in the Cuban National Archives under her name, are: "La participación de la mujer en las ciencias y las artes." "La reinvindicación de los derechos de la mujer," "Consideraciones sobre la educación física e intelectual." and "La mujer en la historia." Published speeches include *La liberación de la mujer por la educación* (Havana: Oficina del Historiador de la Cuidad, 1955).

5. Antonio G. Zamora, "La mujer en Cuba: El Colegio 'Isabel la Católica' y María Luisa Dolz," *El Hogar* Año 13 (September 27, 1896). 1–4. *El Hogar* also contains photographs of the school and the students.

6. de Velasco, *Aspectos nacionales,* 17.

7. Mary Elizabeth Springer, "The Feminist Movement in Cuba," *Bulletin of the Pan American Union* (December 1923): 580. "Una ultímisima institución femenina," *Bohemia* (July 18, 1926): 25. Medardo Vitier, "En torno a la enseñanza en Cuba durante la República," *Diario de la Marina, Siglo y Cuarto* (Havana: Diario de la Marina, 1925), 78.

8. Extrapolated from: U.S. War Department, Office, Director for the Census of Cuba, *Report on the Census of Cuba, 1899* (Washington, D.C.: U.S. Government Printing Office, 1900), 166. The change in the midcentury statistics comes from Republic of Cuba, *Informe general del censo de 1953* (Havana: Fernández 1953).

9. Republic of Cuba, Law of August 3, 1917, *Gaceta Oficial,* 1942–43.

10. Ricardo M. Alemán y Martín, *La capacidad de la mujer en el derecho civil* (Havana: Imprenta Avisador Comercial, 1917), 29–31.

11. Cuba, Laws and Statutes, *El código español de Cuba* (Havana: Imprenta Avisador Comercial, 1889).

12. This was Morales's interpretation of the word "hombres," which other legislators argued meant "men" and not "humankind."

13. República de Cuba, *Diario de Sesiones del Senado, May 24, 1916* (Havana: Imprenta de Rambla, Bouza), 18. The *Diario de Sesiones del Senado* hereafter will be referred to as *DSS*.

14. *DSS,* May 12, 1917, 5.

15. *DSS,* May 2, 1917, 8.

16. *DSS,* May 2, 1917, 9.

17. *DSS,* May 12, 1917, 8.

18. *DSS,* May 14, 1917, 5.

19. *DSS,* May 2, 1917, 11.

20. *DSS,* May 11, 1917, 15–17.

21. *Gaceta Oficial,* Año 16, no. 19, tomo 1, (July 23, 1917): 1205–6.

22. Interview with Elena Mederos de González, September 20, 1980.

23. Dulce María Borrero de Luján, *El matrimonio en Cuba* (Havana: Imprenta Siglo XX, 1914).

24. de Velasco, *Aspectos nacionales,* 75.

25. Eliseo Giberga, *El problema de divorcio* (Habana: Librería y Imprenta "La Moderna Poesía," 1911), 64.

26. Giberga, *El problema,* 65.

27. de Velasco, *Aspectos nacionales,* 75.

28. de Velasco, *Aspectos nacionales,* 75.

29. *DSS,* July 9, 1918, 5.

30. Giberga, *El Problema,* 40.

31. de Velasco, *Aspectos nacionales,* 78.

32. Dulce María Borrero de Luján, "Protección de la madre" (Speech delivered at the public session of the Second National Women's Congress, April 16, 1925). Published also in *Cuba Contemporánea* 12, (May 1925): 5–18; and *Repertorio Americano, Semenario de Cultural Hispánica* (Costa Rica) 10, no 12 (May 25, 1925): 179–81. Aurelia Castillo de González wrote three articles supporting divorce: "Maternidad—Infancia," *Cuba Contemporánea 17* (May–August 1918), 341–46; "Mujeres antes que hombres," *Cuba Contemporánea* 17 (May–August 1918), 89–94; and "El divorcio," *Cuba Contemporánea* 17 (May–August 1918), 417–18.

33. Francisco G. del Valle, *El divorcio y los hijos* (Havana: Imprenta "Militar" de Pérez Hermanos, 1915), 13.

34. Ibid., 12.

35. Ibid., 14.

36. Mario Nin y Abarca, *El divorcio ante el derecho internacional privado en la doctrina y en la legislación jurisprudencia cubana* (Havana: Imprenta y Papelería de Rambla, Bouza 1926), 8.

37. *The Havana Post,* September 11, 1913, sec. 1, 1.

38. Bryan to Gonzales, May 18, 1914, as cited in Louis A. Pérez, *Cuba Under the Platt Amendment* (Pittsburgh: University of Pittsburgh Press, 1986), 337–38.

39. Mario Nin y Abarca, *El Divorcio,* 10.

40. For a statistical analysis of the use of the divorce law in Cuba, 1917–25, see K. Lynn Stoner's "In Defense of Motherhood: Divorce Law in Cuba During the Early Republic," *Women and Politics in Twentieth-Century Latin America* (special issue of *Studies in Third World Societies*), edited by Sandra F. McGee, no. 15 (March 1981), 1–32.

Chapter 3

1. María Collado, Archivo Nacional de Cuba. Fondo: Donativos y Remisiones, caja 661, no. 7, n.p.

2. Collado, Archivo Nacional.

3. Pérez, *Cuba,* 214–18.

4. Ibid., 231–35.

5. Ibid., 241.

6. Ofelia Domínguez Navarro, *50 Años de una vida* (Havana: Instituto Cubano del Libro, 1971), 81–82.

7. Federación Nacional de Asociaciones Femeninas (FNAF), *Memoria, del Primer Congreso Nacional de Mujeres, Abril 1–7, 1923* (Havana: n.p.), 19–21.

8. Ibid.

9. Dulce María Borrero de Luján, "La mujer y la degeneración de la sociedad cubana," *Revista Bimestre Cubana* 13: 120–27.

10. FNAF, *Primer Congreso,* 240–44, 431–41.

11. Ibid., 316–30.

12. Ibid., 338–44.

13. Ibid., 368–70.

14. In Cuba there were several degrees of legitimacy. Legitimate children were those children born to a married couple; natural children were those who issued from parents neither of whom was married; illegitimate children were the issue of two people, at least one of whom was married to a third person. In the latter case, the child had no right to shelter, protection, recognition, or inheritance of the married partner.

15. Ibid., 275–82.

16. FNAF, *Primer Congreso,* 474.

17. FNAF, *Memoria del Segundo Congreso Nacional de Mujeres, Abril 12–18, 1925* (Havana: n.p.), 279–89.

18. FNAF, *Segundo Congreso,* 284.

19. See Ofelia Domínguez Navarro, letters from Hortensia Lamar dated March 29, 1927, and May 21, 1927. Correspondencia dirigida a Ofelia Domínguez Navarro por diversas personas, 1920–62, y sin fecha, Archivo Nacional, caja 673, no. 1.

20. For newspaper coverage on this incident, see *Heraldo de Cuba,* April 17, 1925; Mariblanca Sabas Alomá, "Paso a las izquierdas," *La Prensa,* April 19, 1925; *El Sol, Hoy, El Fígaro,* and *Diario de la Marina,* April 17–25, 1925.

21. For the resolutions to the Second National Congress, see FNAF, *Segundo Congreso,* 646–48.

22. Domínguez, *50 Años de una Vida,* 84.

23. The CNOC, the Directorio Estudiantíl Universitario, and members of such intellectual associations as the Grupo Minorista all understood that their membership was on lists of disagreeables who were subject to arrest, incarceration, exile, and disappearance.

24. Alianza Nacional Feminista, *Vigésimo aniversario* (Havana: n.p., 1948), 5.

25. Rosa del Bosque, "Rumores del feminismo militante: La Conferencia Interamericana de Mujeras," *La Mujer* 1, no. 10 (March 15, 1930), 3.

26. Ofelia Domínguez Navarro came from the lower-middle class; she studied to be a lawyer and became a member of the intelligentsia.

27. Unión Laborista de Mujeres, *Informe de la Secretaria* (Havana: n.p., 1932). Ofelia Domínguez Navarro, *A las sufragistas y a la opinión pública* (Havana: Central Committee of the Unión Laborista de Mujeres, 1932).

28. The founding membership included María Collado, Rosario Sigarroa, Ana María González viuda de Arroyo, Frances Forcada viuda de Barba, Florinda Castro viuda de Ochotorena, Mina Oltmans, Clemencia Medina de Ramírez Ross, Aurora Blanco, María Luisa Pellón de Cortes, Consuelo Nieto, Juana Diez de Molinet, Paula Núñez, Petronila Stincer de Soto, Petrona Pérez, Isolina Dobal, Mercedes Parez de González, Juana Alonso Amor, María Pepa Martínez, Rosita Añon, and Petra Segoviano.

29. María Collado wrote many articles in *La Mujer* exposing firms that mistreated their female employees, and she refuted the more radical feminists on their complaints about violations in the Woolworth's stores (called el Ten-Cent). The reports she submitted to the Ministry of Agriculture and Industry are in her archival collection. Expediente que contiene informes rendidos por María Collado mientras desempeño el cargo del trabajo de la mujer en la Secretario de Agricultura Comercio y Trabajo. February 1926 to August 1933. Donativos y Remisiones, caja 662, no. 24.

Chapter 4

1. To test my hypothesis that feminist leaders came from the privileged classes and that their social status affected their objectives for the Cuban feminist movement, I conducted a survey that collected biographical data about their position in society. The survey consisted of twenty-six questions that indicated marital status, number of children, levels of education, profession, husband's and father's occupations, number of servants, political contacts, and organization memberships. I selected sixteen women who had living relatives both in Cuba and the United States and who represented the leadership in five feminist organizations (the Club Femenino, the Alianza Nacional Feminista, the Partido Demócrata Sufragista, the Lyceum Lawn and Tennis Club, and the Unión Laborista de Mujeres). Two other subjects were feminist writers who were not affiliated with the organizations. Although sixteen leaders cannot represent the entire membership of feminist organizations, they indicate the statuses of leaders. To verfiy the responses given to me by informants, I consulted social directories, obituaries, and homages for corroborating information. All of the women were long-time activists and therefore were influential in shaping the objectives of the Cuban feminist movement.

Class designations follow characteristics of social groups. The upper class, for example, consisted of landholders, major merchants, bankers, and urban landlords. Members of the middle class owned their own homes or rented pleasant apartments and were trained and employed as well-paid professionals such as doctors, professors, pharmacists, or writers. Both groups had access to political authorities through family connections or friendship. None were hourly workers without skills, members of the informal work force, or even members of syndicates. Those who were unemployed did not have to work; they were either independently wealthy or their husbands or families supported them.

2. My estimate is made by adding together the annual membership lists of the Lyceum Lawn and Tennis Club, the Alianza Nacional Feminista, the Club Femenino de Cuba, the Unión Laborista de Mujeres, the Partido Demócrata Sufragista, and the Partido Nacional Sufragista and determining an annual average. Membership in feminist organizations was highest in 1932 when 947 were registered in these organizations. The figure 1,000 allows for the possibility of membership in independent provincial or municipal organizations for which there is no information. It also includes unaffiliated feminist intellectuals. I counted only once the women who belonged to more than one organization.

3. Because consensual union was given a legal status under the 1940 constitution, the census could no longer identify the nature of matrimonial unions.

4. Cuba, Dirección General del Censo, *Census of the Republic of Cuba* (Havana: Maza, Arroyo y Caso, 1912), 385.

5. Cuba, Dirección General del Censo, *Informe general del censo de 1943* (Havana: P. Fernández, 1945), 998.

6. Some feminists had more than one career. One woman, for instance, was a lawyer and a diplomat.

7. Although my survey did not ask about relatives in the extended family who held public office, a number of my informants pointed out that cousins and uncles of the feminists were also politicians, and one of the feminists had President Zayas in attendance at her wedding.

Chapter 5

1. Luz Gay established the journal *La revista blanca*. Laura G. de Zayas Bazan was a correspondent for many foreign newspapers, and she later published in *El Fígaro, Bohemia, Cuba y América,* and *Letras*. For women, she presented her revolutionary appeals as well as household advice in *La mujer y la casa*. Rosa Trujillo from Güines established a literary magazine, *Letras Güineras,* which espoused the philosophies of self-rule. Rosario Sigarroa, a patriot and and advocate of women's rights, founded *Cuba Libre*.

2. María Urzais of Guanabacoa founded *La Golondrina,* María Radelat developed *Grafos,* an art review, and Isabel Margarita Ortex produced *Vanidades,* one of the leading women's magazines with reputable social commentary. The Catholic journal *La crónica religiosa* that favored conservative principles was founded by the religious writer Angela López Récio.

3. See *La Mujer* of the Partido Demócrata Sufragista, 1929–50; *La Mujer*

Moderna of the Club Femenino de Cuba, 1925–40; *Lyceum* of the Lyceum Lawn and Tennis Club, 1936–39 and 1949–58; *Boletín* of the Alianza Nacional Feminista, 1931–33; *El Sufragista* of the Partido Nacional Sufragista, 1922–34; *Aspiraciones* of the Asociación Femenina de Camagüey, 1912–18.

4. *Heraldo de Cuba*, March 19, 1923, 1.

5. Jorge Mañach, "Nuestros Colaboradores los Minoristas," *Social*; "Los minoristas sabáticos escuchan el gran Titta," *Social*, February 24, 1924, 24–27.

6. During the colonial period Cuban commentary appeared in *La Revista Bimestre* (1830), *La Revista Cubana* (1885), *Hojas Literarias* (1891), and *La Habana Elegante* (1849–1905). At the beginning of the twentieth century, positivist journals such as *Arpas cubanas* and *Cuba Contemporánea* invited provocative essays.

7. *Bohemia*, *Carteles*, and *Vanidades* were Cuba's most popularly read journals.

8. For an excellent treatment of the Grupo Minorista, see Ana Cairo, *El Grupo Minorista y su tiempo* (Havana: Editorial de Ciencias Sociales, 1978).

9. See Mariblanca Sabas Alomá, *Carteles*, 1927–29; Ofelia Rodríguez Acosta, *Bohemia*, 1929–32. Ofelia Domínguez Navarro also wrote for journals and magazines, but she made her living as a lawyer, and she did not have a regular column with a single publication. She was a visiting editor for socialist papers, however, when the regular publishers were in jail. Her essays appeared in *El País*, *El Mundo*, *Carteles*, *Bohemia*, *Villaclara*, *El Cubano Libre*, *La Palabra* (a clandestine communist paper), *Mediodía*, and *Notícias de Hoy*. She also had regular radio programs on station CMO, Radio Salas, the Ministry of Education station, and Mil Diez.

10. Literary analysts have disregarded Sabas Alomá's work to the extent that she should be called the most forgotten Minorista.

11. Mañach, "Los minoristas," 24–27.

12. A collection of Sabas Alomá's columns on feminism was published in *Feminismo: Cuestiones sociales—Crítica Literaria* (Havana: Editorial "Hermes," 1930).

13. Ibid., 31–32.

14. Ibid.

15. Ibid., 35.

16. Ibid., 48.

17. Ibid., 80.

18. Ibid., 53.

19. Ibid., 53–54.

20. Ibid., 37.

21. Ibid., 118.

22. Ibid., 38.

23. Ibid., 56.

24. *Evocaciones* (Havana: Graphical Arts, 1922). *Apuntes de mi viaje a Isla de Pinos* (Havana: Montiel, 1926). *El triunfo de la débil presa* (Havana:

Rambla, Bouza, 1926). *La vida manda* (Madrid: Biblioteca Rubén Darío, 1929). *Dolientes* (Havana: Editorial "Hermes," 1931). *En la noche del mundo* (Havana: La Verónica, 1940). *Europa era así* (México: Ediciones Botas, 1941). *Sonata interumpida* (México: Ediciones Minerva, 1943). *La dama de arcón* (México: Ediciones Estela, 1949). *Hágase la luz* (México: Ediciones Estela, 1953).

25. Ofelia Rodríguez Acosta, *La tragedia social de la mujer* (Havana: Editorial Genesis, 1932).

26. "Anticipándonos a la vida futura," *Bohemia* 22, no. 42 (October 19, 1930), 13.

27. "La responsabilidad personal," *Bohemia* 23, no. 3 (March 15, 1931), 9.

28. "Los deberes de la mujer para con el hombre," *Bohemia* 22, no. 44 (November 2, 1930), 17.

29. Ofelia Rodríguez Acosta, *La vida manda,* 85.

30. "Rebasando el feminismo," *Bohemia* 23, no. 22 (September 27, 1931): 24.

31. María Collado's bibliography includes: *Havana: Comité central pro-estatua Emilia de Cordoba* (Havana: Imprenta Caraso, 1928). Archival and library holdings of her work in Cuba are extensive. A full run of *La Mujer* can be found in the José Martí National Library. María Collado donated her vast collection of feminist materials to the national archives. Found under her name in the donations and gifts nomenclature, her collection contains memorabilia from women's congresses and club functions, letters, notes on a book about Cuban women, and her reports to the Department of Agriculture on the working conditions of women.

32. "La mujer," *La Mujer* 1, no. 1 (April 4, 1929): 2.

33. María Collado, "Palpitaciones del feminismo militante" *La Mujer* 1, no. 14 (May 31, 1930): 9.

34. Ibid.

35. Collado, "Palpitaciones del feminismo militante," *La Mujer* 1, no. 12 (April 15, 1930): 6–7. And María Collado, "Habla la directora: Las feministas pasadas," *La Mujer* 1, no. 14 (May 31, 1930): 1.

36. María Collado, "Habla la directora: Políticas, no; revolucionarias, sí," *La Mujer* 2, no. 38 (July 1, 1931): 1.

37. María Collado, "Datos de nuestro archivo," *La Mujer* 1, no. 14 (May 31, 1930): 6.

38. María Collado, "Reparémonos para el 1 de noviembre," *La Mujer* 1, no. 8 (January 30, 1930): 1–2.

39. Orquidea [pseud.], "Cartas para todos," *Revista Protectora de la Mujer* (June 25, 1915). Original essay found in the Archivo Nacional, Donativos y Remisiones, caja 661, no. 7.

40. María Collado, "Expediente que contiene informes rendidos por María Collado mientres desempeño el cargo del trabajo de la mujer en la Secretaria De Agricultura, Comercio y Trabajo," February 1926 to August 1933, Donativos y Remisiones, caja 662, no. 24.

Chapter 6

1. Archivo Nacional, Fondo Especial, legajo 3, no. 49.

2. On May 13, 1927, the London police took over the offices of the Soviet consulate and claimed to have discovered documents that linked Soviet diplomats with international anti-imperialist organizations. Britain immediately broke diplomatic relations with the Soviet Union. In Latin America, right-wing governments began arresting or threatening leftists for being a part of the "proceso comunista," or creeping communism.

3. Gerardo Machado, *Acuerdos del Congreso de la República de Cuba sobre reforma de la constitución y manifiesto del honorable señor Presidente General Gerardo Machado y Morales al país* (Havana: n.p., 1927), 26–28.

4. *Diario de Sesiones de la Camara Cubana,* May 9, 1928, 7.

5. Domínguez Navarro, *50 Años,* 116.

6. *Gaceta Oficial,* Extraordinary Edition, May 11, 1928.

7. Ofelia Domínguez Navarro remembered the members as: Pilar Jorge de Tella, Hortensia Lamar, Dulce María Borrero de Luján, María Ignacia Matheu, María Luisa Julio de Lara, Veneranda Martínez, Rosa Pastora Leclerc, Josefina Pedroso, Rosario Guillaume, and Ofelia Domínguez Navarro.

8. Roberto Padron Larrazábal, *Manifiestos de Cuba* (Havana: Editorial Lex, 1952), 148.

9. The full contents of the speech can be found in Domínguez Navarro's *Cinquenta Años,* 126–29. An open letter from the Alianza to President Machado asking for his support of the vote can be found in the "Alianza Nacional Feminista: Una Carta Abierta al Presidente Machado," *La Mujer* 1, no. 5 (December 15, 1929): 4 and 16.

10. Mariblanca Sabas Alomá, "Efectivamente, Sra. Chapman Catt . . . ," *Feminismo* (Havana: Editorial "Hermes"), 165–70.

11. "Lutgarida Machado," *La Mujer* 1, no. 3 (October 28, 1929): n.p.; *La Mujer* 1, no. 9 (February 29, 1930): front cover; *La Mujer* 1, no. 7 (January 30, 1930): 3.

12. María Collado, "Cordialidad femenina," *La Mujer* 1, no. 3 (October 28, 1929): 7; and "Políticos de talla: Ldo. Antonio Bravo y Corresos, Senador por Oriente," *La Mujer* 1, no. 12 (April 15, 1930): 3.

13. María Collado, "Habla la directora: El momento es decisivo," *La Mujer* 1, no. 19 (August 15, 1930): 1.

14. The ABC was a secret resistance group that was established to violently oppose Machado's *porra.* Organized in cells, much like communist revolutionary groups, the ABC attacked members of the police as well as Machado supporters. The ABC held to no particular political ideology, and its membership consisted mainly of middle-class and professional people. After the defeat of Machado, the ABC dissolved itself.

15. Alianza Nacional Feminista, *Vigésimo aniversario* (Havana: n.p., 1948), 17.

16. Hortensia Lamar, "Sumner Welles, liberador romántico," *Bohemia* 25, no. 42 (December 10, 1933): 8.

17. Alianza, *Vigésimo aniversario*, 17, and María Collado, "Habla la directora: Acotaciones del momenta actual," *La Mujer* 2, no. 25 (November 30, 1930): 29.

18. Ofelia Domínguez Navarro, "A las sufragistas y a la opinión pública," n.p., 1.

19. María Collado, "No estamos de acuerdo," *La Mujer* 2, no. 26 (December 15, 1930): 3. Also in *Essays by María Collado,* Archivo Nacional, Donativos y Remisiones, caja 661, doc. 7.

20. Rafael García Barcena, "Rafael Trejo," *Bohemia* 25, no. 46 (November 16, 1930): 19.

21. *El Mundo* 1, (October 2, 1930). See also a full description of women's involvement in the Trejo incident in Pablo de la Torriente Brau's "Las mujeres contra Machado," *Pluma en ristre* (Havana: Ministerio de educación, Dirección de Cultura, 1949), 32.

22. Ofelia Rodríguez Acosta, "El homenaje a Rafael Trejo," *Bohemia* 22, no. 45 (November 19, 1930): 17.

23. "La historia de un homenaje," *Bohemia* 25, no. 46 (November 16, 1930): 19.

24. María Collado, "La hora sombria," *La Mujer* 2, no. 22 (October 10, 1930): 3.

25. Domínguez, *50 Años*, 177.

26. Ibid., 193.

27. Collado, "Habla la directora: Acotaciones del momento actual," *La Mujer* 2, no. 25 (November 30, 1930), 1.

28. Piedad de la Maza. Unpublished diary that ran from 1926 to 1948, n.p.

29. Domínguez, *50 Años*, 205.

30. Ibid.

31. Ibid.

32. Domínguez, *50 Años*, 11 and 210.

33. "La mujer opina," *Bohemia* 23, nos. 1 and 2 (January 4 and January 11, 1931): 26–28 and 26–27, respectively. Also "Debe concederse el voto a la mujer," *Bohemia* 24, no. 24 (June 12, 1932): 36–38.

34. "El voto a la mujer," *Bohemia* 24, no. 21 (May 15, 1932): 21.

35. Alianza, *Vigésimo aniversario*, 18.

36. Alianza, *Vigésimo aniversario*, 19.

37. "Discurso en pro del sufrágio universal," *Heraldo de Cuba* (July 14, 1933): 1–5.

38. Dr. Manuel Dorta Duque, a professor of law at the University of Havana and a member of the Committee in Opposition, confirmed this report while speaking to the Lyceum Lawn and Tennis Club.

39. "Se entrevisitaran hoy los políticos con Mr. Sumner Welles," *Heraldo de Cuba* (July 14, 1933): 1–5.

40. Alianza, *Vigésimo aniversario*, 19.
41. *Gaceta Oficial*, Extraordinary Edition, No. 10, February 3, 1934.
42. Alianza, *Vigésimo aniversario*, 20.
43. The electoral code of the Constitution was rewritten and reaffirmed on a number of occasions between 1934 and 1936. The June 11, 1935, law superseded the constitutional law of February 3, 1934, and Electoral Code No. 663 of October 5, 1934, brought the law more into line with the Constitution's intent. Article 3 of that law corresponded exactly to Article 38 of the constitution. Finally, a new electoral code, adopted by Decree-Law 54 of July 3, 1935, determined the conditions under which all Cubans could vote.
44. *Gaceta Oficial*, Extraordinary Edition, No. 10, February 3, 1934.
45. Ofelia Domínguez Navarro, "El desenvolvimiento político-social de la mujer en Cuba," *Bohemia* 26, no. 30 (August 26, 1934): 74.

Chapter 7

1. For a detailed description of a country school setting during the 1910s, see Domínguez, *50 Años*, 35–50.
2. Commission on Cuban Affairs, 130–40.
3. Manuel Góngora Echenique, "En la universidad," *Bohemia* 19, no. 29 (July 17, 1927): 19.
4. Medardo Vitier, "En torno a la enseñanza en Cuba durante la República," *Diario de la Marina, Siglo y Cuarto* (Havana: Diario de la Marina, 1955), 78.
5. Elena Mederos de González, "Acción Social," *Lyceum* 3–4 nos. 9 and 10 (June 1938–39): 52–55.
6. Alianza, *Vigésimo aniversario*, 27 and 23; and Isabel Margarita Ordex, "El camino recorrido por la mujer cubana en medio siglo de República," *Carteles* (May 18, 1952): 191.
7. Mirta Aguirre, *Influencia de la mujer en Iberoamérica* (Havana: Imprenta P. Fernández, 1947), 86.
8. *DSS*, January 10, 1927, 3.
9. *Gaceta Oficial*, April 7, 1913.
10. *Gaceta Oficial*, January 10, 1934.
11. Alianza, *Vigésimo aniversario*, 34–35.
12. María Teresa Bernal, "Feminismo y feminidad," *Bohemia* 22, no. 37 (September 14, 1930): 11.
13. Graziella Barinaga y Ponce de León, *El feminismo y el hogar, conference de propaganda de la Alianza Nacional Feminista, 25 de abril, 1930* (Havana: Talleres Tipográfricos Carasa, 1931), 30.
14. Ofelia Rodríguez Acosta, "La maternidad transcendente," *Bohemia* 23, no. 26 (October 25, 1931): 11.
15. María Collado, "Habla la directora: La mujer no debe ser juzgada por su fortuna, sino por su conducta," *La Mujer* 1, no. 20 (August 30, 1930): 1.

16. Mariblanca Sabas Alomá, "Un año de feminismo," *Social* 14 (January 1929): 26 and 74. Unión Laborista de Mujeres, *Unión Laborista de Mujeres* (Havana: Talleres Tipográficos Carasa, 1931), 30.

17. Founders were: Matilde Gobel de Pelayo, Aguida Malpica de Rosell, Belen González de Demestre, Pepa Zaldo de Zaxon, and Manuela Picabia de Plá.

18. Women-run charity organizations included: Asociación Católicas Cubanas, Order of the Eastern Star, Sociedad Humanitaria, Damas Isabelinas, and Liga de Mujeres. The Sisters of Charity ran orphanages for girls and exemplified the Church's provision for the poor.

19. Lowry Nelson, "The Social Class Structure," in *Background to Revolution,* edited by Robert Freeman Smith (New York: Alfred A. Knopf, 1966), 199.

20. *Havana Post,* September 7, 1913, sec. 2, 11.

21. Jorge I. Domínguez, *Cuba: Order and Revolution* (Cambridge: Belknap Press, 1978), 27. While Domínguez admits that the table of real wages for 1903 to 1933 is imprecise, it nevertheless demonstrates approximate fluctuation of real wages during the first thirty years of the Republic.

22. Alianza, *Vigésimo aniversario,* 32.

23. Anita Aroyo, "Presencia de la mujer en la vida cubana," *Diario de la Marina: Siglo y cuarto* (Havana: Diario de la Marina, 1955), 192–99.

24. Elena Mederos de González, "El Lyceum y su mundo interior," *Revista Lyceum* 11 (February, 1954): 41 and 44.

25. Interviews with Elena Mederos de González, Washington, D.C., September, 1980.

26. Ofelia Domínguez Navarro, *De seis a seis* (México: 1937). Edelmira González, *Estampas de la carcel* (Havana: n.p., n.d.).

27. "Acción Social," *Lyceum* 2, no. 8 (December 1937): 53–55.

28. In 1938 Dra. García Tudurí de Coya, a member of the Lyceum, performed that duty.

Chapter 8

1. For discussions of men's public sexual domination of women in Spain and Latin America, see: Julian Pitt-Rivers, *Honor and Shame: The Values of Mediterranean Society* (Chicago: University of Chicago Press, 1966); Octavio Paz, *Labyrinth of Solitude* (New York: Grove Press, 1985); and Glen Caudill Dealy, *The Public Man* (Amherst: University of Massachusetts Press, 1977).

2. Conversations with Donna Guy, director of the Latin American Studies Center, University of Arizona, informed some of this analysis. Her forthcoming book, *Sex and Danger in Buenos Aires: Prostitution, Family, and the Nation* (Lincoln: University of Nebraska Press), contains arguments that link social control and statecraft with the direction of family life and moral standards in early twentieth-century Buenos Aires.

3. Commission on Cuban Affairs, *Problems of the New Cuba* (New York: Foreign Policy Association, 1935), 87.

4. República de Cuba. *Código Penal vigente en la República de Cuba* (Havana: Casa Editora, Librería e Imprenta "La Moderna Poesía," 1906), pp.191–96.

5. Rosa Anders, "Igualdad en la legislación sobre el adulterio," in FNAC, *Primer Congreso,* 337–44.

6. In fact, in 1914 seventeen men were tried for killing their wives, and only one was sentenced. In 1915 twenty-one men were tried, and three were sentenced. There is no way to know how many men killed their wives for committing adultery and were not brought to trial. Statistics come from República de Cuba, Secretaria de Justicia, *Anuario de estadística judicial y penitenciaria, Bienio de 1914–1915* (Havana: Imprenta "La Propagandista", 1917), xiii and xx.

7. *Anuario de estadística judicial,* 341.

8. Leonor Martínez de Cervera, "¿Hasta cuándo?" *La Mujer* 1, no. 10 (March 15, 1930): 9.

9. Sabas Alomá, *Feminismo,* 60, 75.

10. Manuel Secades, *Tesis, leído el día de mayo, 1902, en la Universidad de la Habana* (Havana: Tipográfia de "El Fígaro," 1903). In the introduction no less then twenty-two jurists, legislators, and law professors wrote their responses to Dr. Secades's thesis. The names were well known: Dr. Ricardo Dolz, Ldo. Rafael Cruz Pérez, Ldo. José María Gálvez, Ldo. Manuel Sanguily, Dr. Evelio Rodríguez Lendian, Ldo. Fernándo de Freyre Andrade, Dr. Leopoldo Cancio, Ldo. Gaston Mora, Dr. Ignacio Remírez, Ldo. Raimundo Cabrera, Ldo. Jesús Romeu, Dr. Luis Estévez y Romero, Ldo. Cristóbal de la Guardia, Dr. Antonio L. Valverde, Ldo. Rafael Montoro, Ldo. Isidoro Corzo y Príncipe, Ldo. Manuel S. Pichardo, Dr. Antonio Gonzalo Pérez, Dr. Antonio S. de Bustamante, Ldo. Félix Iznaga, Dr. A. González Lanuza, and Ldo. Manuel Rafael Angulo.

11. Secades, *Tesis,* 138.

12. Ibid.

13. Ibid., 154–55.

14. Ibid., 201.

15. Emilio Roig de Leuchsenring, "El delito en adulterio debe desaparecer de nuestro Código Penal" *Carteles* 9, no. 9 (September 28, 1926): 16. "Un asesinato que la ley provoca y sanciona," *Carteles* 9 no. 10 (May 7, 1926): 10. "Sobre el divorcio: Lo que es hoy en Cuba; lo que debe ser," *Carteles* 9, no. 13 (March 28, 1926): 16. "¿Casarse para descasarse?" *Carteles* 15, no. 8 (February 23, 1930): 30.

16. For more statistical details regarding the cause for divorce brought by women and men and the incidence of divorce brought by women and men, see my article "In the Defense of Motherhood," 1–32.

17. Sabas Alomá, *Feminismo,* 93.

18. Ibid., 84.

19. Emilio Roig de Leuchsenring, "Ley de divorcio . . . antidivorcio," *Carteles* 15, no. 7 (February 16, 1930): 18; and "Uniones libres, y los hijos, todos iguales ante la ley," *Carteles* 15, no. 24 (June 15, 1930): 34 and 46.

20. Secades, *Tesis,* 11.

21. Ibid., 209.

22. Alianza, *Vigésimo aniversario,* 29.

23. María Collado, "Habla la directora: La primera cocina gratuita de La Liga Nacional Contra Tuberculosis Infantil," *La Mujer* 2, no. 39 (August 1, 1931): 1; and "La exposición de labores en el colegio 'María Corominas,'" *La Mujer* 1, no. 18 (July 30, 1930): 3.

24. *Diario de Sesiones de la Camara Cubana,* May 21, 1928, 13–24.

25. "Congreso Nacional Femenino," *Lyceum* 3, nos. 11 and 12 (September–December 1938): 74–77. Piedad Maza, "La tragedia de la juventud cubana," *Lyceum* 3, no. 13 (January–March 1939): 18–26.

26. *Diario de Sesiones del Congreso Constituyente,* May 18, 1940, 6.

27. Ibid., 9.

28. Ibid., 11.

29. *Diario de Sesiones de la Convención Constitucional,* May 18, 1940, 20.

30. Interview with Eusebio Mujal, August 4, 1981.

31. Ibid.

32. *Diario de Sesiones del Congreso Constituyente* May 20, 1940, 20.

Chapter 9

1. Antonio Bravo Correoso, "Debe ser socialista-conservadora," *Bohemia* 30, no. 23 (June 5, 1938): 4.

2. Extrapolated from: U.S. War Department, *Report on the Census of Cuba, 1899* (Washington, D.C.: Government Printing Office, 1900), 16; and Rebública de Cuba, *Informe general del censo de 1953* (Havana: Fernández, 1953).

3. Medardo Vitier, "La vida de la mujer cubana en su relación con la historia de Cuba," *Cuba Contemporánea* 14 (May–August 1917): 335.

4. Dulce María Borrero de Luján, "Protección de la madre," *Cuba Contemporánea,* 13, no. 38 (May 1925): 14.

5. Alianza, *Vigesimo aniversario,* 14.

6. Eusebio Mujal, letter listing female representation in the CTC.

7. Jean Stubbs, *Tobacco on the Periphery: A Case Study in Cuban Labour History, 1860–1958* (New York: Cambridge University Press, 1985), 93.

8. Republic of Cuba, "Law Protecting the Woman Worker," *Gaceta Oficial,* November 19, 1925, 12,842.

9. Her speeches at the Alianza appeared in *El Cubano Libre,* a radical newspaper.

10. Domínguez, *50 Años*, 148–50.

11. Sabas Alomá, *Feminismo*, 171–77.

12. María Collado, "Justicia para la mujer que trabaja, sí: Difamación injusta para los que le dan empleo, no," *La Mujer* 1, no. 3 (October 28, 1929): n.p.

13. Sabas Alomá, *Feminismo*, 171–78.

14. Stubbs, *Tobacco*, 93.

15. Ofelia Rodríguez Acosta.

16. *DSS*, April 25, 1917, 7.

17. Dulce María Borrero de Luján, "Protección de la madre," in FNAF, *Primer Congreso*, 241.

18. Ibid.

19. Ofelia Rodríguez Acosta, "El derecho materno," *Bohemia* 30, no. 17 (May 6, 1938): 17.

20. "El hospital de maternidad," *Bohemia* 30, no. 33 (August 14, 1938): 41.

21. Republic of Cuba, "Maternity Law, 1934," *Gaceta Oficial* (December 28, 1934): 11,456. Decree-Laws 405 of November 12, 1935, and 503 of January 8, 1936, amended the first decree-law, adding to the regulatory legislation only.

22. Eugenio Flamand Montero, *Disposiciones legales Cuaderno No. 2 sobre maternidad obrera*, (Havana: El Lápiz Rojo, 1937), 1–10.

23. Osvaldo Valdés de la Paz, "36 mil madres obreras son amparadas," *El País* (March 6, 1940): 3.

24. Interamerican Commission of Women, *Report on the Legal Status of Women* (Washington, D.C.: Organization of American States, 1957), 14.

25. Alianza Nacional Feminista, *XX Aniversario de la Alianza Nacional Feminista* (Havana: n.p.), 24–25.

26. *Gaceta Oficial*, October 19, 1934, 2.

27. Ibid.

28. *Gaceta Oficial*, April 1, 1937, 1.

29. Partido Comunista de Cuba, *Bases para el proyecto de constitución* (Havana: Partido Unitario Revolucionario, 1939). Blas Roca, *Por la igualdad de todos los cubanos, conferencia pronunciado en los salones del Club "Atenas," March 27, 1939* (Havana: Ediciones Socialist, 1939). Francisco Calderio [Blas Roca], *El pueblo y la nueva constitución, informe ante la reunión plenaria del Comité Ejecutivo Nacional de la Unión Revolucionaria Comunista, June 23, 1940* (Havana: Ediciones Sociales, 1940).

30. Partido de Acción Republicana, *Programa constitucional acordado y aprobado por la Asamblea Nacional en su sesión del día 24 de agosto de 1939* (Havana: Molina, 1939).

31. *DSCC*, May 26, 1940, 8.

32. Ibid., June 3, 1940, 11. Diario de Sesiones del Congreso Constituyente.

33. Ibid., 7.

34. Mariblanca Sabas Alomá, "Atayala: Bestias de carga," *El avance criollo* (March 29, 1941): 3.

35. Mariblanca Sabas Alomá, "Atayala: Aspectos de la lucha feminista," *El avance criollo* (March 3, 1941): 3.
36. Cubano de Investigaciones Económicas, *A Study on Cuba* (Coral Gables, Fla.: University of Miami Press, 1965), 431.

Chapter 10

1. Married women had no legal personality separate from their husbands'. They lost control of their own property upon marriage, husbands governed family matters, both financial and personal, and male authority was inviolate.
2. Sabas Alomá, *Feminismo*, 54.
3. Rodríguez Acosta, "¿Cúya es la culpa?" 11, 16, 70.
4. Ricardo Sarabosa, "El código civil ante el Congreso Jurídico," *Cuba Contemporánea* 2 (May–August, 1916): 10.
5. Ibid.
6. Ibid., 6.
7. Interamerican Commission on Women, *Reseña histórica sobre reconocimiento de los derechos políticos a la mujer de América* (Washington, D.C.: Pan American Union, 1965), 3–4.
8. *Interamerican Conference for Maintenance of Peace, Final Act,* December 1936 (Washington, D.C.: Pan American Union).
9. Pan American Union, Eighth Assembly, Lima, Peru, "Lima Declaration in Favor of Women's Rights Resolution XX" Washington, D.C.: n.p., 1939.
10. Full bill outlined in *DSS,* November 8, 1927, 20–21.
11. A dictamen is a legal opinion rendered by a legal body (in this case a constitutional assembly) that has juridical weight and influences court rulings. It is not a law, however, and it can be overruled by laws that it contradicts.
12. Lyceum Lawn and Tennis Club, "Congreso nacional feminismo," *Lyceum* 3, nos. 11 and 12 (September–December 1938), 74–77.
13. Gustavo Gutiérrez Sánchez, *Constitución de la República de Cuba* (Havana: Editorial Lex, 1941), 37.
14. Eighty-one delegates went to the assembly, forty-four of them from the opposition block led by ex-presidents Ramón Grau San Martín, Mario G. Menocal, and Miguel Mariano Gómez along with Joaquín Martínez Sáenz. These forty-four delegates came from the following political parties: eighteen delegates belonged to the Partido Revolucionario Cubano, a left-wing group not to be confused with the Communist Party; seventeen delegates were from the Partido Demócrata Republicano, a conservative party; six were from the Partido Acción Republicana; and four were from the ABC. The Social Democratic faction led by Colonel Fulgencio Batista elected thirty-seven delegates whose members belonged to the following

political parties: seventeen to the Liberal Party, nine to the Partido Unión Nacionalista, six to the Fusión Unión Revolucionaria-Comunista, three to the Conjunto Nacional Democrático, and one to the Partido Nacional Revolucionario. Taken from Gutiérrez Sánchez, *Constitución,* 65.

15. Lawyers, 31; doctors, 14; landowners, 5; ranchers, 2; businessmen, 3; retired military, 1; ex-military, 1; journalists, 4; solicitors, 2; dentist, 1; refinery owners, 2; industrialist, 1; cattle rancher, 1; pharmacist, 1; farmer, 1; doctors of science, 2; architect, 1; engineers, 2; notary publics, 2; brick mason, 1; copper miner, 1; teacher, 1; shop worker, 1; cobbler, 1. Taken from Gutiérrez Sánchez, *Constitución,* 66.

16. Nor, for that matter, did the male delegates represent the average male population in terms of social or economic position or interests.

17. *Convención Constituyente* 1, no. 26 (April 27, 1940): 21.

18. Ibid., 23.

19. Ibid., 26.

20. *Convención Constituyente* 1, no. 27 (May 2, 1940): 14–16.

Bibliography

Primary Sources: Official Documents

One of the first indications that a study on the legal status of Cuban women was feasible was the wealth of government records in the United States dating from 1902 through 1958. The Library of Congress is the main repository for Cuban documents with materials ranging from a nearly complete set of the congressional debates, complete records of the laws, deliberations of the 1940 constitutional assembly, speeches of General Gerardo Machado encouraging the passage of the 1927 constitution, microfilmed newspapers and magazines, and a complete set of Cuban censuses. The Organization of American States Library, and especially the Office of the Interamerican Commission of Women, has numerous studies on the legal, economic, and work statuses of women, which provide comparisons of women throughout Latin America. Other government agencies such as the U.S. Department of Labor and international bodies such as the United Nations also conducted special reports on women.

Congressional Debates

A full collection of the Cuban congressional debates is shared by a number of U.S. libraries with the majority deposited in the Library of Congress. The *Diario de Sesiones de la Cámara* along with an index for promulgated laws is complete and in the Library of Congress. The Hoover Library and the Library of Congress share the volumes for the *Diario de Sesiones del Senado* with a volume spread as follows—Library of Congress: 1–35, 43–52, 54, 57–; Hoover Library: 36–42, 53, 55–56. (One drawback to using the congressional debates is that there is no index of the contents of daily floor debates.)

The Organization of American States Documents

The Pan American Union established the Interamerican Women's Commission in 1928. Since then the commission has both lobbied for and written studies on the legal and economic statuses of women in Latin America. The Cuban delegation was particularly active in these efforts before 1958, which resulted in rich materials on Cuba. The Organization of American States Library contains all records from the commission as well as records of the general assembly proceedings affecting women. The library also contains other precious documents such as summaries of the national Cuban's women's congresses, and it contains political manifestos of the Unión

Laborista de Mujeres. Additionally, the Pan American Union *Bulletin* offered occasional articles on women in Cuba.

Laws and Statutes

The *Gaceta Oficial* announced legal decrees to attorneys and the general public. The date of publication in the *Gaceta* and not the date of legal passage marked the moment when the law took effect. Milo Borges's indexing of Cuban law aids in finding specific legislation in the *Gaceta,* which makes it the most reliable source of the law. In time, of course, various agencies or legal authors compiled laws with interpretations on a particular subject. Most legal works can be found in the Hispanic Law Division of the Library of Congress.

Cuban Censuses

Beginning with the North American Census of Cuba in 1899, Cuban censuses were comprehensive and fairly sophisticated. They include both tabulated and untabulated statistics, which give the researcher raw figures as well as analyzed studies. Units of classification remain fairly constant throughout the first fifty years of the Republic, which enhances the results of long-range studies. Cuban censuses occurred in 1899, 1909, 1919, 1931, 1943, and 1953. The 1931 census contains only information on regional populations and voting districts. Other data can be found in the 1943 census in comparative tables.

Various government departments, also referred to as *secretarías* or *ministerios,* published annual statistical analyses with information about women. The Secretaría de Justicia, for example, reported crimes, convictions, and sentences in a given year, noting which offenders were women and which were men. The Secretaría de Educación and the Casa de Beneficiencias also published helpful statistical studies.

International Agencies

International agencies besides the Pan American Union published material on Cuban women. Their work tended to draw cross-cultural conclusions.

Cannon, Mary. "Women in Latin America: Legal Rights and Restrictions." Women's Bureau, U.S. Department of Labor. Reprinted from the *Women Lawyer's Journal* (Winter, 1948), with revisions.
Commission on Cuban Affairs. *Problems of the New Cuba.* New York: Foreign Policy Association, 1935.
Employment of Women Before and After Childbirth. London: International Labor Organization, Legislative series, November, 1935.

"Protection of Women Workers in Cuba." *Industrial and Labour Information* (Geneva) (June 3, 1935): 325–26; and (June 10, 1935); 362–63.

United Nations Secretary-General. Commission of the Legal and Social Condition of Women. "Condición jurídica de la mujer casada." *Informe.* New York, 1958.

United Nations Department of Economic and Social Affairs. *The Convention on the Political Rights of Women: History and Commentary.* New York, 1955.

U.S. Department of Labor. *Political Status of Women in the Other American Republics.* Washington, D.C.: U.S. Government Printing Office, February 1958.

"Women in Industry," *U.S. Review of Labour Statistics, Monthly Labour Review* 48 (May 1939): 1071–72.

Materials on Women in the Cuban Wars of Independence

Literature on women during the Cuban Wars of Independence is largely biographical and lacks analysis of women's contributions to the struggle against Spain. Two exceptions are Paul Estrade, "Les Clubs Feminins dans le Parti Révolutionaire Cubain (1892–1898)," *Femmes des Amériques* ii, series B. Vol. ii (Toulouse, France: Publication Services of the University of Toulouse–Le Mirail, 1986), 85–105; and Ann Waggoner, "The Role of Women in the Cuban Wars of Independence, 1868–1898," Master's thesis, Arizona State University, 1988. Estrade's is a statistical study of women's work in revolutionary clubs that enumerates which clubs were run by women, their positions within the umbrella organization, and a review of the activities of several of the clubs. Waggoner's thesis, based upon biographical sources, assesses the various activities women undertook during the wars and compares activities of the Ten Years War with those of the War of 1895. Nancy A. Hewitt gave a paper on Cuban patriots in Tampa and Ibor City between 1895 and 1901 at the American Historical Association meeting in Washington, D.C., December 1987. Using club records and newspaper accounts, Hewitt demonstrates how women defied U.S. disapproval of unionization to enunciate the social reform objectives of José Martí and how they raised funds for the independence movement.

Primary documents for women independence activists include:

Borrero de Luján, Dulce María. "Protección a la mujer madre, pobre o abandonada." *El Fígaro* 42, no. 10 (n.d.): 204–7.

Davis, Richard Harding. *Cuba in War Time.* New York: R. H. Russell, 1898.

Dolz, María Luisa. *La liberación de la mujer cubana por la educación.* (Homenaje de la Ciudad de la Habana en el centenario de su nacimiento, 1854–1954.) Havana: Oficina del Historiador de la Ciudad, 1955.

Domínguez Navarro, Ofelia. *Cinquenta años de una vida.* Havana: Instituto Cubana del Libro, 1971.

Flint, Grover. *Marching with Gómez.* Norwood, Mass.: Norwood Press, 1898.

de Merlín, La Condesa. *Mis doce primeros años e historia de Sor Inés.* Havana: Imprenta "El Siglo XX," 1922.

————. *Viaje a La Habana.* Havana: Imprenta El Siglo XX," 1922.

Núñez Jiménez, Antonio. *Cuba as Portrayed in Nineteenth-Century Cigarette Lithographs.* Havana: Ediciones turísticas de Cuba, 1985.

O'Kelly, James J. *The Mambi-Land or Adventures of a Herald Correspondent in Cuba.* Philadelphia: J. B. Lippincott, 1974.

Quesada, Gonzalo de, and Henry Davenport Northrop. *Cuba's Great Struggle for Freedom.* Washington, D.C.: J. R. Jones, 1898.

Torriente, Loló de la. *Testimonio desde dentro.* Havana: Editorial Letras Cubanas, 1985.

Villaverde, Cirilo. *Cecilia Valdés or Angel's Hill.* Translated by Sydney G. Gest. New York: Vantage Press, 1962.

Correspondence

Cabrales, Gonzalo. *Epistolario de Héroes, Cartas y Documentos Históricos.* Havana: "El Siglo XX," 1922.

Lara Mena, María Julia de. *La familia Maceo, Cartas a Elena.* Havana: ALFA, 1945.

Government Documents

Correspondencia Diplomática de la Delegación Cubana en Nueva York Durante la Guerra de Independencia de 1895 a 1898. 5 vols. Havana: Publicaciones del Archivo Nacional de Cuba, 1943.

Documentos para servir a la historia de la Guerra Chiquita. 3 vols. Havana: Publicaciones del Archivo Nacional de Cuba, 1949.

U.S. War Department. Office, Director of Census of Cuba. Lt. Col. J. P. Sanger, inspector-general, director. *Report on the Census of Cuba, 1899.* Washington, D.C.: U.S. Government Printing Office, 1900.

Biographical sources appeared as speeches, books, and articles.

Speeches

García Baylleres, José L. *La mujer cubana en las luchas por la independencia: Concha Agramonte y Boza.* Havana: Imprenta La Milagrosa, 1951.

Homenaje a Bernarda Toro de Gómez. Havana: Imprenta del Ejército, 1932.

Homenaje a la mujer periodista. Havana: Cuaderno no. 9, 1944.

Homenaje a los mártires de 1851. Havana: Administración del Alcalde Sr. Nicolás Castellanos Rivero, 1951.

Marquina y Angulo, Rafael. *La Ciudad de Marta y Marta de la Ciudad.* Havana: Imprenta "El Siglo XX," 1950.

Mesa Rodríguez, Manuel I. *María Luisa Dolz, Educadora y Ciudadana.* Havana: Academia de la Historia de Cuba, Imprenta "El Siglo XX," 1954.

Ponte y Domínguez, Francisco. *La mujer en la Revolución de Cuba.* Havana: Imprenta Molina, 1933.

Books

Aguirre, Mirta. *Influencia de la mujer en Iberoamérica, Ensayo.* Havana: P. Fernández, 1947.

Boloña, Viuda de Sierra, Concepción. *La mujer en Cuba.* Havana: Imprenta "La Prueba," 1899.

Bueno, Salvador. *Figures cubanas del siglo XIX.* Havana: Unión de Escritores y Artistas de Cuba, 1980.

Caballero, Armando O. *La mujer en el 95.* Havana: Editorial Gente Nueva, 1982.

Casasus, Juan J. E. *La emigración cubana y la independencia de la patria.* Havana: Editorial lex, 1953.

Caturla Brú, Victoria de. *La mujer en la independencia de América.* Havana: Imprenta La Milagrosa, 1945.

Comité Provincial del PRC en la Habana. *La mujer cubana en los cien años de lucha: 1868–1968.* Havana: Instituto del Libro, 1969.

Jiménez, Dora. *Las revoluciones del feminismo.* Havana: Molina, 1930.

Lagomasino A., Luis. *Patriotas y Heroinas.* Havana: "Boletín Nacional de Historia y Geografía," 1912.

Mujeres en Revolución. Havana: Sección de Historia de la Direccion Política de las FAR, November, 1974.

Padrón, Albelardo. *Mambisadas.* Havana: Editorial Gente Nueva, 1985.

Ponte y Domínguez, Francisco J. *Historia de la Guerra de los Diez Años (Desde la Asamblea de Guáimara hasta la destitucide Céspedes).* Havana: Imprenta "El Siglo XX," 1958.

Raggi, Carlos M. *Sociedad, democracia, trabajo.* Havana: La Casa Montalvo Cárdenas, 1938.

del Río, Pastor. *En honor de la mujer espirituana y de la sociedad "El Progreso."* Havana: Imprenta Ramiro F. Moris, 1947.

Rodríguez de la Cuesta, Vincentina Elsa. *Patriotas Cubanas.* Pinar del Río: Talleres Heraldo Pinareños, 1952.

Rodríguez García, José A. *De la Revolución y de las Cubanas en la época revolucionaria.* Havana: Academia de la Historia de Cuba, Imprenta "El Siglo XX," 1930.

Santovenia, Emeterio S. *Una Heroina Cubana.* Havana: Imprenta Seoane y Fernández, 1918.

————. *Huellas de Gloria: Frases históricas cubanas.* Havana: Imprenta "El Siglo XX," 1928.

Sarabia, Nydia. *Ana Betancourt.* Havana: Editorial de Ciencias Sociales, 1970.

————. *Historia de una familia mambisa: Mariana Grajales.* Secretaría de Trabajo Ideológico Comisión Nacional de Historia, Unión de la Juventud Comunista. Havana: Editorial Orbe, 1975.

————. *María Cabrales.* Havana: Editorial Gente Nuevo, 1976.

Servicio Femenino Para la Defensa Civil. *Gertrudis Gómez de Avellaneda.* Havana: n.p. 1947.

Zaldívar, Angela M. *¿Es la mujer cubana subdita o ciudadana?* Havana: Imprenta y Papelería La Universal, 1926.

Articles

Aguirre, Mirta. "Marta Abreu (1845–1909)." *Mujeres Cubanas* 13 (November–December 1951): 5.

Alvarez Conde, José. "Marta Abreu, El Naturalista y Villaclara." *Magazine Social* 4 (April 1951): 8–9, 28–29.

Alvarez Estévez, Rolando. "Los clubes femeninos en la emigración." *Mujeres* 10 (February 1970): 43–47.

Aparicio, Raúl. "Escorzo de Mariana." *Juventud Rebelde* (March 5, 1969): 2.

Castillo de González, Aurelia. "Para un héroe una belleza, la viuda de Agramonte." *Social* 3 (February 1918): 13–14.

"Colegio María Luisa Dolz." *El Hogar,* no. 7 (March 27, 1904): 4–6.

"Directiva del Asilo 'Huerfános de la patria.'" *El Hogar,* no. 28 (October 1, 1899): 10.

Duvallón, Georgina. "En el centenario de la Guerra de 1868: Nuestras Mambisas." *Mujeres* 7 (December 1967): 56–58.

"La enseñanza en Cuba." *El Hogar,* no. 14 (June 9, 1901): 2–3.

Horrego Estuch, Leopoldo. "Patriotas cubanas: Marta Abreu y Magdalena Peñarredonda." *Bohemia* 57 (October 29, 1965): 105–7.

Martín, D, "Rosa, 'La Bayamesa.'" *Mujeres* (September 1968): 81.

Martínez Guayanés, Maria A. "Martí y las cubanas en la emigración." *Mujeres* 9 (March 1969): 44–47.

Méndez, Graziella. "Adela Azcuy." *Mujeres* 5 (August 1965): 43.

————. "Amalia Simoni de Agramonte." *Mujeres* 8 (October 1968): 65.

————. "Amparo Orbe." *Mujeres* 1 (September 1969): 65.

————. "Bernarda Toro de Gómez." *Mujeres* 8 (July 1968): 67.

————. "Carmen Cancio Bello." *Mujeres* 7 (October 1969): 51.

————. "Emilia Casanova." *Mujeres* (August 1968): 67.

————. "Evangelina Cossío." *Mujeres* 1 (March 1969): 71.

————. "Isabel Rubio, (1837–1898)." *Mujeres* 8 (June 1968): 67.

————. "Julia Zapatero de González." *Mujeres* 8 (November 1968): 65.

———. "Magdalena Peñarredonda." *Mujeres* 9 (February 1969): 65.

———. "María Cabrales de Maceo, (1849–1905)." *Mujeres* 8 (December 1968): 65.

———. "María Hidalgo Hidalgo." *Mujeres* 1 (August 1969): 65.

———. "Rosario Collazo." *Mujeres* 9 (January 1969): 59.

Méndez Capote, Renée. "Mariana Grajales." *Mujeres* 8 (June 1968): 42–43.

Morales, Salvador. "Ana Betancourt Mora." *Revolución y Cultura* 27 (November 1974): 74–75.

Ortíz, Fernando. "Elogio postumo de Marta Abreu." *Revista Bimestre Cubana* 7 (March–April 1912): 91–99.

Quiñones, René Carles. "La educadora cubana María Luisa Dolz." *Revista Parlamentaria de Cuba* 3 (January 1924): 113–14.

Ravelo, Aloyma. "Lusía Iñiguez." *Romances* 38 (November 1974): 67.

Rexach, Rosario. "Las mujeres del 68." *Revista Cubana* (January–June 1968): 123–42.

Rodríguez Calderón, Mirta. "Evangelina Cossío, la muchacha quinceañera." *Bohemia* 59 (July 21, 1967): 16–20.

Roig de Leuchsenring, Emilio. "La muerte de una gran patriota." *Social* 10 (July 1925): 7.

Santos, Nelly E. "Las ideas feministas de Gertrudis Gómez de Avellaneda." *Revista Interamericana Review* 5 (Summer 1975): 276–81.

Sarabia, Nydia. "Mariana Grajales." *Mujeres* 12 (June 1972): 61–71.

———. "Páginas para el centenario, Ana Betancourt, maestra." *Mujeres* 8 (October 1968): 38–39.

"La vida de Doña Bernardina Suárez de Durete." *Marta Abreu* 1 (September 1959): 8–9.

Vignier, Enrique. "Cronología, Apuntes de las primeras rebeldias y luchas patrioticas de la mujer en Cuba." *Revolución y Cultura* 26 (October 1974): 66–79.

Zamora, Antonio G. "La mujer en Cuba, El Colegio 'Isabel la Católica' y María Luisa Dolz." *El Hogar* (September 27, 1896): 1–4.

Cuban Feminism

Cuban feminists used the printed word to convey their arguments and objectives. They published their ideas in popular newspapers, feminist journals, memoirs of conferences, literature, and organizational annual reports. Most of these primary documents are found only in the José Martí National Library and the Cuban National Archives. I have microfilmed seventeen rolls of film containing these sources, and Scholarly Resources, Inc. has distribution rights for the films. The Cuban National Archives has the personal papers of Ofelia Domínguez Navarro and María Collado, which contain personal correspondence and memorabilia from feminist gatherings. It also has substantial documents on the life of María Luisa Dolz, which are being compiled by Dania de la Cruz, Cuban archivist, for a biographical study. Ana Betancourt's speech is also in the archives, as is scattered information on the Alianza Nacional Feminista.

Good tools for beginning a study on Cuban feminism are:

de la Cruz, Dania. *Movimiento Femenino Cubano: Bibliografía.* Havana: Editora Política, 1980.

Fernández Robaina, Tomás. *Bibliografía de la Mujer Cubana.* Havana: Ministerio de Cultura, 1985.

Stoner, K. Lynn. *Latinas of the Americas: A Source Book.* New York: Garland Publishing, Inc. 1989.

Valdéz, Nelson. *Cuban Women in the Twentieth Century: A Bibliography.* New Mexico: Latin American Studies Association, 1978.

Feminist Organizational Records

Alianza Nacional Feminista. *Alianza Nacional Feminista.* Havana: Imprenta y Librería "La Propagandista," 1930.

———. *Boletín de la Alianza Nacional Feminista* (1931–35).

———. *Homenaje de la Alianza Nacional Feminista.* Havana: n.p., 1929.

———. *Vigésimo aniversario.* Havana: n.p., 1948.

Asociación Femenina de Camagüey. *Revista de la Associación Femenina de Camagüey* (1926–).

Club Femenino de Cuba. *La mujer moderna.* 1926.

Federación Nacional de Asociaciones Femeninas. *Memoria del Primer Congreso Nacional de Mujeres: Abril 1–7, 1923.* Havana: Imprenta de La Universal, 1923.

———. *Memoria del Segundo Congreso Nacional de Mujeres: Abril 12–19, 1925.* Havana: n.p., 1925.

———. *Primera Série de Conferencias Divulgación Cívica.* Havana: Talleres Gráficos "Cuba Intelectual," 1927.

Lyceum Lawn and Tennis Club. *Lyceum Lawn and Tennis Club* (the journal published by that organization).

———. *Memorias 1930–1959.*

———. *Statutes,* n.p., n.d.

El Partido Demócrata Sufragista. *La Mujer.* 1929–31.

El Partido Feminista. *Aspiraciones.* 1918–?

El Partido Sufragista. *La Sufragista.* 1922–34.

Unión Laborista de Mujeres. *A las sufragistas y a la opinión pública.* 1930. (Flier from the Central Committee of the Unión Laborista de Mujeres. Located in the Organization of American States Library.)

Unión Laborista de Mujeres. *Unión Laborista de Mujeres: Informe de la Secretaria.* Havana: n.p., 1932.

Articles and Statements about Feminism by Cuban Feminists

The issue of women's changing social, economic, cultural, and political roles fascinated intellectuals and the general literate public. Radical feminists were often writers who, from the comfort of their studies, wrote stunning essays on the direction of feminism and criticisms of activist strategy. These thinkers wrote for the popular press and therefore influenced basic premises of the women's movement. Moderate feminists often responded to radical change in print, thus opening a heated debate for at least fifteen years. Between 1926 and 1940 *Bohemia* and *Carteles* gave regular space to radical feminist journalists Ofelia Rodríguez Acosta and Mariblanca Sabas Alomá, respectively. A number of feminist writers published in newspapers such as *El Mundo, El País,* and several short-run periodicals including *El Avance Criollo, Ahora,* and *Alma Mater.* After 1940 feminists continued to write about the movement in an attempt to preserve its history. Rich sources for feminist rhetoric appear in feminist journals (cited above) and the following published materials:

Aguirre, Mirta. *Influencia de la mujer en Iberoamérica.* Havana: Imprenta P. Fernández, 1947.

Amando Blanco, Isabel. "La mujer es una flor." In *Exposición de flores,* edited by Lyceum Lawn and Tennis Club, 164. Havana: Imprenta "El Siglo XX," 1954.

"Aquellos Años." *Cuba Internacional: Mujer Como Protagonista.* Special issue dedicated to the Second Congress of the Federation of Cuban Women. (November 1974).

Arocena, Berta. "Un congreso nacional de mujeres." *Bohemia* 30, no. 20 (May 15, 1938): 23, 32, 45, 48, and 52.

———. "Una voz de mujer: De asistencia social." *El Mundo* (April 1, 1941): 1.

Arroyo, Anita. "Presencia de la mujer en la vida cubana." *Diario de la Marina. Siglo y cuarto.* 192–99. Havana: Diario de la Marina, 1955.

Barinaga y Ponce de León, Graziella. *El feminismo y el hogar.* (Conference given at the Alianza Nacional Feminista on April 25, 1930.) Havana: Talleres Tipográficos Carasa, 1931.

Behar, Cariña. "Problemas sociales de la protección familiar del menor en Cuba." *Revista de Servicio Social* (January–March 1956): 20–25.

Borrero de Luján, Dulce María. "Protección de la madre." *Cuba Contemporánea* 13, no. 31 (May, 1925): 119–23; and in *Repertorio Americano, Semanario de Cultura Hispánica* (Costa Rica) 10, no. 12 (May 25, 1925): 179–81.

———. *El matrimonio en Cuba.* Havana: Imprenta "El Siglo XX," 1914.

———. "La mujer y la degeneracion de la sociedad cubana." *Revista Bimestre Cubana* 13: 120–27.

Collado, María. "La agitación actual y las feministas." *Revista Parlamentaria de Cuba* 2, no. 10 (January 1923): 491–92.

————. Complete archive of personal papers are located in the Archivo Nacional de Cuba in the *donativos* and *remisiones* catalog.

————. "El error de María Maeztu." *Bohemia* 19, no. 23 (June 5, 1927): 21.

————. "La mujer cubana en el parlamento." In *Album del Cincuentenario,* published by the Asociación de Reporteros de la Habana, 123–25. Havana: Editorial Lex, 1953.

————. "La revolución femenina en Cuba." *Bohemia* 19, no. 50 (December 11, 1927): 13, 56, 58, and 63.

"Con delegadas de todos los lugares de Cuba se inició ayer el Congreso Femenino." *Hoy* 2, no. 92 (April 19, 1939): 1–6.

"Delegadas al Congreso Nacional Femenino." *Hoy* 2, no. 92 (April 19, 1939): 11.

de la Maza, Piedad. *Diary: 1925–1947.* Was in the personal possession of Elena Mederos de González. Washington, D.C.

de la Torriente, Loló. *1 defensa y 2 comentarios.* Havana: Ediciones Lucha CNOC, 1932.

————. *Testimonio desde dentro.* Havana: Editorial Letras Cubanas, 1985.

de Nevero, Florisa. "Evolución feminista." *Bohemia* 18, no. 37 (September 12, 1926): 7.

————. "El feminismo y una feminista." *Bohemia* (July 18, 1926): 8.

de Vera Lens, Amelia [Alianza Nacional Feminista]. *Pro la mujer cubana.* (Radio talks of under fifteen minutes.) Havana: Editorial Alberto Soto, 1930.

Dolz y Arango, María Luisa. *La liberación de la mujer cubana por la educación.* Havana: Oficina del Historiador de la Ciudad, 1955.

Domínguez Navarro, Ofelia. *50 Años de Vida.* Havana: Instituto Cubano del Libro, 1971.

————. "El desenvolvimiento político-social de la mujer en Cuba." *Bohemia* 26, no. 30 (August 26, 1934): 74 and 155–56.

————. *De Seis a Seis: La vida en las prisiones cubanas.* México: n.p., 1937.

————. "Entrevistas." *Bohemia* 30, no. 40 (October 2, 1938): 38–39.

————. "Protección mutua y mutuo respeto." *El Cubano Libre* (August 1, 1928): 6.

————. Complete personal papers of Ofelia Domínguez Navarro are located in the Instituto de Historia in Havana, Cuba.

Fernández Sanz, María. "Temas Femeninos: La pseudo frivolidad de la mujer." *Cuba y América* 1, nos. 8 and 9 (August–September 1934): 6 and 18.

Gómez Carbonell, María. "Orientaciones Femeninas: La posición de la mujer cubana frente a los males presentes." *Cuba y América* 2, no. 14 (February 1935): 11.

Jara de Zelaya, Elena. "Mujeres contra nuestra propria abulia, prejucios y remoras." *Cuba y América* 11, no. 20 (August 1935): 23.

Jiménez, Fora. *Las evoluciones del feminismo.* Havana: Molina, 1930.

Lamar, Hortensia. "El Club Femenino de Cuba." *Carteles* 9, no. 13 (March 28, 1926): 16.

Martínez Márquez, Berta. "El Día de las Madres es patentado en Norteamérica." *Bohemia* 27, no. 20 (May 14, 1935): 9, 51, and 52.

Martínez y Martínez, Julia. *Necesidad de la educación en la mujer como medio de preparación para el desempeño de sus deberes civiles y políticos.* Havana: Imprenta y Papelería "La Universal," 1927.

Mederos de González, Elena. "Desenvolvimiento femenino en Cuba." In *Almanaque del Mundo: El libro de la vida nacional,* 359–64. Havana: La Companía Editora "Almanaque del Mundo," 1931.

———. "El Lyceum y su mundo interior." *Revista Lyceum* 6 (February 1954): 32–46.

———. "La posición de la mujer en Cuba." Unpublished paper, 1975. In possession of Mederos family. Washington, D.C.

Mederos Vda. de Fernández, Rafaela. *La mujer en el frente social de Cuba: Recopilación de 44 años de labor, 1894–1938.* Havana: Impresa Editora de Publicaciones, 1939.

Morel, Isabel. "Orientaciones femeninas: Hable, mujer de América." *Cuba y América* 2, no. 20 (August 1935): 6–7.

"Opiniones de 'Hoy'. Congreso de Mujeres." *Hoy* 2, no. 92 (April 19, 1939): 1–6.

Ortex, Isabel Margarita. "El camino recorrido por la mujer cubana en medio siglo de República." *Carteles* (May 18, 1952): 84–91 and 191–93.

Palaez de Villa-Urrutia, Aida. *El sufragio feminino.* (Representing the Partido Nacional Sufragista, Pelaez de Villa-Urrutia gave this speech before the First National Women's Congress on April 6, 1923.) Havana: Imprenta "El Siglo XX," 1923.

Pozo Gato, Catalina. "La negra cubana y la cultura." *Diario de la Marina,* sec. 3 (November 30, 1930): 6.

"Primer Congreso Nacional de Mujeres de Cuba." *Fígaro* 40, no. 13 (April 1923): 166–72.

Puga de Losada, Amalia. "El voto." *Cuba Contemporánea* 33 (September–December 1926): 322.

Rodríguez Acosta, Ofelia. "Comentarios a un folleto feminista." *Bohemia* 22, no. 18 (May 7, 1930): 15, 66, and 70.

———. "Concepto del patriotismo." *Bohemia* 22, no. 43 (October 26, 1930): 17.

———. "Los deberes de la mujer para con el hombre." *Bohemia* 22, no. 44 (November 2, 1930): 17.

———. "El derecho de amar." *Bohemia* 24, no. 21 (May 22, 1932): 13.

———. "El feminismo en la universidad." *Bohemia* 22, no. 17 (April 27, 1930): 9.

———. "El gobierno de las mujeres." *Bohemia* 24, no. 23 (June 5, 1932): 13.

———. "Letter to Mariblanca Sabas Alomá." In *Feminismo,* edited by

Mariblanca Sabas Alomá, 19–22. Havana: Editorial "Hermes," 1930.
———. "La maternidad transcendente." *Bohemia* 23, no. 26 (October 25, 1931): 11.
———. "Matrimonio y amor libre." *Bohemia* 21, no. 36 (September 8, 1929): 19.
———. "La mujer cubana y la hora actual." *Bohemia* 22, no. 41 (October 12, 1930): 11.
———. "Piedras en el camino de la mujer." *Bohemia* 23, no. 7 (April 7, 1931): 17.
———. "El porvenir de las guerras." *Bohemia* 24, no. 25 (June 19, 1932): 11.
———. "Preocupémonos del niño." *Bohemia* 24, no. 18 (May 1, 1932): 13.
———. "La propia ruta." *Bohemia* 24, no. 22 (May 29, 1932): 13.
———. "¿Qué mueve al hombre en oposición al feminismo?" *Bohemia* 21, no. 24 (June 16, 1929): 11.
———. "Rebasando el feminismo." *Bohemia* 23, no. 22 (September 27, 1931): 24.
———. "Sobre el niño, otra vez." *Bohemia* 24, no. 20 (May 15, 1932): 13.
———. "Sobre la pena de muerte." *Bohemia* 22, no. 39 (September 28, 1930): 9.
———. "El voto a la mujer española." *Bohemia* 23, no. 24 (October 11, 1931): 19.
Rubio, Luz. *Consideraciones sobre feminismo*. Havana: Imprenta Molina, 1914.
Sabas Alomá, Mariblanca. "Un año de feminismo." *Social* 14 (January 1929): 26 and 74.
———. "Atalaya: Aspectos de la lucha feminista." *El Avance Criollo* (March 3, 1941): 3.
———. "Atalaya: Bestias de carga." *El Avance Criollo* (March 29, 1941): 3.
———. "Atalaya: Carta sobre la hermana del apostol." *El Avance Criollo* (April 10, 1941): 3.
———. "Atalaya: La mujer de solar." *El Avance Criollo* (March 19, 1941): 3.
———. "Atalaya: Palabras a las mujeres cubanas." *El Avance Criollo* (April 24, 1941): 3.
———. "Concepto de la feminidad." *Bohemia* 26, no. 41 (November 20, 1934): 20.
———. *Feminismo: cuestiones sociales—crítica literaria*. Havana: Editorial "Hermes," 1930.
———. "La mujer fuerte." *Bohemia* 26, no. 43 (December 9, 1934): 26.
———. "Negras en el Congreso de Mujeres," In *Por qué se publica este folleto,* edited by Angel Césea Pinto Albiol. Havana: n.p., 1941.
Sobavilla, Lesbia. "Las que no iríamos a la guerra." *Bohemia* 28, no. 23 (October 25, 1936): 21 and 44.
Unión Cristiana Feminil de Temporancia de Cuba. *Una sesión de temporancia en el Club Rotario de la Habana*. Havana: Unión Cristiana de Temporancia de Cuba, 1931.

Articles and Statements about Cuban Feminism by Men

Men also wrote about Cuban feminism, often from a different perspective than that of feminists. Although they were not always .conservative, men often wished to preserve the sanctity of the home by maintaining the image of the protected and dependent woman. They expressed a respect for women which came from their reverence for women's moral superiority. Some men attacked feminism for attempting to destroy women's social virtue; others tried to endorse the woman's movement and tie it into another political effort, such as the socialist or trade union movements. Few men supported a feminist struggle against the Cuban patriarchy. Emilio Roig de Leuchsenring was an exception to this rule.

Alemán y Martín, Ricardo M. *Capacidad de la mujer en el derecho civil.* Havana: Imprenta Avisador Comercial, 1917.
Arango, Rodolfo. "Mujeres de ahora." *Bohemia* 27, no. 5 (February 3, 1935): 24 and 61.
"Aspiraciones femeninas." *El Mundo* (February 12, 1954): A-6.
Carrera Justiz, Francisco. *El feminismo y el efebocracia.* Santa Clara: Times of Cuba, 1929.
Coyula, Miguel. "La mujer cubana." *Bohemia* 27, no. 17 (April 26, 1936): 38.
"Club Feminino de Cuba." *Bohemia* 21, no. 11 (March 17, 1929): 28.
"Club Feminino de Cuba." *Cuba Contemporánea* 19 (January–April, 1919): 447–48.
"Del concurso para glorifican a la mujer cubana." *Bohemia* 24, no. 26 (June 26, 1932): 18.
del Río, Pastor. *María Luisa Dolz: El Maestro y su apostado.* Havana: Imprenta de "El Fígaro," 1929.
del Valle, Francisco Gerardo. "Mentir es el encanto y una necesidad en la mujer." *Bohemia* (March 28, 1926): 13.
———. *El divorcio y los hijos.* Havana: Imprenta "Militar de Perez Hermanos." 1915.
de Velasco, Carlos. *Aspectos nacionales.* Havana: Jesús Montero, 1916.
———. "El esfuerzo femenino," *Cuba Contemporánea* 19: 97–107.
———. "La mujer y la hembra." *Bohemia* 21, no. 26 (June 30, 1929): 23.
———. "La negra cubana," *Diario de la Marina,* sec. 3 (November 2, 1930): 5.
———. "El siglo de la mujer." *Bohemia* 23, no. 32 (December 6, 1931): 11–12.
de Velasco, Carlos. *A las mujeres cubanas.* Havana: Sociedad Editorial Cuban Contemporánea, 1919.
"Disuelta la sección feminina de PRC Auténtico." *El Avance Criollo* (April 2, 1941): 21.
don Ramir [pseudo.]. "Variedades." *La Unión Constitucional* 1, no. 282: 2–3.
Dumas, Alejandro. "La cuestión de divorcio," *Cuba Contemporánea* 20: 304–6.

Editorial, Congreso Nacional de Mujeres. "Brillante Alarde de la Cultura y el Avance Femenino en Cuba." *La Discusión* (April 4, 1923): 2.

"La emancipación de la mujer." *Cuba Contemporánea* 16 (January–April 1918): 359–60.

Ferrer y Picabia, Emilio. *Capacidad jurídica de la mujer casada.* Havana: Imprenta Militar de la Viuda de Soler, 1881.

García Garofalo y Mesa, M. *Marta Abreu Arengibia y el Dr. Luis Estévez y Romero.* Havana: Imprenta y Librería "La Moderna Poesía," 1925.

García Montes, Oscar. "La reforma del Código Civil," *Cuba Contemporánea* 11: 177–88.

Giberga, Eliseo. *El problema de divorcio.* Havana: Librería e Imprenta "La Moderna Poesía," 1911.

Godoy, Armando. "A la mujer cubana." *Cuba Contemporánea* 41 (May–August 1926): 212.

Homenaje a la mujer periodista. Cuaderno No. 9. Havana: Comisión de Cultura, 1944.

Lazo, Raimundo. *El feminismo y la realidad cubana.* Havana: Imprenta y Librería "La Propagandista," 1931.

Lobo y Sagarra, Adolfo Gómez. *Breve reseña de la asociación de las hijas de María.* Santiago de Cuba: Imprenta y Librería de Eduardo Beltrán, n.d.

Machado, Manuel. "El voto femenino." *Adelante* 1, no. 2 (1932): 7.

Mañach, Jorge. "El Lyceum y la conciencia nacional." Speech given at the Lyceum, Havana, Cuba, March 5, 1954. *Revista Lyceum* (April 1954); 32–46.

"El mejor feminismo." *Bohemia* 20, no. 51 (1928): 3.

Menéndez Menéndez, Emilio. *El divorcio.* Havana: Cultural, Sociedad Anonima, 1932.

Padrón, Pedro Luis. *La mujer trabajadora.* Havana: n.p. 1972.

Prevost, Marcel. "La emancipación de la mujer." *Bohemia* 21, no. 11 (March 17, 1929): 21 and 55.

"Primer Congreso Nacional de Mujeres." *Cuba Contemporánea* (September–December 1923): 437.

Prío Socarrás, Carlos. *Homenaje nacional de las asociaciones femeninas al honorable presidente de la república Dr. Carlos Prío Socarrás.* Speech given at the Vedado Tennis Club, Havana, July 9, 1949. Havana: Imprenta P. Fernández, 1950.

Ramos, José Antonio. "El sentido económico de la emancipación de la mujer." *Cuba Contemporánea* 28 (January–April 1922): 5–33.

Roig de Leuchsenring, Emilio. "Un asesinato que la ley provoca y sanciona." *Carteles* 9, no. 10 (May 7, 1926): 10.

———. "¿Casarse para descasarse?" *Carteles* 8, no. 15 (February 23, 1930): 30.

———. "La explotación de la mujer." *Carteles* 9, no. 8 (February 21, 1926): 16.

———. "Esas . . . también son mujeres." *Carteles* 9 (May 21, 1926): 16.

———. "Encuesta sensacional: ¿Qué opina Ud. sobre el matrimonio y el divorcio?" *Carteles,* no. 18 (May 2, 1937): 34.

———. "Ley de divorcio . . . antidivorcio." *Carteles* 15, no. 7 (February 16, 1930): 18.

———. "Matrimonio civil." *Carteles* 15, no. 28 (July 13, 1930): 34.

———. "El delito de adulterio debe desaparecer del nuestro Código Penal." *Carteles* 9, no. 9 (September 28, 1926): 16.

———. "Prólogo." In *Feminismo,* edited by Mariblanca Sabas Alomá, 1–5. Havana: Editorial "Hermes," 1930.

———. "El resultado de la encuesta sobre el matrimonio y el divorcio." *Carteles,* no. 26 (June 27, 1937): 44.

———. "Sobre el divorcio: Lo que es hoy en Cuba: lo que debe ser." *Carteles* 9, no. 13 (March 28, 1926): 16.

———. "Uniones libres, y los hijos, todos iguales ante la ley." *Carteles* 15, no. 24 (June 15, 1930): 34 and 46.

"Una asamblea sufragista en el Club Femenino de Cuba." *Bohemia* 20, no. 5 (January 29, 1928): 30.

"La Unión Radical de Mujeres contra una postergación." *Ahora* (October 21, 1933): 12.

Velasco, Carlos de. "A las mujeres cubanas." *Cuba Contemporánea* 19 (January–April 1919): 345–52.

Vitier, Medardo. "La vida de la mujer cubana en su relación con de la historia de Cuba," *Cuba Contemporánea* 14: 323–40.

Prescriptive Literature for Women

The turmoil of the early republican period created confusion about acceptable behavior for women. Women still wanted to marry and have families, but they were also challenged to find work and enter politics. Advice columns existed in most of the popular journals such as *Bohemia, Carteles,* and *Vanidades.* To contrast with these modern columns, one might look in nineteenth-century journals for women, such as *Album Cubano de lo bueno y lo bello,* edited by Gertrudis Gómez de Avellaneda. Domitila García de Coronado, a nineteenth-century poet, wrote a book of advice to her daughter entitled *Consejos y Consuelos de Una Madre a su Hija,* which won literary prizes in 1881, 1889, 1890, and 1900.

Feminist Literary Writing

A number of feminists wrote novels, poetry, essays, and journal articles. Some considered themselves writers; others believed they wrote only to make a point and not to create art. Their works were mostly ignored or forgotten. Critics were kinder to women writers in the nineteenth century, and their art as well as analysis of their pieces abound.

Domínguez Navarro, Ofelia. *De seis a seis.* México: n.p., 1937.

Figarola-Caneda, Domingo. *Correspondencia íntima de la Condesa de Merlín.* Madrid and Paris: Industrial Gráfica, 1928.

Gonzáles, Edelmira. *Estampas de la carcel.* Havana: n.p., n.d.

González Curquejo, Antonio. *Florilegio de escritoras cubanas.* Havana: "La Moderna Poesía," 1910.

————. *Florilegio de escritoras cubanas.* Havana: Aurelio Miranda, 1913.

————. *Florilegio de escritoras cubanas.* Havana: Imprenta "El Siglo XX," 1919.

Rodríguez Acosta, Ofelia. *Evocación.* Havana: Graphical Arts, 1922.

————. *La tragedia social de la mujer: Conferencia.* Havana: Editorial Genesis, 1932.

————. *La vida manda.* Madrid: Editorial Biblioteca Rubén Darío, 1929.

Sabas Alomá, Mariblanca. *La Remora.* Havana: Imprenta "El Siglo XX," 1921.

Sansores Pren, Rosario. *El Breviario de Eros.* Havana: Tipos Molina, 1930.

Soravilla, Lesbia [Gipsy]. *El dolor es vivir.* Havana: n.p., n.d.

Valdéz Roig, Giana. *María Luisa Milanes: Su vida y su obra.* Santiago de Cuba: Ediciones Archipiélago, 1930.

Legal Treatises and Documents

Creating law generated discussion from legal theorists and legislators about the nature of law in general as well as about the suitability of specific legal changes. These treatises provided insight into legal as well as social considerations identified by lawmakers.

Alemán y Martín, Ricardo M. *Capacidad de la mujer en el derecho civil.* Havana: Imprenta Avisador Comercial, 1917.

Alfonso, Ramón María. *La reglamentación de la prostitución, breves apuntes sobre como deber ser en Cuba.* Havana: Imprenta "El Siglo XX," 1912.

Ashby, Margery Corbett. "En favor del sufragio femenino." *Revista Parlamentaria de Cuba.* 3, no. 22 (January 1924): 272.

Azcuy, Aracelio. *El derecho de la mujer.* Havana: Editorial Lex., 1951.

Cabrera, Raimundo. *La Casa de Beneficencia y la Sociedad Económica.* Havana: Imprenta y Papelería "La Universal," 1914.

del Valle, Francisco G. "Los derechos de los hijos ilegítimos." *Cuba Contemporánea* 23 (May–August, 1920): 281–318.

————. *El divorcio y los hijos.* Havana: Imprenta "Militar" de Pérez y Hermanos, 1915.

Duque, Matías. "La mujer." *Nuestra Patria: Lectura para hombres.* Havana: Imprenta y Librería Nueva, 1928.

————. *La prostitución, sus causas, sus males, su higiene.* Havana: Imprenta y Papelería de Rambla, Bouza, 1914.

Fernández Pla, Francisco. "La mujer y sus derechos." *Bohemia* 24, no. 49 (December 4, 1932): 11 and 54.

Ferrara, Orestes. "El matrimonio en Cuba." *Cuba Contemporánea* (June 1914): 52–57.

Ferrer y Picabia, Emilio. *Capacidad jurídica de la mujer casada.* Havana: Imprenta Militar de la Viuda de Soler, 1881.

Figueras, Jesús. *La posición jurídica de la mujer.* Havana: Jesús Montero, 1945.

Figueroa, Ana. *La mujer ciudadano: Sugestiones para la educación cívica de la mujer.* Paris: UNESCO, 1954.

Flamand Montero, Eugenio. *Disposiciones legales cuaderno No. 2: Maternidad Obrera.* Havana: Imprenta "El Lápiz Rojo," 1937.

Gibergo, Eliseo. *El problema del divorcio.* Havana: Librería e Imprenta "La Moderna Poesía," 1911.

Gutiérrez, José Margarito. *La mujer: Defensa de sus derechos e ilustración.* Havana: Imprenta y Papelería de Rambla, Bouza, 1929.

Gutiérrez Sánchez, Gustavo. *Constitución de la República de Cuba.* Havana: Editorial Lex., 1941.

Hernández Corujo, Enrique. *Lecciones de derecho constitucional cubano.* Havana: Editora O'Reilly, 1942.

Huertas y Gorostiza, Eduardo de. *La mujer casada: Sus derechos pecuniarios.* Buenos Aires: Casa Editorial Hispano-Americana, 1942.

"Intrigas y secretos del Machadato: La porra de mujeres." *Bohemia* 26, no. 7 (March 18, 1934): 12–13, 52–53, and 57.

Lazcano y Mazon, Andres M. *Las constituciones de Cuba.* Madrid: Ediciones Cultura Hispánica, 1952.

Le Riverend, Eduardo. *El derecho de la mujer casada.* Havana: n.p., 1940.

López Castillo, Raúl. *El divorcio,* vol. 3. Havana: Biblioteca Jurídica de Autores Cubanos y Estranjeros, 1932.

Martínez, José Agustin. *La mujer en el código nuevo.* Based on a conference given at the Alianza Nacional Feminista. Havana: Jesús Montero, 1950.

Menéndez Menéndez, Emilio. *El divorcio.* Havana: Cultural Sociedad Anónima, 1932.

Montori, Arturo. "La inferiodad jurídica de la mujer." *Cuba Contemporánea* (May–August 1922): 106–36.

Nin y Abarca, Mario. *El divorcio ante el derecho internacional privado en la doctrina y en la legislación y jurisprudencia cubana.* Havana: Imprenta y Papelería de Rambla, Bouza, 1926.

Núñez y Núñez, Eduardo Rafael. "Domática de las causales de divorcio." In *Libros que escribe la jurisprudencia.* Havana: Jesús Montero, 1947.

Sáenz, José Manuel. *El negro y la constituyente y la constitución.* Havana: Jesús Montero, 1944.

Sarabasa, Ricardo. "El código civil ante el Congreso Jurídico." *Cuba Contemporánea* 2 (May–August 1916): 5–13.

Scott, James Brown. *Nacionalidad.* Speech given as the opening session of the International Law Academy at the American Institute, November 3, 1929. Havana: Imprenta "El Siglo XX," 1929.

Secades y Japón, Manuel. "Defensa de los derechos de la mujer y de la prole en las uniones legítimas." Law thesis. Havana: Tipografía de "El Fígaro," 1930.

Velasco, Carlos de. *Aspectos nacionales*. Havana: Biblioteca de Autores Cubanos, Jesús Montero, 1915.

———. "El esfuerzo femenino." *Cuba Contemporánea* 19 (January–April 1919): 97–107.

Zaldívar, Angela M. *¿Es la mujer cubana súbdita o ciudadana?* Havana: Imprenta y Papelería "La Universal," 1926.

Zamora, Juan Clemente. *Estudios sobre el proyecto de reforma constitucional.* Havana: Imprenta y Papelería de Rambla, Bouza, 1927.

Zayas Rodríguez, Ramón D. *Derechos de la mujer casada: Legislación y jurisprudencia.* Trinidad: Topografía Venus, 1957.

Index

About the Author

K. Lynn Stoner, Assistant Professor of History at Arizona State University, is the editor of *Latinas of the Americas*. She is currently working on a collection of biographical sketches of Latin American feminists in cooperation with a number of Cuban historians.